Loisaida as Urban Laboratory

Loisaida as
Urban Laboratory

PUERTO RICAN COMMUNITY ACTIVISM
IN NEW YORK

TIMO SCHRADER

THE UNIVERSITY OF GEORGIA PRESS
Athens

© 2020 by the University of Georgia Press
Athens, Georgia 30602
www.ugapress.org
All rights reserved
Designed by
Set in 10.25/13.5 Minion Pro Regular
by Classic City Composition, LLC

Most University of Georgia Press titles are
available from popular e-book vendors.

Printed digitally

Library of Congress Cataloging-in-Publication Data

Names: Schrader, Timo, author.
Title: Loisaida as urban laboratory : Puerto Rican community activism in New York / Timo
    Schrader.
Description: Athens : The University of Georgia Press, [2020] | Series: Geographies of justice and
    social transformation ; 51 | Includes bibliographical references and index.
Identifiers: LCCN 2020024736 | ISBN 9780820357980 (hardback) | ISBN 9780820357973
    (paperback) | ISBN 9780820357997 (ebook)
Subjects: LCSH: Puerto Ricans—New York (State)—New York—Politics and government—
    20th century. | Puerto Ricans—New York (State)—New York—Social conditions—20th
    century. | Puerto Ricans—New York (State)—New York—Ethnic identity. | Hispanic American
    neighborhoods—New York (State)—New York—History—20th century. | City planning—
    Political aspects—New York (State)—New York—History—20th century. | Lower East Side
    (New York, N.Y.)—Politics and government—20th century. | New York (N.Y.)—Ethnic
    relations.
Classification: LCC F128.9.P85 S36 2020 | DDC 305.868/72950747—dc23
LC record available at https://lccn.loc.gov/2020024736

For all the women who have
raised, inspired, and empowered me.

CONTENTS

ILLUSTRATIONS

FIGURES

TABLES

ABBREVIATIONS

ORGANIZATIONS

AAB	Adopt a Building
CAW	Cityarts Workshop
RGS	The Real Great Society

ARCHIVES

CAWA	Cityarts Workshop Archive, New York
CP	Charass, Centro Library and Archives, Center for Puerto Rican Studies, Hunter College, City University of New York
FP	Carol Bernstein Ferry and W. H. Ferry Papers, 1971–1997, Ruth Lilly Special Collections and Archives, University Library, Indiana University—Purdue University Indianapolis
PPP	Pedro Pietri Papers, Centro Archives and Library, Center for Puerto Rican Studies, Hunter College, City University of New York
RLRF	Ronald Lawson Research Files for the Tenant Movement in New York City, TAM 214, Tamiment Library/Robert F. Wagner Labor Archives, New York University
TDCM	Timothy Drescher Community Murals
VAFR	Vincent Astor Foundation Records, Manuscripts and Archives Division, New York Public Library

ACKNOWLEDGMENTS

First and foremost I want to thank Zoe Trodd and Stephanie Lewthwaite, my two amazing supervisors, who not only provided invaluable and continuous feedback on my thesis work and my PhD program but also balanced out my own self-critical personality with their positive, aggressive encouragement. Additionally, I want to thank Christopher Phelps and Jonathan Bell for examining my PhD thesis and providing important feedback to publish this monograph. I also want to thank the rest of the staff at the Department of American and Canadian Studies and the School of Cultures, Languages and Area Studies as well as everyone I have worked with outside of the school at the University of Nottingham. This includes the wonderful support from the University of Georgia Press and the editors of the Geographies of Justice series: Mathew Coleman, Sapana Doshi, and Mick Gusinde-Duffy.

I want to pay a tremendous amount of respect to all the wonderful archives and archivists who have helped me on my various trips to New York. I truly admire their work, and they have inspired me to think more consciously about the way scholars—especially historians—use, create, and depend on the "Archive" for everything. I am grateful to the Centro Library and Archives at the Center for Puerto Rican Studies (City University of New York), the Columbia Center for Oral History (Columbia University), the Tamiment Library and Robert F. Wagner Labor Archives (New York University), the New York City Municipal Archives, the Brooklyn College Library (City University of New York), CITYarts, and the New York Public Library.

I am grateful to the University of Nottingham for awarding me the Vice-Chancellor's Scholarship for Research Excellence, and I also want to thank the following organizations for awarding me various types of travel and research grants: the School of Cultures, Languages and Area Studies; the British Association for American Studies; the European Association for American

Studies; the Economic History Society; the University of Nottingham Graduate School; the Royal Historical Society; Historians of the Twentieth Century United States; and the Midlands3Cities Doctoral Training Program.

Lastly, I want to thank my two interviewees, Maria Domínguez and Adál Maldonado, for being so generous with their time and so passionate in their responses. I have come to realize how sparse and uneven the archival records can be, and their insight as Loisaida artists and activists proved tremendously helpful in tracing the history of Loisaida community activism in all its breadth. Equally, I want to thank Libertad Guerra at the Loisaida Center for offering me a space for the interview with Maria and for welcoming me to Loisaida.

Loisaida as Urban Laboratory

INTRODUCTION

Viva Loisaida

> Loisaida came into my life; it was in the back of a van, you know, and I said Chino I found
> the name and I came back to the Lower East Side and there was the whole parallel
> between Don Quijote in the 15th Century and Chino and I 'cause we think we're in love
> with this community that nobody wants. So there, how could there be decay and there
> could be growth in the same place? It's because *creativity* is taking place here.
>
> —Bimbo Rivas, *Viva Loisaida* (1978)

On the weekend of April 15–16, 1967, an unprecedented event took place on the corner of East 56th Street and 2nd Avenue at the High School of Art and Design in New York. New York Puerto Ricans of various stripes—politicians, social workers, community leaders, parents—had been working for months to organize a conference in cooperation with Mayor John V. Lindsay's administration titled Puerto Ricans Confront Problems of the Complex Urban Society: A Design for Change. The purpose of this gathering "was to develop a design for change [and] that a copy be forwarded to the mayor with the request that prompt action be taken on these recommendations by the City Council, Board of Estimate, and the appropriate city, state, and federal agencies."[1] Lindsay himself attended the conference and stressed in his opening remarks that "what Puerto Ricans have accomplished in our city is largely the result of their own initiative and reflects the wellspring of creativity and drive which is so manifest on the island where they have their roots."[2] A cynic might point out, rightfully so, that Mayor Lindsay was hoping to secure the Puerto Rican vote, which he had lost in his 1965 election, by assembling representatives from all Puerto Rican neighborhoods and seemingly offering them a direct channel to the city's administrating agencies. However, Lindsay scholars such as Vincent J. Cannato, Nat Hentoff, and Daniel E. Button regarded him as a progressive mayor who sought educational reform and supported

President Lyndon B. Johnson's Great Society and its antipoverty and social service programs. Making out Lindsay's true motivations for organizing the conference, in hindsight, is impossible; what is far more important is that this conference took place in New York.

According to a *New York Times* article, the city had organized several similar conferences with the government of Puerto Rico prior to this—but all of them in Puerto Rico. Another conference involving the island government and the city was scheduled for December 1966, but "objections from New York Puerto Ricans led to its replacement by yesterday's [April 15, 1967] self-help effort here instead."[3] By voicing their objections and making the city cancel its plans with Puerto Rico's government, New York Puerto Ricans, mostly those raised in the city rather than on the island, demonstrated a determination to focus on and participate in solutions to problems that affected them in the city—including poor public education, a changing job market, and absentee landlords.[4] As Alfredo Nazario, Puerto Rico's secretary of labor, pointed out in his speech at the conference, "All discussions about the problems that the Puerto Rican New Yorker confronts in the adaption to the ways of such a complex urban society as New York City, ought to be held here . . . and not back in San Juan."[5] In the wake of the fiftieth anniversary of this conference, it is appropriate to chart the history of activism in the then-emerging Puerto Rican neighborhood of Loisaida (Spanglish for the Lower East Side) to assess the effects and influence of this conference, which saw the Puerto Rican communities of New York initiate a dialogue between the city administration and a politically underrepresented but significant minority. How did Loisaida activists mobilize otherwise largely apathetic residents? More important, what did they achieve both during a phase of pro-community support at the city and federal levels that lasted until the end of the 1970s and during a subsequent phase of pro-developer and pro-corporate policies that severely hindered neglected urban neighborhoods such as Loisaida from keeping their community development efforts alive?

The 1967 conference serves as a good starting point to answer the first question. The keynote speaker was the highest-ranked Puerto Rican politician in New York, Bronx Borough president Herman Badillo, who focused on two key subjects in the speech he gave following Lindsay: the roles of education and institutions in improving the lives of New York Puerto Ricans.[6] One of the overarching subjects of the conference was education, and the recommendations of the conference to Lindsay's administration strongly underscore Badillo's statement that "education is the most important single area in need of help at once. . . . Therefore the greatest effort has to be spent in insuring that we and our children receive that degree of education, because with the education we can take advantage of the opportunities."[7] As his subsequent involvement as a U.S. congressman with the Committee on Education and Labor; the Banking, Finance and Urban Affairs Committee; and the Small Business Committee shows, Badillo was a fierce supporter of vocational education for children and young adults with a non-English-speaking background. He anticipated a turning point in the way Puerto Rican communities would deal with this problem in subsequent decades, when a large number of community organizations would spring up in Loisaida and other New York neighborhoods to confront the issues surrounding education—and to find solutions. These solutions were strongly tied to a more sustainable form of activism pioneered by Loisaida activists, many of whom had been members of Puerto Rican gangs before they decided to channel their energy through community development instead. Turning Loisaida into an urban laboratory, these activists experimented with and developed strategies that they employed as effective activist tools to mobilize the community and claim a stake in the life and design of the neighborhood: *youth engagement, network building*, and the *human right to the city*.

The term "Loisaida" was coined, and then widely adopted, by the activist and poet Bittman "Bimbo" Rivas in an unpublished 1974 poem, "Loisaida," to refer to a part of the Lower East Side. The use of this Spanglish term instead of other common labels honors the name that the residents chose themselves to counter real estate developers who called the area East Village or Alphabet City in an attempt to attract more artists and ultimately gentrify the neighborhood.[8] The physical boundaries of Loisaida run loosely from East Houston Street to East 14th Street and from 1st Avenue to the East River. However, the term really refers to the Puerto Ricans who were so dominant in the area in the mid-1970s. Drawing the boundaries in such a way merely helps to situate the core of the Puerto Rican residents in the Lower East Side. Many institutions and groups worked beyond and in between these boundaries, especially those that worked with Puerto Ricans in various New York areas to coordinate and publicize such cultural activities as festivals and fairs, plays, and poetry performances. So the term "Loisaida" is not so much a label for a physical area as it is a state of mind.

That Loisaida residents created this activist laboratory to find solutions to urban problems facing them is significant because despite the horrendous state of the housing stock, most Puerto Ricans wanted to stay and improve their environment according to their own ideas. As Jack J. Olivero, lawyer and Puerto Rican civil rights advocate of the Puerto Rican Legal Defense and

Education Fund, summarized in his recommendations on housing at the conference, "We [Puerto Ricans] do oppose a system that seeks to make gypsies of us by moving us from slum to slum; we do oppose the kind of thinking whereby we become the 'expendables' in any neighborhood."[9] The panel on housing agreed that gentrification was very much tied to the displacement of Puerto Ricans living in such lower-income areas as the Lower East Side. The discourse of displacement through public and urban policies goes back to the early twentieth century and specific policies such as "segregation and repatriation . . . slum clearance, public housing," as Stephanie Lewthwaite notes, writing on reform policy and Mexican communities in Greater Los Angeles.[10] Like their Mexican American counterparts in Los Angeles, Puerto Ricans in New York faced enormous threats due to urban deindustrialization and neighborhood disinvestment beginning in the 1950s, which spawned a surge in community activism projects with a conscious focus on the role that institutions needed to play. If Loisaida activists were to become the architects of their own neighborhood, they had to learn how to coordinate effectively to tackle a range of systemic urban ills simultaneously. While these activists sought to work with, not against, the city and governmental institutions as much as possible, by fighting for the rights of their community, they were radicals in their own right, "sustained by the view that a great range of social problems are tied together and must be addressed *holistically*," as Howard Brick and Christopher Phelps write.[11]

To show how Loisaida activists mobilized and worked toward sustainable community activism, this book offers the first in-depth analysis of the network of community activism in the Lower East Side from 1964 to 2001. Based on an amalgam of unprocessed organizational archives, oral histories, ephemera, and neighborhood publications, it traces the cultural urban history of activism in Loisaida. Focusing on key institutions and community groups that mobilized the neighborhood residents and built a lasting activist network demonstrates how community groups pioneered a methodology for community activism: *sustainable activism*. Examining the interplay of community activism, urban politics, and Puerto Rican history in this urban laboratory of Loisaida provides three crucial insights: (1) the necessity for grassroots organizations to adapt their activism to the changing needs of the community, (2) the creativity of urban communities to transform and design their immediate environment, and (3) the root causes that keep activist campaigns from reaching their full potential. This book illuminates the consequences for an urban neighborhood in a major transitional phase in U.S. history: the shift from 1960s antipoverty programs to 1980s neoliberal policies. More important, it shows the ingenuity and strength of activists to handle this shift in the political and socioeconomic landscape of New York by devising strategies to continue their service to the residents of the Lower East Side at all costs.

Manuel Díaz Jr. was one of the earliest community leaders who showed his ingenuity in neighborhood work, which he discussed at the 1967 conference.[12] Díaz reiterated Badillo's point about the role of community institutions from an activist's street-level point of view: "Institutions are the instruments through which a community speaks and sets goals. It is through *an interplay of these institutions* that conflicts emerge, are defined, and get resolved. It is through these institutions that a minority community can address its grievances in a complex urban society as we know it in the United States. In other words, power, whether it be black, white or brown, is not power until or unless it is organized."[13] Díaz focused on how a community can channel its political and economic power through institutions to improve aspects of the lives of its members.[14] In speaking of a "community," he did not overlook the vagueness of such a term when he suggested that "seven hundred thousand Puerto Ricans in NYC, however, does not per se make a community . . . the real test of a complete community is the degree to which it develops a set of functioning social organisms through which it can express its cultural strengths, define its problems, and confront relevant social and economic issues."[15] It is precisely this notion of a network of community institutions that lies at the heart of this book because a network of functioning institutions was necessary for community activism to be *sustainable*. Moreover, for a network of community institutions to be considered sustainable, some institutions need to emerge as activist hubs that coordinate efforts of other organizations in the area—be it support for funding applications, workshops on keeping institutions running, or just partnerships for projects and campaigns.

In 1967, Díaz already demanded that the Puerto Rican communities in New York engage in sustained *and* sustainable community development: "The organizations which existed in the late 1940s and early 1950s were concerned more with life on the Island than life in New York City. . . . early migrants tended to see New York as only a temporary experience, with the idea always on the surface of returning to the beloved Island, such desires not to confront New York were only natural expressions of felt reality."[16] Subsequent generations growing up in the city, then, shifted their focus from island politics to political and economic power in New York, thereby shifting their perception of the city as their permanent, rather than temporary, residence—without ever losing their cultural connections to the island.

A Town Called Loisaida

In order to understand the significance of Loisaida's activism, we first need to trace the emergence of this community. Following Manuel Díaz's comments on the ambiguities of the term "community," this book roots the definition of community in a shared territory, the neighborhood, where "territoriality is presumed. Solidarity is left problematic."[17] Accepting that solidarity between members or institutions of a community is problematic does not mean it is not a key aspect of the community; rather it highlights the fact that we cannot presume this solidarity outright. Key aspects of communities such as "shared meanings, sentimental attachments, and interpersonal networks of recognition and reciprocity" are "*slowly established* among the proximate inhabitants of a common territory," according to John E. Davis.[18] A community is always rooted in territory—physical, spiritual, or imaginative—but social networks are constantly negotiated. In defining community this way, we can avoid the highly problematic and romantic connotations of community as a positive "alternative to negative labels for the present: mass society, capitalism, the acquisitive society, industrialism, the modern age."[19]

The Puerto Rican community of Loisaida, then, refers to a network of institutions or social organisms—to borrow Díaz's term—located in a shared but contested territory, through which Puerto Rican residents and community members organized and acted on various aspects relating to the improvement of life in that neighborhood and beyond. The neighborhood of Loisaida was shared and contested because the residents were not all Puerto Rican and did not all share the same vision for the neighborhood or believed in the same philosophy of activism. Even Puerto Ricans were not a single unit that moved together. Different generations of Puerto Ricans—those born and raised on the island, those born on the island and raised in New York, and those born and raised in New York—had varying degrees of attachments to the island and the city.

So why examine Loisaida as opposed to East Harlem, for example, which has a longer history of Puerto Rican migration and settlement going back to the early twentieth century? In *Barrio Dreams: Puerto Ricans, Latinos, and the Neoliberal City* (2004), Arlene Dávila examines the cultural politics of urban space in East Harlem, analyzing the simultaneous Latinization and gentrification of El Barrio. She makes a compelling case for focusing on the various actors—politicians, residents (with varying ethnic backgrounds), and investors—who fought over urban space and the cultural representation of specific neighborhoods. Despite the fact that East Harlem has always had

TABLE 1. Comparison of Puerto Rican population and total population for East Harlem and Loisaida, 1970–2010

	1970	1980	2010	1970–80 change
East Harlem				
Total population	186,745	140,371	115,921	−25%
Puerto Rican population	60,291	45,856	29,352	−24%
As a percentage of total population	32%	33%	25%	
Ratio of total population to Puerto Ricans	3:1	3:1	3:9	
Loisaida				
Total population	61,664	41,652	45,608	−34%
Puerto Rican population	22,407	18,105	8,722	−19%
As a percentage of total population	36%	45%	19%	
Ratio of total population to Puerto Ricans	2:8	2:2	5:2	
Census tracts, 1st Avenue to East River and from Houston Street to East 14th Street				
20	3,105	4,405	2,101	+42%
22.02	1,453	729	232	−50%
24	3,851	4,414	2,254	+15%
26.01	3,818	1,807	844	−53%
26.02	3,058	970	232	−68%
28	2,746	2,094	1,883	−24%
30.02	564	569	354	+1%
32	868	1,019	387	+17%
34	2,944	2,098	435	−29%

Source: United States Bureau of the Census, 1970, 1980, and 2010.
Note: The data is taken from the following specific sources for the three different years: Table P-7 General and Social Characteristics of Persons of Puerto Rican Birth or Parentage: 1970, Table P-7 Race and Spanish Origin: 1980, and New York City Census FactFinder (NYC CFF): 2010.

more Puerto Rican residents than Loisaida, the actual ratio of Puerto Rican residents to non–Puerto Rican residents in 1970 and 1980, the decade when Puerto Ricans emerged as a dominant demographic in Loisaida, is smaller than that of Loisaida. As table 1 shows, East Harlem's ratio of total population to Puerto Rican residents remained stable, with the latter making up only a third in both years. In Loisaida, on the other hand, Puerto Ricans were already stronger with 36 percent in 1970 compared to East Harlem's 32 percent. A decade later, Puerto Ricans made up almost half of the entire population of Loisaida, which means that they had a much stronger influence in this small neighborhood on the Lower East Side—Loisaida's area is approximately 0.90 square kilometers compared to East Harlem's 4.20 square kilometers.

Table 1 also shows that between 1970 and 1980, both East Harlem and Loisaida lost a substantial number of residents: "by 1976, there were 100 vacant lots and 150 vacant buildings" in Loisaida, and the number of residents in the area between Avenues B and C from 3rd and 12th Streets dropped from 14,908 to 4,597.[20] While East Harlem lost almost 15,000 Puerto Rican residents, Loisaida lost "only" about 4,000 between 1970 and 1980, during the harshest phase of housing abandonment and disinvestment. This attests to a key difference between East Harlem and Loisaida that Dávila points out: Puerto Ricans in East Harlem were more likely to move back to Puerto Rico or other places. As she says, "A key, though less-documented, impetus for this out-migration . . . is the dominant association of El Barrio with urban blight and of upward mobility with moving away from El Barrio to Puerto Rico or the suburbs of Connecticut, New Jersey, Florida, and elsewhere, leading to the decentralization of the Puerto Rican community."[21] Putting it more clearly, she argues that "Upward mobility was synonymous with leaving El Barrio. . . . Many had *no intention of returning*."[22] This was not the case with Puerto Ricans in Loisaida, who were just emerging as a dominant demographic in this part of the Lower East Side and mobilizing residents to improve Loisaida instead of leaving.

Further, table 1 shows a stark decline in non–Puerto Rican residents in Loisaida from 1970 to 1980, many of whom left the neighborhood due to the rise in drug traffic, natural deaths, and the "departure of hippies."[23] However, while Mele in his analysis of demographic changes counts 40,145 total residents in 1970 and 24,093 in 1980, census data for the relevant tracts that make up Loisaida show different numbers. Mele chose to leave out census tracts 30.02, 32, and 34 despite the fact that these account for 3,686 Puerto Ricans in 1980, and there were certainly several key Puerto Rican community institutions in this area that warrant an inclusion of these census tracts.[24] Our conclusions about the data are the same, however: many earlier immigrant communities in the neighborhood—from Ukraine, Germany, or Poland—left, leaving Puerto Ricans as the largest demographic in Loisaida with 45 percent. This is not to say that Puerto Ricans did not also move out, far from it. As Mele notes, Puerto Ricans and other Latino groups were significantly displaced due to disinvestment in the area but, more importantly, they were "forced to leave their homes due to arson or other forms of landlord harassment and victimization . . . others doubled up illegally with friends and families in the public housing projects lining the East River."[25] This is visible in the increase in census tracts 20 and 24 from 1970 to 1980, which encompass these public housing projects.[26]

Considering that, unlike East Harlem, the newly emerging Puerto Rican community in Loisaida housed a significantly larger ratio of Puerto Ricans to other residents in the late 1960s through to the 1980s who decided to stay in their homes rather than seek upward mobility elsewhere, this neighborhood represents a unique opportunity to analyze the beginnings of Puerto Rican community activism during this time. In fact, the great number of institutions that sprang up between the 1960s and 1980s demonstrates that this was the most active and organized—in terms of community development—Puerto Rican community in New York during that time because urban economic shifts, especially the encroaching threat of gentrification from neighboring SoHo and Greenwich Village, affected the real estate market and the social makeup of the neighborhood the hardest. Additionally, an examination of Loisaida demonstrates the effects that larger economic shifts in the United States and New York had on a small urban neighborhood. As scholar William K. Tabb summarizes, "The policies put into practice in the 1960s may be described as redistributive liberalism, and in the 1970s as neoconservative reprivatization."[27] On the national scale, President Johnson's "War on Poverty" turned into President Nixon's and President Ford's "War on the Poor," while on the local level, Mayor Lindsay's support for Great Society programs turned into Mayor Edward I. Koch's effective pro-business and pro-gentrification strategies, which affected black and Latino communities the most.[28] The rapid urban deindustrialization that followed World War II led to neighborhood disinvestment in the early 1970s, culminating in New York's worst fiscal crisis (1974–1975) since the Great Depression, and paved the way for reinvestment and gentrification from the late 1970s onward.

While other Puerto Rican satellite communities such as the Bronx and East Harlem also suffered at the hands of private real estate investors leading to disinvestment, as the drop in numbers in table 1 shows, there was no strong gentrifying push from neighboring areas there. The gentrification frontier in Loisaida encroached "block by block, building by building,"[29] which explains why the highly lucrative land in the Lower East Side presented a huge potential for gentrification, while the more distant areas in Harlem and the Bronx were not affected to the same degree—at least not at this time. Arlene Dávila mentions the construction of public housing projects, initially intended for the "submerged middle classes," as an earlier type of neighborhood revitalization beginning in the 1940s, but these "have since become associated with urban blight, crime, grime, and poverty."[30] The gentrification that emerged out of bohemian neighborhoods such as SoHo, Greenwich Village, or Tribeca was a much more strategic process that presented a bigger threat to Loisaida than East Harlem because of the significant number of public housing projects in East Harlem, which slowed down gentrification. In Loisaida, Neil Smith points out, "especially hard hit was the area south of Houston Street and the Alphabet City area to the east between Avenue A and Avenue D. Urban renewal here simply reinforced the ghettoization of poor residents, especially Latinos, amid the concrete rubble brought on by disinvestment."[31]

While it is certainly true that, eventually, Loisaida "succumbed to this process [of gentrification]," it is precisely this investment rollercoaster and the constant threat of gentrification measures and policies that activated the neighborhood in a way that makes the Puerto Rican community of Loisaida and its vision of urban design so important.[32] Unlike in East Harlem, where residents' confrontation with gentrification was "not a direct challenge," community institutions in Loisaida and their activists did challenge gentrification at every corner.[33] Of course, the fact that artists and activists themselves, even while fighting gentrification, "have long been recognized as pioneers and catalysts of gentrification" remains, unfortunately, relevant for Loisaida and East Harlem alike.[34] By re-creating the history of activism in Loisaida, we can see not only how community efforts can fight against such encroaching threats as disinvestment and reinvestment but also, and more importantly, provide a historical, practical framework that other small urban communities facing similar threats can look to for strategies of small-scale, hands-on activism that succeeded because of its adaptability to the community's needs and its focus on reclaiming control over space.

Improve, Don't Move

It is only recently that scholars have dedicated themselves to documenting the history and migration of Puerto Ricans in the United States, during an era when the Puerto Rican population increased by around 700,000 every decade since 1970 before it jumped from 3,406,178 in 2000 to 4,623,716 in 2010.[35] In the last two decades, studies have provided much-needed macrohistorical insights into the life of Puerto Ricans moving to the mainland United States, their struggles to translate their job skills to urban centers, and their methods of keeping close ties with their island roots both through cultural traditions and practices as well as familiar connections.[36] Other scholars have focused on political and social movements in New York, including the *casita* movement, community gardens, and murals.[37]

Christopher Mele has written most extensively on gentrification and community development in the Lower East Side in *Selling the Lower East Side: Culture, Real Estate, and Resistance in New York City* (2000). By analyzing the political and cultural forces of organizations and groups going back to the late nineteenth century, Mele demonstrates how developers, city officials, and the media co-opted the Lower East Side for their personal agendas in order to sell the cultural history of this neighborhood. Mele provides excellent analyses of Puerto Rican forms of resistance and subcultures between the 1960s and 1990s. For him, representations of the neighborhood "play a central role in the production and reproduction of frequently effective cultural and political resistance, from riots to rent strikes to graffiti and squatting."[38]

What has not really been highlighted prominently enough is how Loisaida was among a growing number of neighborhoods pioneering a new form of urban living. Since the 1980s, urban planners and scholars have discussed strategies of urban development that revisit the pre–World War II idea of neighborhoods as community-driven and ecologically conscious entities. So-called new urbanists formed the Congress for New Urbanism in 1993 to promote their ideas of urban planning: "We recognize that physical solutions by themselves will not solve social and economic problems, but neither can economic vitality, community stability, and environmental health be sustained without a coherent and supportive physical framework."[39] Despite having the right ideas and priorities to turn urban neighborhoods into people-centered communities again, new urbanists generated a paradox of creating universal designs for urban living while attempting to put community life front and center. Jill Grant argues, "While new urbanism acknowledges diversity, its overwhelming preference for identifying universal principles and solutions might suggest that it seeks to reduce or deny difference or 'otherness.'"[40] Essentially, new urbanism is a top-down approach to planning that oftentimes disguises its true nature as the "architecture of gentrification and redevelopment" rather than the solution to urban blight and lack of social interaction.[41]

Gentrification affects predominantly (economically) marginalized groups such as African Americans and Latinos who have historically lived in the most neglected parts of U.S. cities, especially in the wake of increasing suburbanization and white flight in the 1950s and 1960s. Therefore, more recently, a range of scholars have responded to the criticisms levied against new urbanism by highlighting the efforts of activists, artists, planners, and residents of specifically Latino neighborhoods who have pioneered community-based models that are sensitive to each individual neighborhood's particular needs. In 1991, James T. Rojas coined the term "enacted environment" to highlight how residents of East Los Angeles are not just users of their environment but creators as well, using their front yards, streets, and social interactions as driving forces to transform the physical form of their neighborhoods.[42] It was not until the 2000s that scholars began seriously examining and expanding Rojas's ideas.[43] A major evolution of Rojas's ideas came through the work of Rodolfo D. Torres and David Diaz on what they term "Latino urbanism."[44] They argue that planners have not acknowledged the rational and sustainable form of urbanism as it has organically developed in many barrios. This is the enacted environment mentioned by Rojas, which demonstrates Latinos' proven track record of organizing and transforming their neighborhoods—despite racist barriers and lack of governmental support.

However, studies of Latino urbanism focus predominantly on Mexicans and Mexican Americans due to their larger percentage of the total U.S. population—almost 60 million versus 5.5 million.[45] Still, Puerto Ricans used Loisaida as a sort of urban laboratory to design methods of transforming it from a rubble wasteland into a livable neighborhood. Manuel Castells, in his seminal book *The City and the Grassroots: A Cross-Cultural Theory of Urban Social Movements*, argues that "major innovations in the city's role, meaning, and structure tend to be the outcome of grassroots mobilization and demands," which encapsulates what is at the heart of Loisaida's urban laboratory.[46] However, in his analysis of 1960s community organizing across U.S. inner cities, Castells distills the diversity of community action into two camps: "a black-led, overall social protest, and a white, moderate income people's defense against urban decay."[47] He bases this conclusion on John Mollenkopf's work on classifications of 229 community organizations, which include only 14 (or 6 percent) groups with a Spanish-speaking ethnic background compared to the overwhelming majority of black (71 percent) and then white (21 percent) groups.[48]

Loisaida activists have produced a type of community organizing that sits both between the forms Castells identifies and outside of it: a Puerto Rican–led, low-income neighborhood movement that tackled socioeconomic, cultural, and environmental issues through daily do-it-yourself organizing and occasional protest events. Loisaida residents, many of whom participated in community action in some form or another, fought urban decay and urban renewal just as much as they fought for their rights as American citizens. They fought for social, economic, and environmental justice in a network of cross-generational, cross-ethnic, and cross-cultural activists. Each chapter in this book shows a different aspect of this dynamic process of creating a sense of place for the families and children who made Loisaida their home, whether by choice or by necessity. Projects spanning almost half a century, such as the University of the Streets, geodesic domes, windmills, solar walls, murals, El Bohío, and El Puerto Rican Embassy, are all products of this Loisaida

laboratory—manifestations of a network of community organizations planning and designing their ideal neighborhood from the bottom up. Their efforts revise our understanding of Latino urbanism and activism. The groups
in this book have all been instrumental in changing the landscape of Loisaida
and pushing forth their own form of urbanism despite the encroaching gentrification of the 1980s.

Key Issues for Loisaida Activists

While activists in Loisaida organized campaigns on all kinds of community
issues, both big and small, there are four macro issues that galvanized the
neighborhood: housing, employment, education, and culture. With regard
to housing, as Mele points out, real estate developers as well as private and
corporate investors see houses and buildings as "income-generating properties rather than as primary residencies."[49] The human element is ignored or
taken out of the equation in a capitalist system where the monetary value of
an object is the primary, and often only, aspect that matters. Referring to the
period of this project, William Tabb explains why real estate owners might
abandon properties, leaving residents to fend for themselves:

> During the expansionary period of the 1960s, housing demand exceeded sup-
> ply, and those able to furnish the rapidly growing market were rewarded with
> high profits. This led to speculative real estate investment, with little money
> down and the building itself used as security. When the downturn came in
> 1974, these buildings were overleveraged and mortgages, taxes, and utility
> bills fell into arrears. . . . When an owner "walks away" from a building, falls
> into tax arrears, or repeatedly fails to pay fines for housing code violations,
> the city can become the owner. New York City has always been reluctant
> to take over the management of such properties, however, preferring to sell
> them—usually to people who will begin yet another round of milking and
> then abandoning the property.[50]

Mele has analyzed the census data of 1970 and 1980 to show that the number
of occupied private housing units fell 48 percent from 10,944 in 1970 to 5,725
in 1980, while in 1970 11,075 Puerto Ricans of a total 18,031 lived in private
units and only 6,536 of a total of 16,492 lived in private housing ten years
later. At the same time, the number of Puerto Ricans living in public units
increased to 9,957 in 1980 from 6,956 in 1970.[51] This shows that disinvestment and abandonment of real estate in the 1970s forced Puerto Ricans into
public housing, most of which was owned by the city due to an increasing

lack of investors at the time. While other ethnic groups fled this increasing ghettoization, Puerto Ricans stayed and organized in community development groups and institutions to revitalize their neighborhood in their own way, without systematically displacing current residents.[52] This activist form of revitalization, as opposed to gentrification, took on various forms such as buying abandoned buildings in auction, clearing rubble and restoring abandoned buildings, renovating abandoned houses, or even building solar panels to provide energy-efficient heating and insulation.

Abandonment, however, led to cheap property prices, and with the recovery of the economy toward the end of the 1970s, investors and politicians sought to gentrify the neighborhood, a change creeping in from Greenwich Village and SoHo, which were gentrified earlier due to their more central location and the historical connections with alternative and bohemian lifestyles that go hand in hand with gentrification. By analyzing the tax arrears delinquency in property ownership from 1975 to 1985 in Loisaida, Neil Smith has shown that "serious reinvestment in the area as a whole began after 1980."[53] These statistics suggest that the Puerto Rican community at the heart of the Lower East Side held out longer than most other areas in the Lower East Side.

Moreover, urban deindustrialization displaced the largely working-class Puerto Ricans in the 1940s and 1950s who were mainly employed in manufacturing industries. Housing disinvestment in the 1970s displaced Puerto Ricans who were forced to move into housing projects. Lastly, gentrification in the 1980s displaced Puerto Ricans because they were not able to afford the steep increases in rent. It is within this harsh historical and economic urban environment that Puerto Ricans in Loisaida concentrated their efforts to improve their housing situation on a grassroots level, seeking funding from charities or any other source available. Smith regards the type of city in which the middle class takes back slum areas through gentrification as the "revanchist city," which "represents a reaction against the supposed 'theft' of the city, a desperate defense of a challenged phalanx of privileges, cloaked in the populist language of civic morality, family values and neighborhood security."[54] The Puerto Rican community of Loisaida countered this narrative with its own version of a revanchist attitude. For residents in this community, private developers, landlords, investors, and city officials were the thieves who sought to steal *their* neighborhood. Hence, the goal of employing sustainable activism was to create the type of livable housing that would serve the community in the way it deserved.

In another area closely tied to the housing issue, Loisaida activists struggled with the effects of economic oppression, which, Ann E. Cudd explains, "is fundamentally a matter of having reduced economic opportunity, consequent on one's social group membership, compared to a group whose members have relatively more economic opportunities. For it to be a case of oppression ... the inequality must be unfair or undeserved, it must harm, and it must benefit the members of another social group. The oppressed group need not be absolutely poor, but there must be a privileged group relative to which they are economically deprived."[55] The majority of activists in Loisaida can be described as economically oppressed due to existing discriminatory practices at the hands of governmental and municipal institutions, businesses, banks, and schools.[56] This economic oppression mostly affected the younger generation of fourteen- to twenty-four-year-olds who had grown up in New York and whose parents likely moved to the city as part of the great migration of Puerto Ricans from the island following Operation Bootstrap—a U.S. initiative beginning in 1948 to transform the Puerto Rican economy from a largely agricultural one to an industrial one.

Based on census data from 1960 and 1970, just under half of all Puerto Ricans (by birth or parentage) in New York between the ages of twenty and twenty-four completed high school (45 percent in 1960 and 40 percent in 1970), while for both years just under a third of all Puerto Ricans between the ages of fourteen and nineteen earned an income ($1,383 median annual income for this group in 1960 and $1,116 in 1970).[57] The 1970 census report even provides a special entry on the exact number of Puerto Ricans between the ages of sixteen and twenty-one not enrolled in school (51 percent) and unemployed or not in the labor force (25 percent), which means the U.S. Census Bureau felt it was important to highlight the high number of young Puerto Ricans in New York not enrolled in school *and* unemployed.[58] Juxtaposing these data sets makes it clear that a large number of Puerto Rican youth dropped out of high school and earned an income far below the minimum wage for New York in 1960 ($2,000 per year) or 1970 ($3,000 per year).[59] While the loss of manufacturing jobs was already under way, older generations of Puerto Ricans (twenty-five and older) earned on average twice as much compared to the younger generation in 1960 (median annual income $3,000) and four times as much in 1970 (median annual income $5,500), though even the median income for 1970 is far below the median income for New York ($9,504 in 1960 and $12,255 in 1970) and barely above the minimum wage.[60] Overall, census data indicates that many young Puerto Ricans did not attend school, which blocked them from entering a job market that was quickly transforming into a service economy, requiring more and more educated individuals.

Emmanuel Tobier's report on poverty in New York also underlines this development: "halfway suitable employment opportunities are simply not available in sufficient numbers to make it worth one's while to make the effort, even though the alternative options of scratching by on a combination of welfare, illegal and off-the-book activities are bleaker still."[61] This distinguishes young Puerto Ricans from the older generation and at least partially explains the surge in gang affiliation among Puerto Ricans who, having fewer opportunities and little economic incentive, found the social aspects (identity, solidarity, territoriality) of gang and street life more attractive than any attempt at navigating the difficult job market.[62]

A major reason for the lack of job opportunities, and the third issue for Loisaida residents, was the educational landscape for Puerto Ricans. At the 1967 conference, there were two panels entirely dedicated to key areas of education, while almost every other panel touched on certain aspects of education in some way, directly or indirectly. One panel dealt with education, broadly defined, while the second focused more specifically on career development. The recommendations of the education panel focused on bilingual education in school, the employment of bilingual teachers, the implementation of Puerto Rican history, and vocational training in high schools since vocational training used to take place at the college level only during this period.[63] The panel on career prospects recommended to Mayor Lindsay's administration that the city should slash some hurdles for Puerto Ricans to get into civil service jobs, offer more creative and practical programs in job training and vocational courses, and create—or help fund—Puerto Rican–run institutions that would provide career training and vocational skills to its community.[64] While it might seem like a utopian wish to ask a mayor to reform the school system to provide bilingual education to Spanish-speaking students, education reform was actually a key part of Lindsay's political platform. Title VII of the Elementary and Secondary Education Act of 1965—the most expansive education bill in U.S. history—did, in fact, authorize the use of federal funds for bilingual programs. Nevertheless, ten years after the conference took place, less than *one percent* of all public elementary and secondary school employees in New York were Latino teachers.

In one major study on education and Hispanics in the United States, the findings also show that "majority teachers sometimes hold negative attitudes toward minority children and that teachers' expectations can affect student achievement. In addition, teachers and other staff members within a school may provide role models for their students."[65] The study made it clear that Latino students in general lacked role models and teachers who respected or even just understood their cultural background. Overall, then, the city administration did not want education reform, which Lindsay scholar Vincent Cannato attributes to both a lack of political will and legal obstructions to reform: "Neither Lindsay nor minority parents had enough political strength and savvy to bring about such massive changes."[66] These educational issues presented major obstacles for Puerto Ricans trying to become more active members of their city. Loisaida activists understood the importance of education as a remedy for other ills, such as the lack of job opportunities for Puerto Ricans, and focused heavily on including children and teenagers in their work.

The fourth major issue for Loisaida activists was culture. Since the term "culture" is essentially meaningless on its own, in this context it refers primarily to the process of negotiating one's cultural heritage and identity in a new environment—the harsh urban environment of New York in this case. The Puerto Ricans coming to New York were often torn between, at least, two languages, two cultures, two places, and two lives (their island past and their New York present and future). Their new home in Loisaida offered little in the way of Puerto Rican culture as residents with European backgrounds speaking different languages dominated the neighborhood. Thus the panel on cultural affairs at the conference in 1967 recommended the creation of cultural spaces and centers to support creative talent in the community with regard to music, literature, dance, and religion, especially since the early generations of Puerto Ricans feared that subsequent generations growing up in New York would demonstrate a "lack of knowledge of the Puerto Rican about his own cultural heritage, his need for identity, for self-esteem."[67] Loisaida Puerto Ricans had to become ambassadors for Puerto Rican history and culture or else risk having their children grow up without it.

The Puerto Rican community was very willing to work with various agencies despite the fact that these agencies had neglected their community's needs before. As Humberto Aponte pointed out in his presentation for the education panel at the 1967 conference, their effort to work with such agencies as the Board of Examiners or the Board of Education had been "greatly obstructed until recently by rigid requirements, by a 'Pontius Pilate' attitude, and by cold and impersonal treatment of Puerto Rican professionals."[68] This reaching out, which became visible across all presentations of the conference, is significant in highlighting the willingness of Puerto Ricans to participate actively in the life of the city, working with official agencies to get support and funding for their institutions. As it turns out, they had to rely almost exclusively on artistic grants and philanthropic organizations to fund their efforts in the coming two decades.

No matter the source of support or funding, Loisaida exploded with art galleries, community centers, and other cultural centers—the most famous was and remains the Nuyorican Poets Cafe. In some way or another, all of these cultural spaces promoted various forms of cultural and artistic expression, offering safe spaces for children to do arts and crafts or learn instruments. Similarly, such places as the Nuyorican Poets Cafe, El Bohío, or the New Rican Village provided stages for local talent, young and old, to share their experiences and demonstrate their artistic prowess.[69] Through various Puerto Rican or Loisaida-specific traditions, artists and organizations provided cultural and spiritual guidance to the community. All the large and small institutions in Loisaida shared a common interest in offering their community spaces to vigorously negotiate their cultural identity and seek out a dialogue between all those common dualities described above.

Sustainable Activism

Faced with these complex issues, community activists turned Loisaida into an activist laboratory, constantly experimenting with organizing strategies that would achieve their goals in the short term, medium term, and long term. They shared resources, connected their work, and created social spaces to discuss their initiatives. This book is concerned primarily with the *methodology* employed by Loisaida activists and only secondarily with the motivations for organizing. Asking why Loisaida residents turned to large-scale neighborhood organizing beginning in the 1960s is not the most interesting or important question to ask—as significant as it still is for contextual reasons. It is quite a common set of reasons to anyone familiar with the history of protest and social movements in the United States or elsewhere. It is even more familiar to residents and activists who have lived this history, whether in Loisaida or elsewhere in urban America. Asking, and answering, *how* these activists conducted their work and what organizing tools they used, on the other hand, reveals not only the strengths and weaknesses of grassroots campaigns but also a set of strategies that helped sustain their cause for decades—a set of strategies that could be interpreted as a set of lessons for other grassroots campaigns.

The term "sustainable activism" is an umbrella term for three distinct strategies that have emerged from researching the efforts of Loisaida activists between 1964 and 2001: the human right to the city, network building, and youth engagement. These are by no means the only strategies that are pertinent to sustaining grassroots organizing for any period, or group—far from it. These are simply the three most important strategies employed by Loisaida activists in the four decades following 1964—the year when a few gang members decided to become community activists under the name the Real Great Society (RGS). They are part of a larger corpus of activist strategies that will prove valuable both for measuring the sustainability of past grassroots campaigns and for guiding future activists who can learn from, and adapt, these lessons for their own causes. Of course, Saul Alinsky produced many organizing tactics in his books *Reveille for Radicals* (1946) and *Rules for Radicals* (1971). There is no evidence that Loisaida organizers drew inspiration from Alinsky directly, even though some indirect influence is more than likely considering the diversity of Loisaida activists over the decades. Alinsky's guide for community activists also matches the work Loisaida activists adopted. This includes turning Loisaida into a symbol behind which residents could unite; creating common enemies in developers, landlords, and the city; finding joy in activist tactics; and making their activism public through colorful and loud protests. Alinsky's ideas might not have actively guided Loisaida activists, but his ideas were in the air and spread throughout marginalized communities throughout the United States in the 1970s.

Building on Henri Lefebvre's famous idea *le droit à la ville*, David Harvey argues that the right to the city is "a common rather than an individual right since this transformation inevitably depends upon the exercise of a *collective power* to reshape the processes of urbanization. The freedom to make and remake our cities and ourselves is, I want to argue, one of the most precious yet most neglected of our human rights."[70] Puerto Rican organizations in Loisaida were, in fact, defending their human rights when they built community gardens on abandoned lots, created community-controlled bilingual workshops and other educational projects, or reclaimed and renovated decaying properties. Defending one's human rights is defending one's community's human rights, and to achieve some measure of success depends on collective organizing. For Puerto Ricans in Loisaida, this meant channeling their activism through community organizations, as Díaz had already pointed out at the conference in 1967, a year before Lefebvre published his seminal *Le Droit à la Ville*. For the organizations to last and for activism to be sustained, the type of activism in play had to be flexible enough to adapt to changing trends that endangered the neighborhood: from disinvestment and financial crises in the 1970s to gentrification policies in the 1980s and the increasing minority status of the Puerto Rican population from the late 1980s onward. The organizations' members also recognized that their efforts depended on a certain measure of control over space so as to ensure that they could actually transform their environment and ultimately claim their right to the city—in small but significant ways.

Another important strategy Loisaida activists employed was the creation of an activist network. This meant both helping one another out on certain projects or pooling administrative and fund-raising activities for greater efficiency. Adopt a Building and Charas were the two key groups with the most significant budgets and fund-raising experience as well as sheer personnel, which meant they naturally evolved into leading hub groups who worked together on all major Loisaida issues—especially in the 1970s. They were also in the ideal position to work with smaller organizations and to create and nurture Loisaida's growing network of community development organizations. Muralist and activist Maria Domínguez described Loisaida's community groups as a family, demonstrating how important these activists considered this network.[71] The word "family" is perhaps more appropriate than the word "network" simply because it makes it clear that this was not just some purely professional network of organizations, but a close-knit group of friends and families. Sharing resources among this Loisaida family was a core strategy to transform a range of smaller projects, causes, and groups into a Loisaida movement working toward similar goals.

Including and engaging young people in Loisaida has been a driving force for activists from the very start in the 1960s—mostly because the founders of RGS were all young themselves when they turned their gang experiences into community work. The standards for youth engagement set by RGS in the 1960s became a major reason why it was able to reach out to residents and why the majority of subsequent activist groups also incorporated a youth-focused strategy into their overall missions. Whether the goal was to provide a safe and drug-free after-school space, offer a path toward a General Education Development certificate, build playgrounds, or support the artistic talent, Loisaida groups found it vital to either target their work toward young people or allow them to help shape the future of their neighborhood. It became vital for the future of Loisaida to engage with young people and ensure that the work of activists was meaningful and helpful to neighborhood families and the younger generations who were shut out from the English-only public school system and potential job opportunities. In fact, for many groups discussed here, youth engagement became synonymous with youth employment—to provide work experience and a career path for unemployed young adults.

While the term "activism" often conjures images of mass rallies, strikes, or dramatic marches, it is equally applicable to actions and projects on the smallest scale that seem ordinary at first but ultimately protest controversial or negative policies and social trends just the same. As the most famous example, the civil rights movement needed the dramatic and mass-scale marches and protests, but the success of this movement depended equally on grassroots activism.[72] Marching for voting rights was just as important as learning the process of voting itself. The term "sustainable activism" is by no means a replacement for larger national or even global protests. Puerto Ricans in Loisaida, however, did not have the resources to build a much larger movement. Recognizing this, they concentrated their efforts in their own square kilometer. There were limits to the effectiveness of their activism precisely because of the lack of critical mass of protest rallies and dramatic media coverage. Nevertheless, the initiatives of Puerto Rican organizations in Loisaida reveal the power of such seemingly ordinary projects as cleaning up streets and abandoned lots or creating community gardens and street murals.

Moving roughly chronologically from the 1960s to the early 2000s, this book showcases the resilience and creativity of Loisaida activists through the most tumultuous times in the history of American urban life. The first three chapters examine organizations focused more visibly on education, housing, and the urban environment, while the latter chapters examine how Loisaida activists sustained their work in the face of encroaching gentrification, both through the steep incline in rent prices and through the appropriation of Puerto Rican and Loisaida culture by developers.

In her work on Puerto Rican beet farmers in the Midwest, Eileen J. Suárez Findlay argues, "Histories of unsuccessful projects also demand examination of what was imagined but did not come to pass—for both elites and working people. Such an analysis of the past is not highly valued in a discipline such as history, which is deeply invested in empirical evidence—if it cannot be proven to have been historically significant, of what use is it to historians?"[73] In many ways, the work of Loisaida activists was unsuccessful as they did not stop the gentrification of the neighborhood and the subsequent forced displacement of Puerto Rican residents who could no longer afford to live in the area. Their pioneering efforts to push through a Puerto Rican–led urbanism in Loisaida were thwarted by developers, the city, and the great loss of community grants that helped this neighborhood in the 1960s and 1970s. Findlay invokes Ann Laura Stoler's important work on "historical negatives," efforts "absent from the historiography because they appear to be colonial debris, unfulfilled visions discarded in process."[74] These historical negatives are important. Even though the Loisaida dream to create a lasting home for Puerto Ricans in New York became an "unfulfilled vision" to large degrees—though by no means in absolute terms—the work of its activists and residents proved vital to improving the quality of life of this community and fostering young artists and activists. Loisaida's cultural and artistic outputs during the final decades of the twentieth century, unlike the concrete work on housing and education, proved to endure and seep into the larger legacy of Puerto Rican history in New York with artists and activists continuing to keep it alive through festivals, events, and art every year. Beyond this, however, the story of these Loisaida activists pushes beyond the impersonal narratives of gentrification and urban decline to focus on the real power marginalized residents in New York had to shape the city's future.

CHAPTER 1

From Dragons to the Real Great Society

> What can you expect from a group of young men from the Lower East Side who fought
> each other, fought other people, robbed them—even tried to kill them—and sometimes
> went to jail? I'll tell you what you can expect from them. You can expect them to wonder,
> to dream, "Is there anything else for me? What's on the other side of the wall? Can the
> things we speak about ever become a reality?"
>
> —Angelo González, "An Open Letter from The Real Great Society"

In the mid-1960s, when Brazilian educator Paulo Freire was developing the framework for critical pedagogy in exile in Chile, President Lyndon B. Johnson was implementing his antipoverty programs across the United States. At the same time, Marxist philosopher Henri Lefebvre was in the midst of writing his seminal *Le Droit à la ville* (1968) in France. In the context of these global events—all of which helped shape what we now call the capital *S* Sixties—a group of former Puerto Rican gang members founded the social service organization Real Great Society (RGS) on New York's Lower East Side to solve what President Johnson's Great Society programs were unable to fix: educating gang members and poor or at-risk teenagers from the bottom up. This chapter examines the efforts of this community activist group to develop its own educational philosophy, which was both inspired by and a grassroots reaction to President Johnson's programs. It offered a critique of the public school system that inadequately supported Puerto Rican children whose first language was Spanish.

The work of RGS indirectly followed Article 26 of the United Nations' Universal Declaration of Human Rights (UDHR) as agreed upon in Paris in 1948. Paragraph (1) states that "everyone has the right to education," and paragraph (2) specifies that "education shall be directed to the full development of the human personality and to the strengthening of respect for human rights and fundamental freedoms. It shall promote understanding, tolerance and friendship among all nations, racial or religious groups."[1] RGS was an activist community group that adhered to global ideas of human rights in the arena of education.[2] RGS employed a *pedagogy of activism* to educate poor and at-risk teenagers through concrete work and community activism rooted in real-life subject matter.

In an interview with *Life* magazine, founding member of RGS Angelo González stated outright that the group "knew President Johnson was trying to get to [them] . . . but he just didn't know how."[3] So rather than hiding the founders' criminal pasts, González opened a letter used as promotional material for the work of RGS by writing that the founders of RGS "fought each other, fought other people, robbed them—even tried to kill them—and sometimes went to jail."[4] González used this language to demonstrate the credibility of RGS, to say to fellow gang members and youth that RGS members had been involved in gangs themselves and might have a solution that could help those living in impoverished or neglected urban neighborhoods. In this letter, González summarized three key elements of RGS that addressed, implemented, or predated the much larger ideas and programs of Freire, Lefebvre, and Johnson: (1) the right to neighborhood space for economic security, (2) the right to educational space, and (3) the right to be respected as human beings. These represent the group's earliest ideas about claiming the human right to the city and prioritizing youth in its work.

To begin with, RGS established a small business called the Fabulous Latin House, which was used as a headquarters as well as the primary source of income for the group, and also created the University of the Streets in 1967 to provide an educational space with content "that was related to the things [they] wanted to accomplish and was right for the people who couldn't make it in the existing school system." Most importantly, however, González demanded in this letter that "the individual has to really be considered as just that—an individual." While Freire had not yet published his seminal *Pedagogy of the Oppressed* in Portuguese at this time, let alone in English, RGS demonstrated a very conscious awareness of the system of oppression that existed in its own environment—the poor conditions of the Lower East Side caused by urban deindustrialization and governmental neglect.[5]

While RGS eventually failed to achieve its goals to fight systemic oppression in the economic and educational sectors on a larger scale, its educational philosophy, which culminated in the creation of the University of the Streets, was an early example of critical pedagogy before it became a theoretical framework and a necessary foundation for its work ethic at Charas—

the organization spearheaded by the second RGS founding member, "Chino" García, which in many ways built successfully on RGS's experimental ideas and activist methods to serve the neighborhood until 2001. Despite the fact that Freire's work was not yet published when the university opened its doors in 1967, RGS' activities should be contextualized within a discussion of Freire to situate the issues on the Lower East Side within a growing global, radical intellectual movement at the intersection of education and human rights.[6] RGS was pioneering a grassroots, activist pedagogy aimed to improve the neighborhood by putting its younger generations front and center in that struggle. The young members of RGS laid the groundwork for establishing critical youth engagement as a core strategy of their sustainable activism. While similarly radical efforts by Che Guevara, Freire, and the Black Panther Party focused on larger societal changes through revolutionary education (antiglobalization, anticapitalism, and black power), RGS developed and practiced a small-scale, urban community–oriented pedagogy specifically to engage young people.[7] A pedagogy of activism is a useful tool to connect the global ideas of Freire and Guevara with local, urban contexts. It provides a model of building a grassroots, activist pedagogy that can serve to interrogate the important work of community-controlled schools across the United States before the advent of neoliberal education policies in the 1970s.[8] This pedagogy served as the prototype for developing a broader strategy of youth engagement for other Loisaida groups that followed RGS.

To provide a context for the emergence of radical education, this chapter first examines the failings of the public school system in the United States by drawing comparisons to another progressive institution on the Lower East Side: the First Street School (FSS). This short-lived reform school in the 1960s, built on the "mini-school" concept of famous social critic Paul Goodman among others, was located in the Lower East Side and offered another model, one not altogether dissimilar to Freire's later concept, on fighting oppression through education. The FSS existed in close proximity to RGS, was founded in the same year as RGS in 1964, and had a similar, though much younger, audience in poor and at-risk neighborhood children and teenagers, including Puerto Ricans and African Americans. The members who founded RGS were exactly the type of at-risk children that the FSS wanted to reach. The remainder of the chapter focuses on the early projects and initiatives of RGS and its founding members to demonstrate the gradual development of their pedagogy of activism as they toured the United States and established themselves as an organization. They eventually created the University of the Streets, the most successful example of their educational philosophy that transformed and inspired many subsequent community organizations in the neighborhood to put the issue of education, particularly youth education, front and center.

This community-focused pedagogical model offered a far more detailed and nuanced approach to the implementation of Freire's ideas in an urban context. This oppression was not as obvious in the political structure as it was subtly integrated into the economic system and cultural ideas of the United States.[9] RGS fused a version of Freire's ideas with a desire to provide social and economic services to residents of the Lower East Side—to counter the effects of economic oppression and poor education resulting in gang life and crime. Freire's pedagogy of the oppressed "denies that man is abstract, isolated, independent, and unattached to the world."[10] RGS integrated this concept into its own projects, even before Freire's work could reach Loisaida. Beyond this, however, RGS was always concerned with the well-being of its neighborhood and its residents. They felt that President Johnson's plans were flawed, designed from the top down, without the crucial input of precisely those who were supposed to benefit from the antipoverty programs. RGS criticized specific issues that David R. Diaz lists in *Barrio Urbanism: Chicanos, Planning, and American Cities* (2005): overt racism, exclusion from the political arena, elite control over land policy, manipulation of federal programs by local political culture, rational-functional planning practice, and the inability of federal agencies to ensure the transfer of knowledge at the community level.[11] By developing a human rights–centered youth education with an eye on gaining job training, RGS articulated a community-based solution to Johnson's programs. Unlike the short phase of antipoverty programs, first co-opted by local elites and then modified to support wealthy neighborhoods, the RGS model spread throughout its neighborhood in the following decades to influence the work of other organizations.[12]

The U.S. Public School System and Paul Goodman's First Street School

In Paul Goodman's most salient criticism of the U.S. educational system as it existed in the 1950s and 1960s, which is also applicable to the first half of the twentieth century and the twenty-first century, he argues that the school system's purpose "is, by and large, to provide—at public and parents' expense—apprentice-training for corporations, governments and the teaching profession itself," quoting comments by the commissioner of education for the state of New York at that time, James E. Allen Jr., about the role of schools for the young: "to handle constructively their problems of *adjustment to authority*."[13] Goodman dedicated much of his life in the 1950s and 1960s to offering constructive criticism of the educational system. He raised this point in 1962 to demonstrate the extent to which pedagogical methods and their implementation through schools had been appropriated by capitalist institutions since Thomas Jefferson and James Madison spread compulsory education through the United States in their pursuit of the educated citizen, who was to be a "society-*maker*, rather than someone who participated in or adjusted to society."[14]

This is not a new development in the United States but rather a reemergence of the early twentieth-century Progressive Era rhetoric of Americanization programs, which were promoted by private industry and the government in an effort to create a better workforce more adjusted "to the rhythms of industrial life."[15] In his most famous work entitled *Growing Up Absurd* (1960), Goodman contextualizes the issues with the school system, largely a critique of the economic and political forces that co-opt curricula, by focusing on the problems of school dropouts and teenage gang affiliation—situating his analysis in the urban environment with which he was most familiar as an educator. He frames the issue of education as a human rights issue with reference to the role education plays in people's lives: "A man has only one life and if during it he has no great environment, no community, he has been irreparably *robbed of a human right*."[16] He does so not just for dramatic effect, but to emphasize that the system of education failed its students on a very basic level by creating a narrative of "society-adjustment" rather than "society-making." His book, *Growing Up Absurd*, is a book on waste, as Goodman said in a radio interview with Studs Terkel, a "waste of humanity. Waste of the most hopeful part of humanity."[17]

While Goodman's immediate concern was America's youth, Freire famously theorized his notion of students being taught to adjust to authority at the end of the 1960s:

> Education thus becomes an act of depositing, in which the students are the depositories and the teacher is the depositor. Instead of communicating, the teacher issues communiqués and makes deposits which the students patiently receive, memorize, and repeat. This is the "banking" concept of education, in which the scope of action allowed to the students extends only as far as receiving, filing, and storing the deposits. They do, it is true, have the opportunity to become collectors or cataloguers of the things they store. But in the last analysis, it is the people themselves who are filed away through the lack of creativity, transformation, and knowledge in this (at best) misguided system. For apart from inquiry, apart from the praxis, individuals cannot be

truly human. Knowledge emerges only through invention and re-invention, through the restless, impatient, continuing, *hopeful inquiry human beings pursue in the world, with the world, and with each other.*[18]

Here, Freire also frames education as a human right by pointing out two key elements of education: to foster dialogue and action. Freire's own experiences in Brazil and Chile informed his theory, which is steeped in language about political oppression rather than economic oppression, but it nevertheless summarizes the main issue with the educational system that scholars, critics, and educators had been tackling from different angles since the beginning of the twentieth century.[19] In fact, Freire's ideas are perhaps "more relevant than ever" in the twentieth century, as founder of educational neuroscience Bruno della Chiesa mentioned in an event with Noam Chomsky that celebrated Freire's achievements.[20] At the heart of all these progressive or radical analyses lies the idea of education as a humanizing project, rather than, as Goodman puts it, an institutional superstructure that "less and less [represents] *any* human values, but simply adjustment to a mechanical system."[21]

Returning to the urban environment of New York, Goodman's humanist notion of education, properly laid out in *Growing Up Absurd*, "was inspiration for the First Street School," according to family friend, Paul Goodman expert, and literary executor Taylor Stoehr.[22] This school existed as a radical, experimental project for children from lower-income families in the surrounding neighborhood on the Lower East Side. It was founded by Mabel Dennison (at the time still Mabel Chrystie) at the original location on First Street between 1st and 2nd Avenues, before it moved to 6th Street between 1st and 2nd Avenues. While this short-lived project had no known affiliation with RGS, its goal of community-oriented education—based on Goodman's call for the decentralization of urban schools "into small units, twenty to fifty, in available storefronts or clubhouses"—provides a revealing comparison when juxtaposed to the later efforts of RGS from 1967 onward.[23] George Dennison, who recorded parts of the history of the FSS in *The Lives of Children: The Story of the First Street School* (1969), was one of the teachers at the FSS alongside Goodman and frames the purpose of FSS—or any school, for that matter—in a distinctly Freirian way: "the business of a school is not, or should not be, mere instruction but the life of the child."[24] Like Freire, he criticizes this banking model of education—the instruction and deposition of predetermined information and knowledge—and offers a renewed focus on the life of the child, putting the individual's needs for education before the society's needs to educate.

The free school, or mini-school, movement of the 1960s provides the back-drop to the existence and project of FSS, though the movement, or the "revolution of progressive education," as Stoehr called it, "kind of faded."[25] While the influence of FSS is most notable in Goodman's ideas about education in *Compulsory Miseducation* (1964), its pedagogical methods and philosophy are far more interesting since it did not, unlike the majority of mini-schools, address middle-class audiences. George Dennison claims in his account that FSS was "the first of the mini-schools." Whether or not this is true, it certainly was the first mini-school that sought to address the needs of poor children, for "about half of the families were on welfare. The rest were too poor to pay tuition . . . routinely classified as underprivileged, delinquent, rebellious, etc."[26] Most mini-schools that followed the models of Alexander S. Neill, Wilhelm Reich, Paul Goodman, and Elliott Shapiro catered to children from middle- and upper-class homes. Certainly, as Stoehr noted, mini-schools or reform schools today "have solidified as institutions," mostly private, and are too expensive for families with lower incomes. Unlike the public school system, the teachers at FSS were keenly aware of the ethnic and cultural backgrounds of their children and certainly would not have had the easiest time getting parents to agree to send their children to FSS. As Alfredo Irizarry, a former student of FSS and later chronicler of Lower East Side history, mentions in a documentary project: "It was during a time when the gangs were still heavy, so we were very territorial, very territorial, and we would not let white people come into our neighborhood. . . . Paul was the first one that started breaking through that paranoia that we had. . . . He used to come to my house and sit down and eat rice and beans with my father and talk politics with my father."[27] Goodman and other teachers went from house to house and knocked on people's doors handing out information "printed in English and Spanish."[28] Despite their intellectual backgrounds and privileged position as artists, authors, or educators, the teachers of FSS managed to demonstrate their sincerity to parents in the neighborhood.

In his account of FSS, George Dennison details, via diaries and commentary, the developments of individual students. One of the major concerns for the mini-school movement in general, for Goodman specifically and Freire later on, was education that dealt with real-life situations. Freire claimed that "the starting point for organizing the program content of education or political action must be the present, existential, concrete situation, reflecting the aspirations of the people. Utilizing certain basic contradictions, we must pose this existential, concrete, present situation to the people as a problem which challenges them and requires a response"[29] Whereas Freire was thinking about political action by raising the critical consciousness of students early on—Freire called this *conscientização* in Portuguese or "conscientization" in English—Goodman was interested in the idea of using "the city itself as the school—its streets, cafeterias, stores, movies, museums, parks and factories."[30] FSS's program was structured to accommodate and embody this teaching method, to provide children with "the world *as it exists*."[31] In a written report of FSS, Goodman highlighted the importance of "informal education," as he called it: "A trip to the store to buy birthday candles, for example, can lead to an impromptu reading lesson from shop window signs, a discussion of taxes, or a demonstration of the importance of budgeting."[32] In the many activities described by Dennison, one school trip stands out as an example for this philosophy of real-life education, which also became a key element of RGS's pedagogy of activism.

After sneaking into the grandstands during a trip to Central Park to watch the St. Patrick's Day parade in 1965, the FSS pupils Stanley and Michael started yelling, causing a scene in public. They quickly got into a fight, and as George and Mabel Dennison attempted to calm the boys, Stanley repeatedly threatened to kill the seven-year-old Michael: "I'm gonna kill that mother-fucker! You fuckin' faggot, I'm gonna kill you! . . . I'm not gonna hurt 'im, I'm gonna kill 'im!" George Dennison threatened Stanley with expulsion, a tactic to see what the school really meant to him. The fighting stopped, but Stanley's anger returned the next day when he confronted Dennison by asking for his knife back. He brought it to school the day before, and Dennison did not have a chance to return it to him since he walked home with Michael that day. Stanley felt that Dennison did not keep his word to return the knife. After the confrontation between the two in the school, Dennison put the knife in Stanley's hands and threw him out of the school after making it clear that knives were not allowed in the building, and anyone who brought one would get expelled for the day—Stanley tested this on the day of the parade. Stanley, however, tried to get back into the building several times before Dennison resorted to spanking Stanley until he started crying. The following dialogue between the two, as recounted by Dennison, demonstrates that this was all about trust for Stanley:

> "Yeah? You said that yesterday and you didn't give it back to me."
> "Why didn't I give it to you?"
> "I don't know."
> "Because I didn't come back to school that's why. Where did I go?"
> "I don't know."

"Who was walking beside me?"

"Michael."

"Why was he walking beside me?"

A little smile came to his lips. "I don't know."

"Yes, you do know. Because you scared him, that's why."

Stanley "so obviously wanted to stay in school." Dennison then comments on his spanking of Stanley and admits that he did not have "the patience any-more, or the commitment, or—most important—the love. . . . Nor was First Street a school for disturbed children. And so the spanking was wrong, which is tantamount to saying that we must get rid of Stanley."[33]

Dennison's honest admission in his own account of FSS reveals, anecdot-ally, a larger issue with the educational philosophy of the school. Dennison failed to recognize that Stanley was only "disturbed" in as much as he was clearly a product of the oppressive and criminal street culture in which he grew up. In the book, not a single diary entry related to Stanley, of which there are many, hints at any mental health issues he might have had. FSS was created precisely to help children suffering the consequences of economic oppression. Despite the best intentions of the teachers and Goodman's un-derlying concept of a mini-school for poor and at-risk teenagers, FSS was never truly equipped to deal with the more complex psychological issues of some of its pupils. Dennison believed that they "must rescue the individuals from their present obscurity in the bureaucratic heap: the students, because they are what this activity is all about; the teachers, because they are the ones who must act."[34] Paul Goodman, similarly, wrote that society has "failed to achieve integration by trying to impose it from above, but it can be achieved from below, in schools entirely locally controlled, if we can show parents it is for their children's best future."[35] Both these comments display a focus on the lead role of educators to "rescue" the children by convincing parents that their model will work. According to Freire, "Pedagogy which begins with the ego-istic interests of the oppressors (an egoism cloaked in the false generosity of paternalism) and makes of the oppressed the objects of its humanitarianism, itself maintains and embodies oppression."[36] This reveals FSS as a humanitar-ian, *not* humanist, project.

Goodman and George Dennison had the best of intentions to help the children who were suffering the consequences of economic oppression in New York. However, these intentions were still egoistic at the core because both men believed they had found the right educational tools, which they tested out on a few children from the Lower East Side. Staying with Freire's

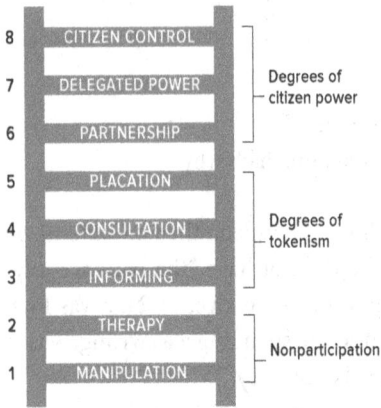

FIGURE 1. Eight Rungs on the Ladder of Citizen Participation

Source: Sherry R. Arnstein, "A Ladder of Citizen Participation," *JAIP* 35, no. 4 (1969): 216–224. Copyright © The American Planning Association, www.planning.org. Reprinted by permissions of Taylor & Francis Ltd., http://www.tandfonline.com on behalf of the American Planning Association.

terminology, these oppressed children and teenagers along with their parents were not allowed to become in charge of their own liberation through education. Using the ladder of citizen participation created by Sherry R. Arnstein (see figure 1), which explains power structures in society from citizen nonparticipation to true citizen power, it is clear that the pedagogical model of FSS fell squarely in the bracket of "therapy"—unsurprisingly Goodman helped develop Gestalt therapy in the 1940s and 1950s, which became the basis of FSS.

Arnstein describes rungs (1) and (2) as levels of nonparticipation: they "have been contrived by some to substitute for genuine participation. Their real objective is not to enable people to participate in planning or conducting programs, but to enable powerholders to 'educate' or 'cure' the participants."[37] Arnstein's model was specifically designed in a 1960s U.S. climate of urban renewal, antipoverty, and growing demands for citizen control in public schools, city halls, and police departments.[38] As such, FSS simply represented another attempt by mostly white, privileged educators and therapists to dictate the rules of the game, imposing a liberal rescue narrative onto poor parents, children, and communities not unlike companies creating their own educational Americanization programs in the Progressive Era.[39] Freire writes, "The raison d'être of libertarian education, on the other hand, lies in its drive toward reconciliation. Education must begin with the solution of the teacher-student contradiction, by reconciling the poles of the contradiction so that both are simultaneously teachers *and* students."[40] The teachers of FSS only marginally attempted this reconciliation by providing a more informal and relaxed learning environment. Beyond this, teachers were clearly teachers and the students were simply students, who would supposedly benefit from the decisions made by teachers—what Freire calls the false generosity of paternalism.

This criticism is only retrospectively applicable in the context of Freire's philosophy several years after FSS closed; FSS was undoubtedly one of the better examples of solving the issues plaguing educational systems at the time. As Peter McLaren notes, mini-schools in the 1960s "had primarily been about creating 'alternative' rather than 'oppositional' educative spaces. . . . Critical pedagogy followed in the wake of the human potential movement as a way of fostering a more oppositional position toward education and schooling practices."[41] George Dennison was certainly aware of the limits of the school and saw it only as a first step for reform:

> I do certainly propose it as a model for the indispensable first step. And since the first step is in fact the continuing foundation, I do propose the kinds of relationships we established at First Street, the kinds of freedom enjoyed by teachers and children and parents, the respect for experience, the absence of compulsion, the faith in the inherent sociability of children; I do propose all these as the environmental model for an entire system, for they belong intrinsically to the educational experience, and not just to the rationale of a school.[42]

At the same time as this school operated, RGS began the slow but gradual development of its own educational model, infused with a strong sense of community identity and activist work. Unlike Goodman and Dennison, who criticized the U.S. educational system for its society-adjustment narrative, which prepared students for jobs rather than for life, the impoverished background of many RGS members required a different approach as their financial situations and harsh environments provided less flexibility to dabble in theories of education. Their upbringings and environments instead demanded a bottom-up design that sought to create critically-thinking students and adults within a job market that was dramatically transforming from an industrial economy into a service economy.

The Early Years of the Real Great Society

In 1961, Angelo González was involved in the murder of an elderly gentleman who was on his way home. At this time, he was a warlord of the Dragons gang in the Lower East Side and only fifteen years old.[43] He was born in New York, and after many run-ins with the police, this crime finally put him in prison.

There González found himself in a unique situation as someone of Puerto Rican descent. There was a strict color line between inmates that was not to be crossed, but González was in a position to get along with both groups fairly well because, as he recalled later, "we have all colors among ourselves," referring to the complex and mixed heritage of Puerto Ricans.[44] He was able to listen to both groups, who frequently started fights with one another, and he came to realize quickly that both sides were dealing with similar issues both inside and outside prison. In this environment, González developed the idea, laid out in the open letter of RGS, of mutual respect as fellow individuals and human beings. González asked, "Aren't we all human individuals?" For him, "That ought to be enough reason for people to get along, to respect each other. What else could these black and white cats really want, except to understand and respect each other?" It is clear that the ambiguity of his ethnic background did not fit the existing system of racial division in this prison environment, which allowed him, for the first time in his adolescent life, to acquire status by preventing fights rather than causing them.[45] He made a decision while in prison that "when [he] got back on the outside, instead of busting heads and making crime, [he] would get people to work together."[46] This scenario is not unlike Freire's own imprisonment in 1964—following the military coup, which "was sufficiently traumatic to teach him a number of things. . . . [T]he relationship between education and politics became even clearer to him and confirmed his thesis that social change would have to come from the masses and not from isolated individuals."[47] Rather than going it alone, González returned to the Lower East Side in 1964 to meet up with long-time sometimes-rival and sometimes-ally "Chino" García and talk about activating the masses in their own neighborhood.

García was born in Puerto Rico and moved to New York at the age of five. He grew up in the same environment as González and adapted easily to gang and street life, first on the West Side (now known as the West Village) and then in the Lower East Side. He had immense trouble making headway in the public school system of New York, "an alien world far removed from the ghetto in which he had to survive, the only real world he knew anything about."[48] The subject matter and lessons of the school system were too vague, too removed from the realities of street life for García. He never learned how to read and write in English, and there was no support for pupils with different language backgrounds to acquire a second language properly. Even Title VII of the Elementary and Secondary Education Act of 1965, when García was already working for RGS, did little to change the integration of bilingual programs and teachers in New York.[49] The 1980 study entitled *The Condition of*

Education for Hispanic Americans also showed that a "majority of teachers sometimes hold negative attitudes toward minority children that teacher's expectations can affect student achievement."[50] García dropped out of school like many other Puerto Ricans at the time.[51] Leaving the public school system behind, García started his life as a gang member at the age of twelve because gang life provided him with a sense of purpose and an alternative model for family and friendship. He soon became a leader in the Assassins and frequently organized and participated in mugging, burglarizing, and gang fights. García explained his shift from protecting his clique as a gang leader to questioning his criminal actions:

> People depended on me. My understanding was to protect myself and my clique. That's what I believed, and I tried to do what I believed. I always considered myself an honest cat. I liked to do my own fighting, not gang up on a guy. I always made it clear to my opponents that even if they got hurt or I got hurt, I was still Chino. Some leaders would lose respect and lose their leadership. I never lost my respect. I never lost my leadership. I said give a guy a chance. Fight hard, but never kick a cat when he is down. People followed me because they could trust me. As I got older I thought more about people getting hurt, and, well, we were always getting locked up in jail. I began thinking maybe we would be better off if we did something else.[52]

However, it was an unusual offer by the police that changed his life dramatically. He became so well known to the police that they visited his parents' home and offered him an alternative: to leave the country or continue his actions and face serious time in prison. At his mother's insistence, García reluctantly accepted the offer and "went into temporary exile in Puerto Rico" in the summer of 1963, staying with his uncle.[53] In Puerto Rico he took a job with a moving van company and traveled the island in a quest, as he put it, "to know what is Puerto Rico?"[54] This brief exile away from street life in urban America was a turning point for García, who faced, like González in prison, his Puerto Ricanness in a different environment: "I began to feel that I knew my people. It was a nice feeling. I saw beautiful things about the people and their culture . . . Puerto Rico showed me a new light. I didn't become an angel overnight, but I knew I had to take a new step. Fighting, robbing, shooting, trouble with the cops, I was sick of all that."[55] This time García made the decision to return to New York, in order to begin "thinking about helping people avoid so much misery."[56] It was a romanticized image of Puerto Rico's tropical landscape and open space and a youthful naïveté about the high level of poverty in Puerto Rico at the time that inspired him to reproduce the sense of freedom he experienced in some capacity in the streets of the Lower East Side.[57] In reality, the U.S. industrialization projects known as "Operation Bootstrap" or *Operación Manos a la Obra* had taken their toll on the economy in Puerto Rico with a move away from agricultural jobs to manufacturing jobs, which ultimately resulted in a net loss in employment. The harsh experiences of RGS founding members García and González as well as their confrontations with their own Puerto Rican roots clearly pushed them toward a life of action and community development.

Once back in the Lower East Side, García and González met up and decided to take action. They reached out to many of their old friends, most of whom were drug addicts, gang members, or petty criminals, and called a meeting in the summer of 1964 to see if people were interested in what they had to say and their vision for improving life in the neighborhood. Their first venture was a clubhouse called the Fabulous Latin House, located on East 9th Street between Avenues B and C. The rundown building was home to the Bonitas Youth Hostel, which provided food and lodging for homeless people. They renovated the basement and created their clubhouse, a multifunctional physical space to use as a headquarters and source of income. Moreover, they wanted this to be a public space that "other guys on the Lower East Side could see and use if they wanted to."[58] From the outset, García and González were concerned with claiming physical space in their neighborhood as a base for future activities and an office for those who were willing to help them. This philosophy of claiming their right to the city remained a persistent element of their future ventures and a core strategy of their sustainable activism.

During the renovation process, the group that had no name but many ideas met Michael "Mike" A. Good, who sought out lodging at the hostel and got involved with García, González, and company. Mike Good was born and raised in the United States, a son of wealthy Belgian parents who had lived a life that could not be further removed from that of the Lower East Side. Mike Good "was a good man for a rich kid," and they all exchanged experiences from their starkly contrasting lives. In early 1965, they considered their future purpose and came up with names for a new organization. They considered Spartican Army, a symbolic name to indicate their small overall numbers yet their strong will and motivation. At this time, Mike Good's brother, Frederic "Fred" W. Good, also became involved in the group. In his interview with Poston, Fred recalled his first encounter with his brother's new friends: "They kept talking about something they called the Spartican Army and how they were going to get rid of poverty, make it possible for everybody to do anything he [*sic*] wanted, stop all racial conflict, do away with juvenile delinquency, create a beautiful and happy world, and take care of all the problems in the Lower East Side."[59] Fred underlined two key goals of RGS: to end poverty and juvenile delinquency. Unlike Goodman and FSS teachers who focused intently on the educational aspect without taking into account the economic realities of oppression in which most of their students were trapped, RGS demonstrated a keen understanding of this economic oppression and designed its early projects to tackle poverty directly rather than simply treating the criminal activities that were largely a result of socioeconomic circumstances.

The final key figure in this founding phase of RGS was former Harvard professor Charles "Charlie" W. Slack, a drug addict who fell from grace in the academic world around the 1960s and who became a born-again Christian in 1980. He worked with some of the gangs in his research as a psychologist and was called up by García one night to visit Mike Good's apartment at 605 East 6th Street and see what they were working on.[60] Charles mentioned his role with the group and described an educational philosophy similar to that of Freire: "You can't get them to reform by telling them anything. You can put ideas into their heads, but the ideas have to be their ideas. Never try to tell them what to do."[61] While his understanding that "they" were the ones who needed reforming was one of the issues Freire criticized most fervently—a lack of trust in the abilities of the oppressed and a lack of knowledge about the system of oppression itself—his humanitarian efforts were very much welcomed by the RGS members-to-be. In a discussion with Slack about the problems with President Johnson's ineffective antipoverty programs, García eventually articulated the name of their group: "We are the *real* Great Society."[62] Slack made contact with some of his professional associates across the United States to schedule speaking engagements for RGS and begin what Poston calls "personal-appearance tours," traveling the nation in a station wagon painted by aspiring artist Fred Good, to visit neglected neighborhoods and talk to young gang members, criminals, and drug addicts about their options to help themselves rather than hold out hope for President Johnson's plan to work.

In September 1966, in an article in the *Oberlin Review*, former Oberlin College junior Marc Landy described RGS as a "proselytizing organization," referring to the reach of the RGS initiatives across the country with "branches in Virginia and New Mexico."[63] Fred Good's written history of RGS activities in the first few years, sent out to the philanthropic Vincent Astor Foundation, mentions its tours to Syracuse University, Albuquerque, Pittsburgh, Madison, Philadelphia, and Boston.[64] RGS also established an exchange program with teenagers from Warrenton, Virginia.[65] All of these talks and mini-projects were certainly efforts to convert at-risk teenagers and gang members as well as teachers and politicians to its version of grassroots antipoverty programs, establishing its *real* Great Society. In fact, most of these trips took RGS to classrooms, universities, and governmental agencies in the hopes of converting decision-makers and the educated class to its humanist way of thinking. RGS visited Syracuse University's Youth Development Center, where it met with students and professors and pointed out "that there was no youth in the Youth Development Center . . . this project wasn't attracting poor, since they were unable to identify with the project and the staff at the Center."[66] RGS also spoke to a criminology class at the University of Wisconsin and a psychologists' convention in Philadelphia.[67] The lack of action resulting from these more academic trips turned RGS away from this type of organizational mission to focusing instead on teenagers in its own backyards in the Lower East Side.

The efforts of RGS in Albuquerque and Warrenton evidence the success of the group's activist philosophy in the early stages of its making. García and Mike Good were invited, through Slack's contacts, "to visit another Westinghouse laboratory studying the use of teaching machines."[68] They spoke to high school students and workers and appeared before the Junior Chamber of Commerce. They also went on local television and radio to share their ideas of developing a project with local Spanish-speaking teenagers. However, a fight broke out one night between locals and street kids, which essentially ended any hope for this project, and the Junior Chamber of Commerce withdrew its support as well. Despite this defeat, García "managed to prevent a serious gang war involving several hundred delinquents" that emerged in response to the fight, which received considerable press attention.[69] While they were unsuccessful in their official mission in Albuquerque, they were the only ones in a position to stop a fight that politicians certainly would not have been able to prevent. Furthermore, "they helped a teenage gang start an ice-cream business," a result of working with the gangs to stop the gang war.[70] Mike Good stayed behind for four months to support this project. Fred Good noted that his brother bought an ice-cream truck to establish a small business, which he then turned "over to two delinquents with the condition that they would return his investment when they had made sufficient money to do so. His $6,000 investment was repaid within a month."[71] This story exemplifies RGS's generally disappointing experiences with many official or governmental institutions throughout its lifespan, while highlighting its success—small as it may seem—in helping members of youth gangs channel their energies into a positive project.

The second early project that explains the development of the RGS approach is the exchange program with teenagers from Warrenton. In August 1966, RGS attempted to set up what Fred Good described as RGS South with the help of William "Bill" Watman.[72] According to a newspaper article, the idea was developed while García, González, and Carlos Troche—another RGS member—were speaking at the Fauquier Community Center in Warrenton with some teenagers who were interested in the ideas of RGS. Watman had worked with RGS members before and sent four teenagers to New York to see what RGS had established on the Lower East Side. They invited RGS members to give a talk in Warrenton, and forty-five teenagers listened to García tell them that they "must do something, and do it now."[73] That's when the teenagers themselves proposed the idea of a "New York–Warrenton cultural exchange program."[74] They then created a football team to pay for another trip to New York. It is unclear what happened to the program, though Vaughan suggested that "local pressures wiped out the entire project," whatever those pressures may have been. However, Watman, who worked for the Office of Economic Opportunity (OEO) at the time, left OEO and joined RGS to help with funding requests alongside Fred Good.[75] Despite their ability to reach out to and inspire local, mostly black teenagers in a remote city, they were not in a position to lead a project there and fight local pressures.

These two cases—indicative of the other recorded projects in these early years—show that Slack's well-meaning support for having RGS tour the country helped to derail it from its original mission to provide antipoverty programs in Loisaida. As Poston writes, the RGS members' speaking engagements "took on the attributes of the theatrical. They developed into productions bordering on extravaganzas which became more skilled, more polished, more grandiose with each performance."[76] Fred Good mentioned to Poston that "the guys [RGS members] got themselves enough sold on the notion that they were doing things they really weren't doing. . . . [T]hey repeated these stories often enough, they really became very convincing, not only to the audience, but to themselves."[77] Fred Good, not having participated in the speaking tours himself, understood that they "had to actually develop the kind of society [they] kept talking about as a living, breathing *human community* on the Lower East Side. And [they] weren't doing that. [They] were just talking about doing it."[78] After an unsuccessful funding bid with the OEO, written by Fred Good and Watman, they eventually secured a grant of $15,000 from the Vincent Astor Foundation in 1967, and the mission of RGS changed, with a renewed focus on the Lower East Side.[79] RGS members finally began work on their original idea: to create an educational space that would facilitate learning based on concrete, real-life experiences. In doing so, they created their own pedagogy of activism at the same time that Freire was writing his *Pedagogy of the Oppressed* in exile many thousands of miles south of the Lower East Side.

Public Education as a Common: The University of the Streets

In 2012, geographer David Harvey published *Rebel Cities: From the Right to the City to the Urban Revolution*, partially revisiting his own comments on Lefebvre's concept of the right to the city and partially discussing its relevance to the 2011 London Riots and Occupy Wall Street. As Pauline Lipman puts it, "the right to the city is both concrete and a metaphor for the transformation of oppressive and exploitative economic, political, and cultural arrangements and a new social imaginary that gives full play to the full development of human beings in relationships of mutuality, respect, solidarity, collective well-being, and joy."[80] Reflecting on the right to the city in the context of education, Harvey's idea of the common becomes particularly useful in understanding the role education plays in the metaphorical and concrete transformation Lipman mentions: "Education becomes a common when social forces appropriate, protect, and enhance it for mutual benefit."[81] RGS members realized that the public education system, especially in economically neglected areas such as the Lower East Side, was not to their benefit, and after their early years of experimenting and touring the country, they opened the University of the Streets on June 26, 1967, at 130 East 7th Street.[82] This educational project, which received almost $200,000 in grants from the Vincent Astor Foundation alone over the span of three years, was the RGS members' version of creating education as a common—a common they built themselves.[83]

With the university, RGS members turned their backs on the largely disappointing experiences of their big U.S. tour and focused on creating a humanist education: "We finally learned that every human being is like a teacher and everybody could teach something to somebody."[84] According to a *New York Times* article from June 27, 1967, "College instructors will join with 17-year-old high school dropouts at the university, which will have neither faculty nor students."[85] In essence, the University paired up people with expertise in one area to teach people interested in that subject, of which some might be teachers in their own right for a topic they felt comfortable teaching. This format still used the student/teacher model of FSS, but what RGS changed was FSS's strict, authoritarian version of this model where teachers are only teachers and students always students. RGS created a platform, an educational space, to strip away the hierarchical model that had become the standard for public schools and instead let "young people from the neighborhood develop a curriculum which is relevant to them, their lives, their experience."[86] The university was geared "to a kid getting a high-school equivalency degree, or to how he could read better, how a community functions. . . . What is community development? What is housing? What is government? What's happening in the world? What's technology?"[87] The university was the site of engaged, democratic education.

RGS's mission was to get those children and teenagers who suffer the consequences of economic oppression the most out of their negative environments—abandonment, rubble, and crime—and into a positive space that offered them a future, as one of the university's students confirmed: "This is a place where you come for any kind of help you need. I first came for a job. They got me one right here."[88] Many of the courses at the university led to the high school equivalency degree (General Education Development or GED), which was initially designed for veterans in 1943, but which "quickly became an exam for civilians rather than returning soldiers. In its over 60-year history, over 15.2 million people have earned the credential."[89] While designed for adults, it has become "a time-honored way for dropouts, immigrants and late bloomers to demonstrate familiarity with educational basics and get a foothold in the job market," as a *Wall Street Journal* article claimed in 2015.[90] However, the university's program subverted the still test-oriented GED exam by offering courses on African American history and Puerto Rican history as well as more praxis-oriented workshops on karate, dance, arts and crafts, computer programming, photography, and media.[91] These practical courses were designed to develop vocational and artistic skills necessary for a new service-oriented job market as well as the general well-being of a person, key components of what later became critical pedagogy: "Knowledge is not only contemplative but practical, sensuous activity."[92]

Unlike FSS, the university's pedagogical philosophy was far more suited as a model to deal with high school dropouts and at-risk teenagers because, as RGS member Bob Rivera explained, "We are trying to supply what the community wants. Kids here are learning to *do* something, achieve something. This builds self-respect."[93] Whereas Goodman and George Dennison's comments reveal a pedagogy built on what they believed the community needed, Rivera's quote shows a focus on what the community actually wanted. They developed the courses in collaboration with community members, a more democratic, grassroots approach, rather than the problematic top-down model of education. The RGS activist pedagogy thus exemplifies another core aspect of what McLaren argues is at the heart of oppositional, not alternative, critical pedagogy: "Opportunities must be made for students to work in communities where they can spend time with ethnically diverse populations in the context of *community activism*."[94]

Returning briefly to Arnstein's ladder of citizen participation, unlike FSS, the university offered participation to its members via the ladder rung (6), partnership, while the RGS creation of the university itself corresponds to a version of rung (8), citizen control. In the latter case, the university represented a community-controlled school that was managed by neighborhood residents. Arnstein, writing in 1969 about ongoing pro-community movements, said that "a neighborhood corporation with no intermediaries between it and the source of funds is the model most frequently advocated. A small number of such experimental corporations are already producing goods and/or social services."[95] There were no intermediaries between RGS and the funding for its projects, and hence it had complete control over the distribution and use of funding—though Arnstein notes that "no one in the nation has absolute control, it is very important that the rhetoric not be confused with intent."[96] While RGS did not have any amount of control over the larger school system to which its projects were responding—a *New York Times* article from 1968 describes only a meeting between RGS members and public school teachers that corresponds to the tokenistic rung (4), consultation, in Arnstein's model—the university did represent an isolated project that put the power of educating youth into the hands of Puerto Ricans, African Americans, and others suffering economic oppression.[97]

Within the university's structure itself, the methodology of having students and teachers negotiate the courses and giving everyone the chance to learn or share expertise demonstrated true partnership in the power structure of the university. Arnstein's rung (6), partnership, explains that "power is in fact redistributed through negotiation between citizens and powerholders."[98] The RGS members managing the university as an organization were, in this instance, intermediaries between the "citizens"—the students and teachers who used the university—and the funding, but the content of the educational program was still based on the actual needs of the community, whether this was learning about Puerto Rican history or teaching people about computer programming. As a report to the Vincent Astor Foundation on the university indicated, "This program will further demonstrate a new form of community organization with the 'educational store front' replacing the political store front as a vehicle for social change. The power of the educated individual will be asserted as the instrument to bring about personal self betterment, and community betterment."[99] Overall, then, the university was a vanguard in organizing community power through true citizen participation in the arena of education on the small-scale, neighborhood level.

From the Real Great Society to the Real Great Neighborhood

While the university started out as a neighborhood project in the Lower East Side, less than a year later, in March 1968, RGS expanded to East Harlem, which suffered similar abandonment and crime.[100] RGS members Angelo Giordani and William Vasquez acquired, with the help of funding from the Vincent Astor Foundation, two buildings on East 110th Street and started expanding on the idea of the university in this area.[101] However, this branch had a more overtly political undercurrent that represented again a political storefront rather than the educational one that RGS sought to establish with the university in the Lower East Side. "In terms of method and style and purpose, it was far more revolutionary, more conscious of race and Puerto Rican nationalism, and much more attuned to the militancy of current minority revolt."[102] Just a couple of months later in May, RGS established another branch of the university in Bedford-Stuyvesant with the help of another Vincent Astor Foundation grant.[103] In essence, RGS became unmanageable in 1969, and with chapters in Harlem and Bedford-Stuyvesant, the group "developed almost into a superstructure, like a really big organization, really a lot of people." As González said, "[We were] dealing with the government and dealing with people all around the country and businessmen. They wasted all our time, we were duplicating what was happening in the outside society so we decided to start CHARAS."[104] RGS members were not interested in—nor equipped to deal with—the administrative and bureaucratic processes necessary to work on a citywide, let alone national, level. RGS and Charas were activist community organizations, not social or governmental institutions. The members realized that they could only affect real change in a manageable, small-scale environment such as the Lower East Side, particularly with the economically oppressed residents of this neighborhood.

RGS's pedagogy of activism, which confronted economic oppression via a truly humanist pedagogy in a Freirean framework, was a significant step for this neighborhood toward participating in the creation of a humanist urbanism described by Harvey in his seminal *Social Justice and the City* (1973): "A genuinely humanizing urbanism has yet to be brought into being. It remains for revolutionary theory to chart the path from an urbanism based in exploitation to an urbanism appropriate for the human species. And it remains for revolutionary practice to accomplish such a transformation."[105] The community organization RGS, unlike the humanitarian philosophy of FSS, developed this revolutionary practice from the ground up in a challenging urban environment: this practice involved tackling the faulty public school system by establishing an *oppositional* education project that proclaimed the *human* right to education—a major component of what Harvey famously argued is "the most precious yet most neglected of our *human* rights: the right to the city."[106]

In *The New Political Economy of Urban Education* (2011), Lipman outlines a few philosophical principles to transform urban education—the result of her analysis of the neoliberalization of education in Chicago. RGS already developed and implemented these principles back in the 1960s, especially the notions that education should be (1) structured as "participatory democracy," (2) connected to its "community and the environment," and (3) a "tool for liberation" that teaches "oppressed people's true histories . . . and draw[s] on their communities' culture, languages, experiences, and social contributions and support their self-determination."[107] More than anything, this is a testament to the radical and powerful ideas that RGS developed, which scholars are now redefining in a new neoliberal urban landscape. The members of these community organizations were activists who wanted to clean up abandoned lots, renovate derelict buildings, create community gardens, reclaim public space for their neighborhood, and build community centers for cultural programs and art, which García described as the "flower growing in between fence wire."[108] When RGS members rebuilt themselves as Charas, they left behind the notion of changing U.S. society at large. Instead, they expanded on their repertoire of sustainable activism and continued, in the following three decades, to engage, teach, and inspire neighborhood youth and involve them in the life of their community—raising future gardeners for those flowers between fence wire. *This* is the lesson RGS members took with them when they became Charas: youth engagement as a core strategy to improve the neighborhood.

CHAPTER 2

Charas as Pioneers of Urban Environmental Activism

> We want to investigate communal life. . . . That's what we want to do this coming decade. Put this experience into action. We are now at a stage when we have to look at things—economically, politically, and culturally from different ways. We have to see what we can do as a community and deal with it. We have to see the different things people can do as communities.
>
> —Chino García, *Charas: The Improbable Dome Builders* (1973)

Back in March 1968, before the founding of Charas, Fred Good of RGS contacted the visionary philosopher-architect Richard Buckminster "Bucky" Fuller because RGS members were fascinated with his idea of solving housing problems through architectural design. Fuller responded and came down to the Lower East Side that same month, according to Charas member Angelo González, to give a talk on East 7th Street in a "meeting hall across Tompkins Square Park from the University of the Streets headquarters."[1] As González mentioned in an interview with Syeus Mottel, who recorded the first project that defined what would become the vital activist community development organization Charas, many RGS members at the meeting were distrustful of this old white man "coming in to tell us what to do," but subsequent Charas director Chino García "told everybody to shut the hell up and listen."[2] And some people did listen, those who later formed the initial members of Charas to whom the name of the group is dedicated.[3] Fuller's talk focused on "the development of a world community," which struck a chord with many in the audience who were already involved in creating an engaged, less apathetic community on the Lower East Side with the University of the Streets.[4] At this time, Fuller did not even mention the geodesic domes that became the focus of Charas's activities for a great deal of the 1970s.

Beyond the vision of building a community, what really captured the attention of the audience was *how* this could be achieved. In the foreword of the book by Mottel, which is dedicated to documenting the geodesic dome project from 1970 to 1973, Fuller writes that "within the community on these streets I find leaders emerging who don't just want to take the law into their own hands, who don't just want to protest, but who, with a very deep and intuitive earnestness and dawning awareness, want to *make things work*."[5] This is exactly what García referred to in the epigraph at the beginning of the chapter; Charas and many other organizations in Loisaida had little interest in just complaining about their situation. As one helper on the dome project said, "Well, I came to see that things I did before, like going on demonstrations and screaming, did nothing concrete. Here I find I am working with something that is very important—housing. . . . We want the community to be less apathetic about their conditions. We want them more involved."[6] Early on, Charas understood the importance of involving the community—of building connections between neighborhood institutions and members—to improve their living situation. Charas was one of the key hub organizations in the neighborhood network of activist institutions in Loisaida, and no history of housing, education, or culture on the Lower East Side during this period is complete without placing Charas at the center or close to the center of various projects, campaigns, and events.

The initiatives of Charas in Loisaida mirror larger trends on the city, national, and global levels surrounding the growing environmental movement at the time, including the Hudson River Environmental Movement, the passing of the National Environmental Policy Plan in 1969, and disasters such as the Santa Barbara oil spill in 1969. Charas not only participated in but also shaped the activist culture in Loisaida. It is important to turn toward smaller urban neighborhoods and communities to understand larger economic, cultural, and political trends in this period of U.S. history. Charas was founded out of a desire to solve the urban housing issues plaguing the local neighborhood with a focus on environmental concerns. Toward the end of the 1970s, the group's members also became increasingly concerned with offering cultural spaces and platforms, which they recognized as playing a vital role in helping the community. Throughout the decades, they always emphasized the importance of offering workshops and educating the community in practical matters such as recycling, consistently giving young people and children opportunities to become more active and engaged members of their community—a remedy against growing gang activity, drug trafficking, and general apathy due to an unwelcoming public school system.

This chapter examines the early environmental phase of Charas in the

1970s, while chapter 5 deals with the more culturally focused period beginning in the 1980s. Using the ideas of Buckminster Fuller and Murray Bookchin, pioneer of social ecology, Charas members were involved in two major projects that stand out in the 1970s: the dome project and the recycling center. With these projects, Charas attempted to solve basic housing problems for its community through a strong commitment to the belief that engaging with environmental technologies was the key to activating the community—particularly black and Puerto Rican children and adolescents struggling in the traditional school system. As such, it continued engaging youth as part of its core method of activism. Additionally, this chapter expands upon the strategy to reclaim urban space, the human right to the city, with the geodesic dome as the object that embodied Charas's vision for grassroots, affordable, and creative housing.

The Probable Dome Builders

The twenty-fifth anniversary flyer for Charas included the slogan "Always doing more with less," which became a symbol for Charas's focus on self-reliance and community development.[7] This vision to improve the neighborhood and build a more engaged community through making use of the resources available to it can be traced back to the dome project and the philosophy of Buckminster Fuller, who inspired Charas at the initial talk in 1968 to think of the environment first because people "will follow the environmental change and improve."[8] Fuller's philosophy did not require great monetary wealth but instead relied on the acquisition of experience, knowledge, and skills to change one's situation.[9] In a speech given at the planning committee for Southern Illinois University on April 22, 1961, Fuller laid out his visionary yet partially utopian plan for education in the future. The speech was published twelve years later as *Education Automation: Freeing the Scholar to Return to His Studies* (1964) and touches on some of the aspects that he talked about when he visited the Lower East Side. The thrust of his life philosophy is summed up in his opening remarks of the speech in 1961: "All thoughts and all experiences can be translated much farther than just into words and abstract patterns. I saw that they can be translated into patterns which may be realized in various *physical* projections—by which we can alter the physical environment itself."[10] The geodesic dome represented just such a physical projection that had the power to alter the physical environment. He must have gotten a sense of this neighborhood's particular issues and needs at the first talk and decided to focus his efforts on the geodesic dome as a structure that Charas would find useful, as it can be quickly and cheaply assembled to return control over housing back to residents who were being hopelessly preyed upon by landlords and private investors doing everything in their power to force out tenants they regarded as undesirable—African Americans, Latinos, and anyone else with low income.[11]

He assigned his assistant Michael Ben-Eli, an Israeli architect completing his PhD project, to go down to New York and introduce Charas to dome mathematics. The idea of being taught mathematics in a classroom setting with a blackboard and an academic teacher did not appeal to many in the group, but they kept going, with García and Roy Battiste emerging as the most resolved to see this project through to completion. They acquired a loft at 303 Cherry Street in the southern part of the Lower East Side thanks to the Housing and Urban Development Corporation (HUD) of New York. With Ben-Eli coordinating the project under the supervision of Fuller, the early phase of the project began. The project attracted media attention and also serious academic attention in the form of the Environmental Research Center of the School of Visual Arts, New York. Battiste was invited to become an instructor there, and Charas became "the resident group at this new division at the School" from fall 1970 through to spring 1971.[12] Charas members were also invited as the prime exhibitor at the Waldorf-Astoria Hotel for a trade show on Recycling Day in February 1971. These early activities demonstrate Charas members' dedication to creating sustainable solutions to basic problems—in this case housing. It was their intention to build these domes out of cardboard (see figure 2) "as an instant answer to disaster area housing or an inexpensive mold for ferro-cement domes."[13]

Early on in the lifespan of Charas, linking the realms of housing and education activism was already a primary focus:

> We looked at housing as something very important. Living in a place, it
> means a whole lot more than just living in a place. It means a whole social at-
> mosphere. It means to a large degree one's education, *real education*. It means
> being able to handle, to cope with the immediate situation and try to relate
> back to the overall because it comes from the house. Okay, you're not satisfied
> with the house, you don't own the house, you live in shitty houses and because
> you live in shitty houses everything else happens after that, you know. How
> you relate to people. How people relate to you. How you feel funny if you
> go into a rich neighborhood, how they feel funny when you're in their rich
> neighborhood. So we thought that housing was basic.[14]

FIGURE 2. Geodesic Dome Exhibition Photograph
Source: Matthew Mottel, *Artwork Assemblage*, original photograph
by Syeus Mottel, from the exhibition Social Imagination: Charas is
Alive on Space Ship Earth, Loisaida Center, New York.

This was the philosophy that shaped Charas in the beginning and the reason why it attracted increasing numbers of community members who were inspired by Charas's hands-on methods of dealing with housing issues. Community member David Lorenzano alluded to this as well in his interview with Mottel: "Before coming down to Charas, I had a different outlook on life. . . . Now I realize that a simple thing like housing can help the oppression people live with."[15]

As with RGS, Paulo Freire's critical pedagogy is a very helpful framework to highlight Charas's conscious efforts to tie housing and education together. Freire advocated for a form of praxis-oriented education that seeks to empower individuals and communities to take concrete action as a means to tackle problems they are facing: "The oppressed must be their own example in the struggle for their redemption."[16] The dome project was exactly such an example. Through a focus on solving housing issues in their neighborhood, Charas members envisioned this kind of project as initiating a larger movement in the community to engage young people and show them a different version of education—one that is useful to them. For Battiste, the dome project was "a more dynamic kind of education. An education that allowed people to learn something new that they could use to help people who have little means. Colleges are supposed to do that. They train people who then are supposed to go out and do something for others. Mostly they do things for themselves."[17] García also recognized Charas's role in this process: "We can be this tool for others," he said. "That's what I see us doing in the '70s."[18] García specifically addressed this in his letter to the Daniel J. Bernstein Foundation (DJB), in which he wrote that "the central concept of self help is aimed at *reducing apathy* in the ghetto and helping people to realize their own potential as productive people."[19] And this is precisely what Charas did in the 1970s and beyond, all of which had its roots in the dome project, which, as described in a *New York Times* article that put the spotlight on Charas, "was a phase in plans leading to the ultimate development of an economically sound enterprise [that] would use all its profits to improve and economically develop not only the Lower East Side but other poor areas as well."[20] Charas members already envisioned how their little community project could be used to help others in similar situations.

At the end of 1971, after receiving substantial funding from Fuller and the New York State Council on the Arts, Charas acquired materials to build its first experimental ferro-cement dome in an East Harlem lot on East 90th Street owned by the Vincent Astor Foundation, which sought to highlight "how urban space could be converted to make it accessible and useful to the people of the vicinity."[21] The founding members of Charas already had a great relationship with the foundation due to the funding it provided for RGS a few years earlier, so this space was an easy choice for the first dome. Despite the harsh December weather, Charas assembled the dome in three days. This inspired Charas to try for a larger, sixty-foot dome, but Charas realized in summer 1972 that this dome was too complex for the group. Instead, Charas acquired permission from the city to use the vacant lot right outside its headquarters on Cherry Street for further dome building activities. It then prepared to build two smaller domes at ten and fifteen feet in height, respectively, to be used in disaster situations for inexpensive, quick assembly. Once the materials arrived and were cut into the proper triangles for the dome, Charas finally erected the ten-foot dome late at night on October 31 along with a polyethylene film sheeting for protection against rain.

"Bucky's dome structures were still an oddity in the architectural vocabulary. But here on the Lower East Side of Manhattan, a group of ex-gang members, ex-junkies, criminals, and just people had created a moment of history."[22] While Mottel regards this event as historic because it seemed improbable that a group of ex-gang members would build an architectural structure after the design of a renowned architect, Charas's dedication in turning an environmental construction project into a neighborhood event with many volunteers is far more noteworthy. Charas consciously "wanted people's involvement to be based on their willingness to cooperate and function rather than the money derived from their efforts" and only used funds for food and materials as well as rent for their loft.[23] In fact, the loft itself became a social space for people to meet, sleep, eat, live, and just hang out. Mottel believed that "continuity of action toward recognizable ends is not easily achieved in this general environment," but it is precisely action-oriented work with recognizable goals that *counteracts* this kind of negative environment.[24] Charas members recognized this as well, which is why they emphasized such an open structure based on volunteer participation, where people, especially children, walking by could join the project so that in the end countless community members had "at one time or another, been part of this event. It belonged to none of them and, yet, it belonged to all of them. The dome touched their lives as surely as they had physically created the dome."[25] This kind of project organization would generally be very difficult to handle, which demonstrates how strong Battiste and García were as leaders in making this work. Sustainable activism is exemplified by precisely this kind of project: passionate people, working toward small-scale and recognizable goals through action-oriented and hands-on work. For RGS it was alternative, or oppositional, education and for Charas it started with building cardboard domes around the city. The joy in the process of building the dome, such as the afterwork hangouts and the inclusion of children in the event, was a key part in driving the motivation of all volunteers through the rough winter and some complications as well.

The dome project went through some rough times following the initial erection of both domes in cardboard. First, the severe weather destroyed the protective sheeting, and then a fire broke out in the smaller dome one night when a homeless person used it for shelter from the weather and made a small fire inside that set the structure aflame.[26] Though it was essentially being used for the very reason for which it was built in the first place, this caused some delay in the project. Focusing on the larger dome, Charas members fitted the cardboard pieces with wooden frames to prepare the dome for cementing, which began in January 1973. The dome was fully cemented on January 14, and as chance would have it, Buckminster Fuller was then in town to give a talk at Carnegie Hall. He cleared his plans for January 15 to come by and see the dome. Mottel's pictures clearly show Fuller's joy at seeing the dome, and he even asked his cab driver, his wife, and neighborhood children playing nearby to join in a photo. Here Mottel's narrative report shows its bias. Mottel, who worked for Fuller as a media person, wrote that Fuller "was the *cause* of their holding together for so long. Here was the *reason* for the change in their lives. This was the man that had affected them very deeply."[27] While Fuller did affect Charas members deeply and was an undeniable influence on the project and Charas's community work and vision, he was not the person holding them together—not least because Ben-Eli was the individual on the ground with Charas. Charas members developed their own motivation to make something positive happen for their lives and the members of their community. This along with the strong bonds of friendship and camaraderie that developed over three years—even more for the leaders who knew each other for much longer—held them together throughout lack of funding, harsh weather, and loose work schedules.

Buckminster Fuller remained a great friend to Charas, as evidenced by his visit to Charas's later community center El Bohío in 1981, where he discussed the history of industrialization and corporatization and even recited a poem that put his world community vision into more poetic language:

> Environment to each must be
> All there is, that isn't me.
> Universe in turn must be
> All that isn't me *AND ME*.
>
> Since I only see inside of me
> What brain imagines outside me,
> It seems to be you may be me.
> If that is so, there's only we.[28]

Although Fuller's environmental vision continued to shape Charas's actions in the decade after the dome project ended in 1973, Charas members deserve the credit for implementing this vision in a neglected urban neighborhood plagued by rising abandonment in the early 1970s. More importantly, Charas built a foundation in community engagement and alternative education fostered by RGS and combined this with solving neighborhood housing problems by emphasizing the role that the environment plays in shaping people's lives: "The environment is where one gets the feeling for mobilization, to move forward, and to relax. A crowded, ugly, uncomfortable environment creates a paranoid person who feels inferior to others. A clean, healthy environment creates a person who feels secure and sees further than just himself."[29] As such, Charas members engaged in conscious activism to create sustainable housing and at the same time find sustainable solutions for educating young people and members of the community more broadly. This is precisely why Charas members defined themselves as "an *education and research program* set up to develop alternatives to existing housing problems" in the letter to the DJB Foundation.[30] In this first decade, they identified themselves first and foremost as an organization dedicated to education.

Dome Land

One specific example of the strong focus on education during the dome project—besides offering children and other members of the community the chance to become a part of the project and hopefully continue on this positive course—was a creative comic book that accompanied the project called *Dome Land*. During the cooperation with the School of Visual Arts in 1971, a student named John Holmstrom started occasionally helping out with and learning about the dome project. He was so intrigued that he created a book that packaged the project into comic form. The comic book essentially narrates a treasure hunt and eventually reveals that the treasure is housing. During this hunt, an anthropomorphized dot, the mathematical depiction of the first dimension, guides the fictional members of Charas to the treasure. This guide serves to teach the characters in the comic book—Charas members and friends—about basic trigonometry and geodesic dome mathematics, just like Michael Ben-Eli did for the group during the project. One of the obstacles that the group in the comic must overcome is the world of the second dimension, symbolizing their earlier, less engaged life as gang members. To reach the third dimension, which stands for both geodesic domes and a philosophy of activism and self-reliance, musician Edgard Rivera, of A Band Called Loisaida and associate of Cuando (Cultural Unidas Aspiran Nuestro Destino Original) and of Charas said, "The only way to get out is—*to work*!"[31] Additionally, the comic book includes Fuller's philosophy of solving global economic and social issues; he explains the significance of the geodesic dome: "I've always seen the dome as more than mere housing! . . . I've hoped the dome would be shared among men, not divided between nations!"[32] The comic depicts the dome as a conceptual space, as envisioned by Buckminster Fuller and Charas, that serves as a solution to urban housing problems. The dome would give its inhabitants a simple but happy life, in which basic needs such as food, shelter, and clothing are provided—something that clearly resonated with Charas and a strong motivation for the group to reach out to the community through a more engaging medium.

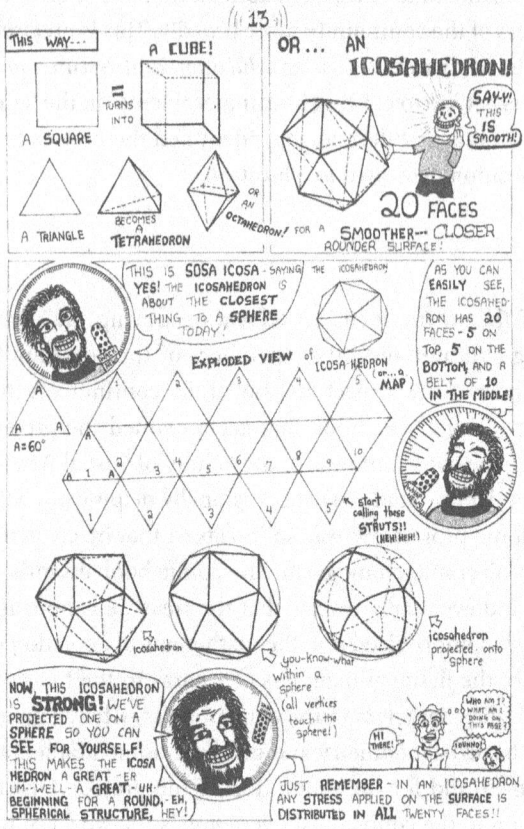

FIGURE 3. *Dome Land* Comic as Educational Tool
Source: John Holmstrom and Charas, Inc., *Dome Land* (1974), 13, Box 4, FP.

This comic was used as an educational tool, which is why it includes several pages of mathematical instructions and explanations (see figure 3). While García admitted in a letter to the DJB Foundation that the comic's "technical descriptions of dome design should be more detailed," it nevertheless served Charas well as a narrative-driven textbook, promotional material, and a small source of income—Charas acquired $175 through sales.[33] Primarily, though, it was used as a didactic tool in weekly dome-building workshops at the Charas loft on Cherry Street as well as at a project in the Bronx with Junior High School 148 and Grade School 110.[34] According to a letter from García to Eileen Fox of the Bankers Trust Company, a private funding sponsor, the Bronx dome project with schools from district 9 was a "prelude to mass-production of domes in the following year for recreation and classroom use."[35] The comic was designed to directly help teach math to school children via a practical tool. Charas members established the workshop at their loft to teach new members and community residents about geodesic domes and dome mathematics. The first session was held between October and December 1974, and almost a dozen participants engaged with this process, which provided opportunity for another session that was planned for early 1975.[36] As in any classroom lesson, Charas provided students with desk spaces and geometry tools, which are also shown in the comic book. Unlike a classroom situation, however, Charas tied the lessons to a practical project when students and veteran Charas members designed greenhouse domes for the community garden at East Houston Street and Bowery. These domes opened in 1973 and were the first urban community garden in New York. Unlike the first prototype domes, this greenhouse dome design required a different structure to serve as an actual greenhouse, which is why Charas members built a pipe dome with clear plastic vinyl for optimal lighting. In a letter to the DJB Foundation, García mentioned that this greenhouse had already been used "for two months and the plants are growing well inside it."[37]

Combining creative education through a more accessible—and joyful—form (the comic) and practical education through hands-on work, Charas members were able to provide local residents with educational lessons that were more relevant and engaging than similar public school subjects. Nevertheless, Charas members fully embraced their new identity as an organization dedicated to researching alternative solutions for urban space and housing. They undertook the dome project because it exemplified a great "productive use of empty space in the city," and because it gave students an immediate sense of achievement that served a vital purpose for their community—and maybe even for their own friends or families.[38] Additionally, Charas built twenty-eight pipe domes for festivals and theater events in the summer of 1974, twenty-four of which were constructed via a contract with the Department of Cultural Affairs.[39] Charas achieved all of this with just five full-time workers and twenty full-time Neighborhood Youth Corps volunteers. Beyond these dome building projects in New York, Charas also engaged in dome-building projects in the Puerto Rican cities Utuado, Cayey, and Playa de Ponce. Charas worked directly with families in these cities to build domes for residential purposes, rather than just for shelter, urban gardening, or cultural events.[40] This use of domes for residential purposes on the island was Charas's intention from the beginning. The organization envisioned the domes as affordable living spaces set among free and public green spaces on the island of Puerto Rico.

While their vision turned into reality for some families in Puerto Rico, domes never became permanent homes that would fully replace apartments or flats in brownstones. More than anything, domes served as symbols that united members of the community—especially Puerto Ricans, other Latino groups, and African Americans—who were tired of absentee landlords and deteriorating properties. Many Loisaidans embraced the idea of the dome to escape the fluctuations of the real estate market and urban renewal patterns that displaced them in favor of young urban professionals and the white middle class. The dome was a tangible and visible symbol of Charas's protest against economic and political forces that threatened to erode their homes on the Lower East Side. Although building permits, land development regulations, and lack of open space in Loisaida prevented Charas from turning the ferro-cement dome into new homes, it found other uses for the domes, as described above, that still served the people of Loisaida even if just as a symbol of pride and protest from which they could draw strength for future initiatives.

During their immediate efforts following this project, Charas members began seeing themselves as an organization rather than just a temporary group for a one-time project. Following the summer of 1974, when Charas built twenty-eight domes across the city, the group reflected on how to become a more efficient organization. As García detailed in his report to the DJB Foundation: "We must develop a mechanism for sharing tasks and work. . . . We lack administrative skills. . . . We lack technical skills. . . . Research of Charas is not articulated."[41] Charas members recognized that they were not yet qualified enough to properly run a nonprofit organization. They particularly required more knowledge of how to raise funds, manage a budget, divide workload, and present their organization's identity and services. This is where their connection with Seven Loaves becomes apparent. Seven Loaves was an administrative superstructure—made up of various cultural organizations throughout its lifespan starting in 1973—that offered workshops and training on how to run a business (for example, planning, budgeting, staff structure, and fund-raising). As one of the founding members, Charas developed a plan with Seven Loaves staff to train Charas members in marketing, fund-raising, bookkeeping, and other administrative tasks from September to December 1975. A detailed outline of the schedule in the report to the DJB Foundation lists items such as creating bylaws, learning about tax exemption for nonprofit organizations, developing an annual administrative calendar for meetings, and developing publicity and brand materials. Charas members were interested early on in building bridges with other community organizations, which

initiated the start of a more developed strategy for a functioning activist network in the neighborhood.

Another early example of network building involved Adopt a Building
(AAB), which helped provide extra space for Charas at 519 East 11th Street.
This place was used as living space, just like the loft at Cherry Street, but
also as a functional space for training workshops and meetings. In return,
two Charas members worked "on the building as volunteers," helping AAB
with renovations.[42] It is precisely this strategy of building activist networks
with other organizations that defined Charas's work for the remainder of its
life on the Lower East Side. This strategy is also visible in the last letter to
Wilbur Ferry and Carol Bernstein Ferry in 1978, in which García mentioned
Charas's cooperation on environmental projects with the Youth Environmental Action (YEA), Loisaida Environmental Action Coalition (LEAC), and the
Plaza Cultural Area Development.[43] At that time in 1978, Charas branched
out into other environmental initiatives beyond domes, the biggest project
being a community recycling center at 340 8th Street between Avenues B
and C, which was a joint project with LEAC that marked a venture into fully
structured environmental education.

Pioneers of Urban Environmental Education

In 1978, the neighborhood magazine *Quality of Life in Loisaida*, which was
founded that same year, published a brief note entitled "Don't Waste Waste,"
which announced the opening of a neighborhood recycling center on East
8th Street.[44] The idea was to inspire cleaner streets by encouraging the community to recycle certain items in containers that were to be positioned on
each block. As an intermediary, the center organized recycling efforts in the
neighborhood, and the profits made from selling paper, glass, aluminum, and
steel were intended to raise funds for community projects.[45] As with the dome
project, Charas employed a layered form of activism that served multiple purposes at the same time. It raised funds (for community projects, not for salaries), solved basic neighborhood problems by removing garbage on streets,
and engaged and inspired the community to improve the neighborhood by
supporting a recycling center "where not only our garbage, but our spirit is
recycled," as an editorial in *Quality of Life in Loisaida* stated.[46] Renovation
work on the garage space at 430 East 8th Street and lack of funding delayed
the opening of the center. Yet the September 1979 issue finally celebrated the
opening of the center, which essentially operated as a fully functional garbage

recycling facility with its own machine to crush aluminum cans. Although Charas remained the driving force for the project, the center was technically spearheaded by LEAC, which consisted of Charas and two other groups operating in the neighborhood and working on environmental projects ranging from finding alternative energy sources to urban gardening: Cuando and the 11th Street Movement.

The community center Cuando was founded in 1971 in tribute to Paul Goodman, who inspired children from lower-income families with his alternative educational model at the First Street School. The 11th Street Movement was essentially a homesteading and building-management group that took over abandoned buildings on East 11th Street with the help of AAB. Although these were separate organizations working on different projects and issues throughout the Lower East Side, their shared goals meant sporadic cooperation, such as the recycling center for which LEAC received a grant of $94,000 from the National Center for Appropriate Technology.[47] Although Charas introduced this trend of environmental activism into the neighborhood with its dome project, both Cuando and the 11th Street Movement had their own projects that stood out as pioneering efforts in Loisaida's environmental movement of the 1970s and 1980s. Members of Charas, Cuando, AAB, and the 11th Street Movement became the pioneering urban environmentalists of New York, focused on solving basic neighborhood problems on the Lower East Side through an environmentally sustainable lens.

One of Cuando's most important projects was a solar wall—another symbol of the environmental movement at the local level. Cuando received money in 1975 from the National Center for Appropriate Technology in Butte, Montana, to develop "energy-related projects, including a passive solar wall" for its building at 92nd Avenue.[48] As a report by the Solar Energy Research Institute (SERI) of the U.S. Department of Energy notes, "The wall was designed by the Energy Task Force and constructed by Youth Corps workers as part of a summer work program sponsored by Cuando."[49] A memorandum to President Jimmy Carter from Graciela Olivarez, director of the Community Services Administration (CSA), in 1978 further indicates that it was New York's first passive solar wall and that the summer project involved black and Puerto Rican young people of the neighborhood.[50] As a passive solar wall, it required no electrical input and was used to heat the building in the winter while keeping the gym cool in the summer. This project provided a low-maintenance, self-help solution to a poorly insulated building in the area—as was typical for houses built in the early twentieth century—and it was wrapped in a well-coordinated program to teach young people practical skills. According to a report on U.S. solar energy development, the designer from the Energy Task Force (ETF), Ted Finch, in cooperation with Cuando personnel Fred Cabrera and Richard Cleghourne, gave a summer-long seminar on energy alternatives attended by young people who put that knowledge into practice when they built the forty-seven-square-meter wall that stretched across the south side of the building between the second and third floors.[51] Although this was only one of various projects of the same ilk—an article in *Quality of Life in Loisaida* mentions Cuando's work with solar gardens—it demonstrated Cuando's strong commitment to both solving housing issues (insulation) and offering young people from the neighborhood a more engaging form of education.[52] Through both practical experience and theoretical lessons, young people were able to add substantially to their curricula vitae as well as recognize the power of community development through hands-on work. This had an immediate positive result on their own living situation as members of a community center that provided a safe space for after-school activities such as "tutorial schools, block parties and camping trips."[53]

While Buckminster Fuller played a large role in turning Charas and other community organizations onto the environmental track, the specific moment in time in the 1970s and 1980s links their environmental projects to a national—even global—concern for the environment. This grew out of the 1960s and 1970s countercultural movements across the United States and such European countries as Germany and the United Kingdom. While many ecological philosophies merely treated symptoms to protect and preserve wildlife—the dominant philosophy being deep ecology—Charas became interested in social ecology, an environmental philosophy built on an anticapitalist foundation. Murray Bookchin, lifelong advocate of anarchism, socialism, and communalism, formulated this philosophy in 1965 with his essay "Ecology and Revolutionary Thought" in the libertarian-socialist periodical *Comment*. In another essay entitled "What Is Social Ecology," published posthumously in the book *Social Ecology and Communalism* (2007), Bookchin reaffirms his position on a movement he started half a century earlier. Social ecology, unlike its defiantly biocentric cousins, "is based on the conviction that nearly all of our present ecological problems originate in deep-seated social problems."[54] For Bookchin, social ecology is well equipped as a critical movement and philosophy to get at the root causes that have affected capitalist societies, such as "trade for profit, industrial expansion for its own sake, and the identification of progress with corporate self-interest."[55] Although social ecology is an admirable environmental philosophy, in its rightful critique that capitalism has transformed from an economic model into a model for organizing one's entire life, the following quote summing up social ecology's mission exposes its utopian nature: "[Social ecology] challenges the entire system of domination itself—its economy, its misuse of technics, its administrative apparatus, its degradation of political life, its destruction of the city as a center of cultural development, indeed the entire panoply of its moral hypocrisies and defiling of the human spirit—and seeks to eliminate the hierarchical and class edifices that have imposed themselves on humanity and defined the relationship between nonhuman and human nature."[56] Bookchin essentially called for the "decentralization of cities into confederally united communities," otherwise known as communalism.[57] However, it is no wonder that Bookchin admits in *The Ecology of Freedom: The Emergence and Dissolution of Hierarchy* (1982) that social ecology is "a radical *utopian* alternative . . . to the present social and environmental crisis."[58] Social ecology's very core goals as both a movement and critique rest on a reversal of capitalism to communalism, a reversal of population growth, a reversal of cities to smaller towns, indeed a reversal of time itself. As naturalist and lifelong pragmatic conservationist Edward O. Wilson puts it so simply, "The world economy is now propelled by venture and technical innovation; it *cannot be returned to a pastoral civilization*."[59] Despite this insurmountable gap between social ecology as a critical theory and social ecology as a new paradigm for societal organization around the globe, its utopian nature does not make it obsolete— far from it. As with the dome project and Buckminster Fuller's vision, Charas found social ecology useful, to some degree, in supporting its own urban environmentalist strategy for Loisaida. Bookchin argues that the "'struggle for existence' . . . explains why increasingly subjective and more flexible beings are capable of addressing environmental change more effectively."[60] Puerto Ricans and African Americans struggled for existence against a backdrop of rampant property abandonment, economic neglect, and cultural discrimination. Charas and other activist organizations fully embraced the idea that they *could* reclaim space in Loisaida and change their environment to reflect their vision of a better life, which is why they initiated projects that gave them more control over neighborhood space and their own lives in general, such as functional community gardens, self-made domes, and small-scale sustainable energy.

The story of the recycling center resembles that of the first erected cardboard dome on Cherry Street in one tragic way: it also burned down in an unknown fire. As with the dome, rather than giving up, Charas went right back to work, attracting funding from various sources such as the Trust for Public

Lands, NYU Graduate School of Business Administration, and the National Consumer Cooperative Bank to repurpose the center as "industrial shop space for carpentry/cabinet making, theatrical scenery shop, and a building supplies cooperative."[61] Before it burned down in 1982, the repurposed center operated for almost three years at 340 East 8th Street and, according to the outline for redevelopment after the fire, employed three paid workers alongside a host of volunteering neighborhood kids and members. In fact, "Requests for warehouse space soon out-grew our storage capacity," as the outline notes. It was a successful project that served its community members by cleaning up streets and giving young people a place to gather useful skills, but it also served community groups such as the city-sponsored Operation Green Thumb, which worked throughout the city on projects for greening urban spaces. Charas, along with members and friends of Cuando, demonstrated its forward-thinking environmental strategies and inspired the neighborhood to recycle its garbage long before the rest of New York caught on.[62] More important, the recycling center represented a more structured version of combining education and environmental concerns. Alongside the center, Charas developed two interesting projects on environmental education: the Charas Bi-lingual Environmental Education Center and the Environmental Internship Program. Both projects were closely linked, being conceived around the same time in early 1979, but also unique in their own right.

In early 1979, Charas and Cuando member, musician, and community activist Edgard Rivera took over responsibilities to coordinate an environmental education program. He submitted an application form to the Department of Health, Education, and Welfare—specifically the Bureau of Elementary and Secondary Education in the Office of Education—to establish the Charas Bi-lingual Environmental Education Center. In essence, as his letter to the bureau indicates, "a core staff member [would] be responsible for coordinating the development of learning programs and materials and involving community residents through the implementation of workshops and the creation of a quarterly environmental newsletter and bi-lingual environmental workshop manuals."[63] As with many similar projects discussed in this book, the center also emphasized "self-help and education as a means for altering these conditions [poverty, housing disinvestment, and monolingual education]."[64] Rivera stressed another hallmark of their community activism: using successful projects and people from the community "as catalysts to encourage and help others."[65] Charas members were these catalysts, as demonstrated by their inclusion of "youth at all levels of program planning and implementation."[66] The proposal lists all the objectives of this program, quoted here in full to give a complete picture of their well-structured education efforts for the community:

1. To develop awareness in the community of the need for environmental action, which can serve as a base for a community conservation program,
2. To motivate community residents to become more aware of and directly involved in environmental action and conservation through the use of media and educational projects,
3. To demonstrate practical means for using community resources for neighborhood conservation and environmental action,
4. To develop a bilingual curriculum dealing with environmental issues, which is relevant and useful for community application,
5. To help community residents plan and administer environmental projects such as recycling centers, community gardens, alternative structures, alternative approaches to the use and distribution of energy and neighborhood park revitalization programs,
6. To integrate environmental concerns with existing and future community planning efforts.[67]

Again, Charas aspired to fight on several fronts by trying to engage the community, offer an alternative education for young people, and investigate solutions to alternative uses of urban space, all with a focus on environmental concerns. This proposal, one of the earliest examples found in the Charas archival collection, also lists the organizations Charas worked with at the time: AAB, LEAC, the 11th Street Movement, and Cuando. Even though some aspects of the Charas Bi-lingual Environmental Education Center never saw the light of day (the quarterly newsletter and the neighborhood directory), it nevertheless enabled Charas to continue to provide alternative means of education and hands-on experience to community children at elementary and secondary school levels.[68]

The second program Charas developed was an Environmental Internship Program for the summer of 1979. As program coordinator, Chino García sent out letters requesting funding from various organizations such as the Ford Foundation, the Field Foundation, and the Robert F. Kennedy Memorial. As García wrote in a letter to the Vincent Astor Foundation, the funds would be used "on partial scholarships and living stipends for a group of five (5) inner-city and low-income Puerto Rican youth to attend the Social Ecology Educational Program of Goddard College in Plainfield, Vermont," Bookchin's institute.[69] With this proposal, Charas expanded its program of using a growing concern for the environment to provide new and engaging opportunities for young people from the neighborhood to do something positive with their lives. As stated in the proposal, the participants in this twelve-week program "would be earning 15 credits towards their Bachelor's degrees and receive training in the emerging fields of social ecology and appropriate technology," but, as García stressed, they would give back to their community by working there, "sharing their knowledge, and helping *reconstruct through productive work*."[70] The courses that Goddard offered for the internship seemed to be tailor-made for Charas's work in Loisaida: "Solar Energy, Wind, Power, Aquaculture, Agriculture, Nutrition, Health Care Ecology, Sociology, Anthropology and Community Development."[71] When participants returned to the neighborhood, Charas had planned volunteer positions for them at the recycling center, community gardens, and solar energy projects that Charas and LEAC were involved in.[72]

A Model for Urban Community Engagement

By giving young people from their neighborhood opportunities to attend a professional educational program at a nationally renowned institute, while at the same time expecting the participants to return to and invest in their own neighborhood, Charas established itself as a pioneering, environmentally conscious group. In fact, García wrote that Charas envisioned this program, much like the center, as "a model for other inner-city neighborhoods, both in New York City and around the country, that are fighting urban decay."[73] It is unclear and doubtful if Charas members ever actively promoted their model to other urban neighborhoods facing similar issues since they had more than enough problems to fix in their own neighborhood. Furthermore, Charas entered a transitional state at the end of the 1970s as it acquired its future headquarters El Bohío and expanded primarily into cultural and artistic community activism. Nevertheless, Charas and other organizations in Loisaida, such as AAB, served as models for other neighborhoods. Their narrow focus on one neighborhood on the Lower East Side allowed them to maximize success within their own community. This early phase during the 1970s enabled Charas to develop key sustainable strategies for its community activism. It expanded upon youth engagement and the human right to the city while taking major steps toward building a large network of Loisaida community groups on the understanding that coalitions forged more organized neighborhoods.

While Charas approached housing issues in Loisaida through a visionary (geodesic dome) and environmental (recycling) approach, it was AAB that contributed directly to the improvement of real homes in the 1970s. AAB was involved in a range of key housing projects that ranged from general information on how to heat water in winter to housing rehabilitation. It helped advocate for tenants' rights, organized buildings and streets to work together against absentee landlords, renovated apartments, supported the squatter movement, and pioneered a program on sweat equity homesteading chosen by the federal Department of Housing and Urban Development as a model for low-income urban communities. Like Charas, AAB was a major force in the community in the 1970s, adopting to the rapidly changing housing and real estate laws as New York was undergoing a financial crisis. AAB's work demonstrates what the *human* right to the city looks like and how residents can be the architects of their own vision for urban living.

CHAPTER 3

Adopt a Building and
Sweat Equity Urbanism

> We chose to stand our ground. Because we know we've got to fight from here—we just
> can't permit (ourselves) to be shoved around from one community and one borough
> into another, one state into another . . . it's time to make a decision if we're going to let
> communities fall apart. That people are going to remain and care enough to continue to
> save their roots . . . their culture . . . and the places where they live.
> —Roberto Nazario (1977)

The New York of the 1970s was a city plagued by an unprecedented level of
housing abandonment and disinvestment both leading up to and following
the city's financial crisis in 1975. Vulnerable and poor neighborhoods such as
Harlem, South Bronx, Williamsburg, Bedford-Stuyvesant, and the Lower East
Side suffered the most. In the midst of this citywide housing crisis, one local
newspaper in Loisaida proclaimed a "Miracle on Avenue C," according to a
headline in the paper's summer issue of 1980.[1] For the largely Puerto Rican
and low-income community in this neighborhood, the process of rehabilitating a building that had been abandoned by its landlord was regarded as a
miracle. By 1980, nineteen of twenty-four apartments at 55 Avenue C, in the
heart of Loisaida, were already completely renovated thanks to tenant and
housing activist Emma Acevado, who worked together with one of the city's
most successful self-help housing organizations: Adopt a Building (AAB).
After the landlord abandoned the building in 1975, discontinuing necessary
maintenance and repair as well as heat and hot water, Acevado organized the
tenants and urged them to stop paying rent. As she recounts in a documentary
on housing efforts in Loisaida, the landlord "threatened to evict us if we did
not pay the rent. . . . I explained to the tenants what rights protected us, for
them not to be afraid. To talk to me if they had problems."[2] Eventually, the
landlord asked Acevado if she would adopt him as well, which meant to live

in the building and contribute to the rehabilitation that followed in the next few years.

As if fighting landlords and dealing with city agencies were not difficult enough for community activists like Emma or groups like AAB, the real obstacle was widespread apathy and hopelessness among residents of Loisaida—something RGS and Charas prioritized in their work as well. Juan Colón, a tenant in 55 Avenue C, described how he turned from apathetic tenant to housing activist:

> I felt the meetings were just talk. They had no strength. I became interested when they began talking about my apartment because I did not have any essential services. My kids were young and they can easily catch pneumonia. So I asked questions and began learning from Emma. She explained what we could do for the building until I fell in love with this movement. . . . Now we are united. If something breaks we fix it. Soon we will put in a new roof. We feel safe. Lately I feel very happy. We can be united. Why shouldn't we be united? Together we can accomplish many things.[3]

In another building, 219 East 4th Street, tenant and community activist Alfredo Irizarry echoed Juan's words: "I just wanted to be part of something. . . . I was tired of moving from district to district. . . . I had never had no confidence in myself. A lot of the times I felt like I was not needed you know? But here I kinda find a sense of need."[4] How did AAB and associated activist groups instill this sense of being needed in Loisaida residents and what became of this burgeoning tenant movement? While RGS and Charas involved residents in educational, cultural, and environmental projects, AAB led grassroots housing projects in various areas of Loisaida. Rather than being equally as important as education centers and cultural programs, it is clear that housing was the key arena for Loisaida activists to unlock a much more wide-scale participation rate among the distressed residents of this neighborhood—at least during the 1970s. This chapter covers the emergence of AAB and focuses on a few specific projects on 11th Street that demonstrate the model of sweat equity, resident-led, and socially engaged housing that AAB envisioned for Loisaida.

Unlike issues such as education, environmental sustainability, and poverty, which the previous two chapters cover, housing was by no means a new space of urban struggle and grassroots action. Tenants worldwide have historically fought for their homes and their rights to fair maintenance, rent, and quality of living. Manuel Castells provides an overview of the Glasgow rent strike of 1915, which included "tenants' committees and women's associations, with the full support of trade unions and left wing parties."[5] There is clear agreement among historians that the rent strike in Glasgow "was organized, led, and enacted by women."[6] Across the Atlantic, New York saw its own rent strike in 1907 with such activists as Pauline Newman, housewives, and the International Ladies' Garment Workers' Union at the helm. Once again, this was a working-class movement organized primarily by women. Clearly, women have played important roles in rent strikes and tenant movements over the past century: from female prostitutes in the Veracruz working-class neighborhood of La Huaca in Mexico in 1922 to the marches of pregnant women in Barcelona's 1931 mass rent strikes.

As such, Loisaida's tenant activism is far from a historical exception; in fact, the urban crisis of the 1960s and 1970s produced many local tenant movements, often led by African Americans. While such organizers as Jesse Gray receive a prominent spot in the scholarship of 1960s and 1970s tenant activism, historians have excavated the leadership roles of women in rent strikes, such as Julia Rabig's study of Newark and Rhonda Y. Williams's study of Baltimore.[7] The work of AAB and Emma Acevado, among others, is both another moment in the long-standing tradition of women-led, working-class tenant activism and another underappreciated campaign of women-led tenant activism in the 1960s and 1970s specifically. Where Loisaida departs from other historical rent strikes or from the tenant struggles of these two decades is the pragmatism of sweat equity urbanism and the intersectionality of housing activism with the environmental movement. Unlike other historical tenant movements, Loisaida residents needed to transform their tactics and organizing strategies to handle the various phases of tenant struggles for this neighborhood from the urban decay of the 1960s to the urban renewal of the 1980s: from tenant organizing and do-it-yourself urbanism (both with and without the help of the city, depending on the administration's politics) to creative antigentrification campaigns and protest marches. Despite the eventual fading away of AAB in the 1980s, this group sparked flames across the neighborhood and produced the foundation for squatters and antigentrification struggles in the 1980s and 1990s.

The Early Years of Adopt a Building

So, who was AAB and how did it get started? The most discernible fact about the history of AAB was that it started out as a 1968 project called One Hundred Worst Buildings of East Harlem. The project, which surveyed deteriorating buildings in another key Puerto Rican neighborhood at the time, was spearheaded by William "Bill" Eddy. The aim was to restore essential services such as hot water and heat to buildings. The project quickly spread to other areas of New York, such as the Bronx and Loisaida. In a speech at Temple Shaaray Tefila in 1971, Eddy articulated what became a core tenet of the group then called Interfaith Adopt a Building: "One day soon, the issue of community control will reassert itself, stronger, more vibrant, and more urgent. I hope that community control will mean local ownership of land, at least as far as housing is concerned."[8] However, Eddy, who later became a Christian minister, claimed, "There is no greater source for this today than that which emanates from our religious institutions." While the civil rights movement had certainly proven the effectiveness and strength of churches in activist efforts, Eddy quickly found himself in a situation where he decided to resign his directorship of AAB due to major differences in direction and philosophy for the organization between himself and colleagues Ruth García and Ibis Marrero.

Both Marrero and García, organizers for AAB in Loisaida, opposed the rapid growth and centralization of AAB within New York. By the time Eddy resigned in November 1973, there had been many issues with internal communication between the local offices and the central headquarters. According to notes taken by a university student who worked with AAB for a few years, "Ibis especially complained that she worked nights and weekends. . . . Bill occasionally takes long weekends, however, and Ibis felt that this was not fair."[9] Aside from personal issues between Marrero and Eddy, Marrero and García also desired more control and independence for the local offices, which finally led to Bill's realization that "his position was no longer viable."[10] This student learned in an interview with Marrero that she grew up in Puerto Rico and came to New York in the late 1960s. Her mother was religious while her father was secular, and she "seemed to find it easier to accept a person [her father] who was self aware than one whose beliefs and actions were contradictory."[11] At the time, Eddy was training to become a minister and had not visited tenants for a while, so it is plausible that Marrero saw Eddy as too "paternalistic [like] missionaries who went out from England and the USA to the rest of the world to carry the true word to the natives."[12]

In essence, Marrero took issue with what she recognized as a growing humanitarian trend of AAB's work ethic and methodology. Rather than tenants and local organizers deciding what was best for each area and building, the central office put forth its plan of action to be adopted across all areas. After Eddy resigned, though he sporadically continued to attend meetings as a friend and adviser, AAB dropped the word "Interfaith" in its title and rescaled efforts to Loisaida, effectively terminating the office in East Harlem. In its new form, AAB stopped advertising that it worked in over 120 buildings—a number greatly embellished by Eddy—and instead focused only on what the organization could realistically accomplish.[13] This mirrors the struggles RGS went through as its members scaled back their mission to focus on achievable goals in their home neighborhood. However, Marrero decided to stay in Puerto Rico after her honeymoon at the end of 1973, and Ruth García became the new director of AAB alongside her future husband, Roberto "Rabbit" Nazario.[14] This first phase in isolation only tells the story of a community organization in flux, figuring out its philosophy, activist methodology, and overall mission and area of operations. Like RGS and Charas, AAB tried to find the best, most sustainable way to serve the tenants of Loisaida's run-down buildings. It demonstrates the desire of Puerto Rican activists in Loisaida to gain more control and involve tenants in organizing activities. Instead of a top-down, humanitarian housing organization, Loisaida representatives wanted AAB to function as a participatory, grassroots group of neighborhood activists and residents.

This first phase of the beginnings of AAB, more isolated and internal, does not, however, fully explain the reasons for a shift toward neighborhood control over a citywide movement. It also does not explain AAB's focus on tackling apathy and hopelessness among residents—to organize and unite them. It is necessary to consider what was already happening in Loisaida, chiefly the efforts of RGS and Charas. AAB organizer Roberto Nazario was involved with RGS, and the story of RGS was certainly known to members of AAB, some of whom came directly from RGS. While the story of the University of the Streets served as a lesson for AAB to limit its actions to a manageable area of operations, Charas's dome project, which was being worked on at the same time as AAB moved toward its big split from the citywide work, demonstrated to the community and its organizers that tackling apathy and inspiring hope needed to be vital parts of any grassroots campaign—including housing. As AAB outlined in its program proposal for 1974: "Since the first winter of 1970 the character of the program has undergone some major changes in the midst of the housing movement in New York. Where we once saw the problem in terms of buildings and lack of services, we now see the attitude of tenants as the major factor in stopping deterioration and providing services."[15] Understanding AAB as not just originating from a religious project on housing in East Harlem but also providing a new climate of hope and action in Loisaida demonstrates the close ties of activists and community groups within Loisaida. AAB made Loisaida its main area precisely because that was where "tenants [had] expressed the most courage in fighting to save their buildings and the future of their neighborhood."[16] In this light, AAB was not just another short-lived and single-issue activist group but, instead, represented one node in a much larger network of sustainable activist organizations in Loisaida during the 1970s and 1980s. Created as a single-issue housing project in East Harlem, AAB and its members quickly became leading activists working on community gardens, playgrounds, parks, murals, and economic revitalization.

How to Adopt a Building

At the outset, in the early 1970s, AAB was chiefly involved in emergency repair programs and working with individual tenants or tenant groups to organize against absentee landlords. According to a description of AAB programs from 1973, "the role of the Adopt-a-Building neighborhood coordinator becomes paramount. He is the person who first responds to a building situation, analyzes it, trains and places a team. . . . It is also the coordinator who develops local resources represented by legal programs, welfare, fire and Emergency Repair."[17] Informing tenants of their legal rights, through the city's Emergency Repair Program (ERP), for example, AAB trained tenants such as Acevado not to passively accept the behavior of absentee landlords but to resist through actions such as withholding rent or going to court for emergency repairs. In the short term, AAB even provided workshops, flyers, and other material to inform tenants, using platforms such as the neighborhood magazine *Quality of Life in Loisaida*. While AAB took on more responsibilities throughout the 1970s and early 1980s, providing residents with do-it-yourself tips, including the use of comic strips humorously called "Loisaida Adventures," became a consistent part of its mission to reach out to the community. The comic strips are especially reminiscent of Charas's *Dome Land* comic, which was also used as an educational tool with a strong dose of humor.

Despite being made up of neighborhood residents, AAB members and coordinators could by no means assume all tenants would just open their doors to them. In a flyer targeted at potential coordinators, AAB stressed the social aspects of working with tenants: "The tenants do not know your motivation or capabilities. In many cases, you are the most recent in a long line of people who have tried to help them. Gaining trust and cooperation takes time and perseverance. . . . Building residents will cooperate with you and with one another to effect changes important to them."[18] The same flyer includes details about the ERP as well as the exact room numbers in the Surrogate

Court Building on Chambers Street where tenants could discuss their land-lord issues and how to adopt a building. This social aspect of gaining the trust of tenants and establishing a relationship with them, emphasizing how AAB could help each individual tenant specifically and not in an abstract sense, was paramount to its overall mission against decaying and rundown buildings. This is the same strategy used by Charas and RGS: to make their work *directly* relevant to residents and offer practical and achievable goals.

One of the earliest housing programs AAB used to directly support tenants was the Article 7A program (7A), part of the New York State Real Property Actions and Proceeding Law (RPAPL). This key program was added to the RPAPL "after successful lobbying by the New York City neighbourhood move-ment," which included AAB at this time.[19] In essence, this article allowed state courts to appoint administrators "to manage buildings where the landlord had failed to do so. This was adapted in the late 1970s to permit tenants living in the buildings to be appointed administrators following a short training run by HPD [the Department of Housing Preservation and Development]."[20] AAB took advantage of 7A to a great extent. Local housing activist Brent Shar-man wrote about one example of 7A action in *Quality of Life in Loisaida*. Patrick Crowe, landlord of 219 East 7th Street in 1978, did not provide heat for the building and demanded rent from tenants as usual. One of these tenants, Thamar Torres, refused to pay rent, and with the help of her mother, Alicia Torres, she contacted AAB's coordinator George Ortega to "document the bad conditions in the building and to go through the proper procedures for an Article 7A court action."[21] Other tenants in 219 feared eviction notices, but Ortega convinced them to go through with the rent strike. The strike was successful, and Crowe did not follow through with his eviction threats. The building went into tenant management, which essentially meant that Thamar Torres collected the rent as the building association's treasurer. The money was then reinvested into the building. This was a common model for success-ful 7A action. As Roberta Gold explains in *When Tenants Claimed the City* (2014), it only took a third of a building's tenants to prove dangerous condi-tions for five days to take advantage of 7A, which essentially "took away the landlord's authority to run the building."[22] In another article, Brent Sharman discussed the dissemination of AAB's work and mobilization with slogans painted on neighborhood walls ("No Heat No Rent") and the key position of AAB in this tenant movement for housing rights: "All tenants should read a small pamphlet called 'Organizing Your Building' published by Adopt-A-Building, 300 E. 4th St. (677–8700). This is the main housing organization in Loisaida."[23]

As these programs and stories suggest, AAB and similar housing organizations across the city and country were largely able to work with government agencies on local, state, and federal levels. They were able to take advantage of a brief period of pro-community and self-help programs designed to shift responsibility for rebuilding distressed areas to these areas themselves, many of which were already demanding more control. As Gold writes, New York "became the national capital of tenants' rights and a kind of *laboratory* for considering what American society might be like if homeownership did not prevail."[24] Fighting to preserve their homes—*mejore, no se mude*—AAB and Loisaida tenants developed, in their urban laboratory, what Gold calls a "distinctive concept of 'community rights,'" or the right to the city: "a kind of democratic say over the uses of capital to shape the urban environment and lives of its inhabitants."[25] Gold further writes:

> The tenants who fought for their homes in postwar New York left a complex legacy. It includes housing laws, rent regulations, and co-op programs that survive in weakened form to this day, making New York a place where working people and people of color still form a vital part of the city's social fabric. It also includes less tangible goods: a history of women's activism; an experience of multiracial and cross-class coalition; an expansive understanding of racial justice; a concept of citizenship based on human relationships rather than property ownership; and an urban vision that celebrates the intense forms of social interaction fostered by dense and diverse city neighborhoods.[26]

This all describes AAB's legacy as well, especially the part about women's activism. A publication by AAB titled "Case Studies for the Preparation of the International Study Day for a Society Overcoming Domination" highlights specifically why women were not just active participants but often leading organizers in this movement—in line with the tradition of women-led, working-class rent strikes over the twentieth century. Emma Acevado, Alicia Torres, and Ruth García are only three examples of this:

> Women, who have in general felt most forcefully the ills of our society: watching their children cold and sick in winter, seeing them go to school and not being educated, not being able to feed their children properly, being treated without dignity by the officials of the social welfare systems, having their men abandon them or be killed by the violence of the streets, drugs and/or alcohol, these women have been in the forefront of the struggle. They fight for bilingual education, are often the forces in the tenant's associations, Parent-Teacher Associations, and community garden projects.[27]

Although women were not as prominent in the earlier work of RGS and Charas, they certainly played key roles in the tenant movement, the mural movement, and the burgeoning cultural and artistic activity in Loisaida.

The remainder of this chapter specifically describes AAB's work with regard to the last two legacy goods Gold identifies: a concept of citizenship based on human relationships and an urban vision that celebrates social interaction. Taken together, these two aspects of AAB's work represent an important strand of sustainable activism: the human right to the city. Suffering the exact same problems as most Loisaida tenants who it ended up helping, AAB became acutely aware of what it was up against in trying to overcome domination:

> We are a community of marginal importance to our society. [We] all share the same problems: landlords who charge high rents for rat-filled, unkept housing with no heat/hot water; lack of education and a system of education which is not bilingual; drugs and alcohol used as escapes from the pressures of life; people who become accustomed to having no rights, being powerless, and victims of every indignity that our society lays on the poor, treating them as nonentities. On the positive side, we have, in the last 5 years witnessed a growing sense of history, pride and community. We now have community leaders [and] tenants are becoming aware of their rights as people.[28]

This was AAB's mission: to make residents aware of their *human* right to the city, their right to be the architects of their own future in Loisaida, their rights as American citizens.

The Tenants of 11th Street

"Their efforts are futile ... they will continue to suffer."[29] According to AAB, this was the response of real estate tycoon Irving Dankner when he met with AAB to discuss the lack of repairs in some of Dankner's buildings—including 509 and 519 East 11th Street. Dankner already had a record of more than sixty years of real estate work when he "watched his empire dwindle from 60 to ten apartment houses, mostly from abandonment or fires."[30] AAB revealed that Dankner owned thirty-four buildings in the Lower East Side alone and purportedly owed around $350,000 on these buildings as well as potentially being a suspect of tax evasion.[31] Tenants in these buildings were not organized and had to endure the suffering as Dankner collected rent but refused to maintain the properties. AAB came along and, not satisfied with Dankner's attitude, made a deal with the city's Department of Real Estate to turn a select number of buildings into co-ops.[32] This included 217 and 519 East 11th Street. Properties with large amounts of unpaid taxes would normally be auctioned off during New York's fiscal crisis years, when the city sped up the process to force tax payment from three years to one year. However, as Susan Baldwin wrote for the major housing magazine *City Limits*, "This policy precipitated a flood not of tax payments but of unwanted property coming into city ownership within the past year [1978]. At the same time, tenant groups have demanded a halt to the city's traditional way of disposing of such property—the auction, on ground that the auction perpetuates slumlords and produces little revenue and less taxes."[33] AAB members were no fans of auctions either, which is why they stepped in and led pilot projects, with funds provided by the city, to coordinate an alternative plan to improve the buildings on 11th Street. Thus began the story of the 11th Street Movement and its grassroots, tenant-led efforts to improve the housing stock on East 11th Street, mobilize residents to fight for their rights as tenants, and become a model action movement that promoted an alternative vision for human-oriented—not profit-oriented—urban living: sweat equity urbanism.

AAB was one of two organizations in New York working together with the federal Department of Housing and Urban Development (HUD) to push through their shared vision of housing reform, as a letter from HUD to Mayor Abraham Beame shows:

> The Department of Housing and Urban Development has received an unsolicited proposal from the Urban Homesteading Assistance Board [UHAB] and two New York City Neighborhood-based Housing Organizations requesting a demonstration of sweat equity homesteading of multiple dwellings. This proposal envisions the use of City job-training programs, under Title I of the Comprehensive Deployment and Training Act, Federal Section 312 rehabilitation loans and private financial sector participation in the self help renovation of abandoned, City-held properties, thereby joining together the resources of HUD, the City of New York and community residents to create much needed low-income cooperative housing.[34]

This demonstration was supposed to take two years beginning in 1975 but ended up showcasing its significance for dealing with the housing crisis. Even as New York plunged into a deeper fiscal crisis, "sweat equity homesteading survived," according to a report by UHAB in 1977.[35] Sweat equity projects—a type of paid, grassroots housing development pioneered by AAB that allowed tenants and neighborhood residents to use their own labor to rehabilitate a building—increased in the midst of New York's financial problems. In her study of homesteading between 1978 and 1993, Malve von Hassell notes that "the homesteading model envisioned that labor would be treated not as a commodity but as a community property to be shared and made available to those in need."[36] However, von Hassell also points out that homesteading is intrinsically "a fragile process of realizing an idea of home or even community in the face of overwhelming external constraints and internal fragmentation."[37] Communities are not static entities like real estate developers or construction companies. They are not bound together by a drive for profit; they are fluid and ever changing. Decentralizing housing rehabilitation to such a large degree comes with at least three requirements: dedicated groups at the local level that have the trust and respect of the neighborhood, support from the city administration, and a steady flow of funds (local, state, and federal). This triangle of complex relationships worked—for the most part—for a brief period in the 1970s. Both the city and HUD committed three million dollars in rehabilitation loan funds. UHAB played the role of a facilitator between neighborhood groups, the city, and HUD. UHAB operated citywide just as AAB did in the beginning; however, unlike AAB's early organizational strategy, UHAB did not interfere directly with the decisions made at the neighborhood level—allowing groups such as AAB to carry out their work while pushing funding and administrative tasks up to a centralized entity.

As mentioned already, AAB worked on numerous properties in Loisaida, but East 11th Street stands out in particular for two reasons: rehabilitation on this street became the de facto model for sweat equity programs, and efforts on this street heavily emphasized the need to go beyond housing-specific issues. East 11th Street was one of the four original homesteading areas, and a graphic produced by AAB shows the concentration of green spaces, renewable energy sites, tenant management, and gut rehabilitation on this block alone. While there are many buildings that illustrate the significance of this street as a model for future projects, number 519 has left the biggest legacy in archival records and newspaper articles. According to a newspaper article from February 11, 1977, number 519 incurred thirteen fires within just three weeks in 1972, a common method to drive out tenants and clear a building.[38] The landlord soon abandoned the building, as many other landlords did for over thirty thousand buildings across New York in just this year. The property was turned over to the city, which enabled a neighborhood group called 11th Street Movement to purchase it in 1974 as part of a loan of $177,000 from the city's self-help housing programs. The majority of the loan was used to pay wages. The group essentially used their own labor to renovate and manage the building. They replaced the early twentieth-century railroad flats with regularly spaced apartments suitable for families, transformed ground floor space into store fronts for community businesses, and overhauled heating and electricity.

The previous chapter describes the activities of the Energy Task Force (ETF) in this area with the building of the Cuando solar wall, and ETF continued its efforts in Loisaida by working with the 11th Street Movement on another iconic and pioneering project: an urban windmill. The Community Services Administration (CSA), a residue of President Johnson's Great Society programs, once again provided the funds for the project, establishing the CSA as an important funding source for Loisaida during this time. An article in *Suburban News* from 1977 explains that this fourteen-foot, three-bladed windmill on top of number 519 was erected to provide two thousand watts of electricity to the thirty-three tenants in the building (see figure 4).[39] Sarah Ferguson, in an article on housing and squatting, points out that the 11th Street Movement was founded by residents and activists from East 11th Street who "teamed up with Interfaith Adopt-a-Building" to work on environmental projects.[40] In fact, an article in a special issue of *WIN Magazine* on Loisaida quotes Chino García, who said that the windmill project was initiated by Charas and AAB, which shows the easy flow of personnel from one organization

FIGURE 4. Windmill on Top of 519 East 11th Street
Source: Travis Price, "The Almost Forgotten Story of the 1970s East Village Windmill," *Gothamist*, September 29, 2014.

to the other.[41] For this particular project, Ted Finch worked alongside architect Travis Price and the 11th Street Movement to get people and children from the neighborhood to erect a large, antiquated windmill and transform it into a cheap and sustainable source of electricity for lower-income families in this building.[42] It was the first windmill of its kind in an urban environment in the United States, putting the 11th Street Movement at the forefront of urban environmental activism alongside Charas and Cuando.[43]

The project also made it into the 1978 documentary *Viva Loisaida*, in which the physical object of the windmill, looming large over the rooftops of Loisaida, "has grown to be a symbol of self-help."[44] Eduardo Standard, business director at ETF, even jokes in the documentary that there are three power companies in New York: "there is Con Ed in Manhattan, there's the Brooklyn power company Brooklyn Union Gas in Brooklyn, and there's a windmill here on 519 East 11th Street."[45] Here, the aspiration to rival these corporate companies that were solely concerned with profits led such groups as ETF and AAB to offer affordable alternatives for lower-income neighborhoods. As with the mass of community domes that sprang from Charas's collaboration with Buckminster Fuller and the solar wall at number 9 2nd Avenue, which inspired more solar walls and collectors in the neighborhood at 519 East 11th Street and 523 East 5th Street, the windmill was a physical manifestation, borne out of hands-on work by community members and children, of the spiritual vigor that grabbed this neighborhood at a peak period during New York's financial crisis of the mid-1970s. These material objects enabled activists to point out to apathetic members of the community, especially young people, what could be achieved with some dedication and cooperation. These iconic environmental projects demonstrated, as the author of the *Suburban News* article suggested accurately, "how urban cooperative groups can *plan their own future*."[46] AAB and Loisaida residents pioneered this community-driven sweat equity urbanism that emphasized social interaction and environmentally sustainable living as a community.

While AAB put human interaction before profit, as the foremost housing organization it had to secure funds and think about the financial viability of its projects. As such, AAB became one of the largest employers in the neighborhood in the 1970s, according to an article in *Quality of Life in Loisaida*: "the group put over 350 people, 98% of them from the neighborhood, through its training and paid for their services in rehabilitating buildings."[47] AAB worked with the city during a brief period of pro-community policies called tenant management by former commissioner of HPD Nathan Leventhal, who was appointed in 1978 by Mayor Koch.[48] Having trained under Mayor Lindsay a

decade earlier, Leventhal was initially able to support pro-community policies. As he stated, "When tenants take control of a building, particularly in a
distressed area, that's the best hope that the building will survive, not when
a private, profit-motivated landlord comes in."[49] Leventhal became deputy
mayor in 1979, the earliest sign of his loss of influence over pro-tenant housing
programs. As Jonathan Soffer explains, "Much of Leventhal's job, no matter
what his title was, was to be a counterbalance to Koch."[50] It was Leventhal who
"had made a reputation as one of the administration's most effective figures,
improving the lives of thousands of people living in housing units taken over
by his department, most often after the owners failed to pay their taxes."[51]
Leventhal supported AAB's vision for sweat equity urbanism in a letter to
Koch: "I am pleased to report that as of August 1, 1979, we have 8,810 units in
alternative management. We have clearly demonstrated that the first phase
of the program—intake—has been a success."[52] However, when Anthony
Gliedman replaced Leventhal at HPD, city support for alternative management programs reversed slowly in the public's eye though Gliedman's letter
to Koch in 1980 shows the city's true attitude toward these programs: "One
of the most difficult issues facing us over the next year will be to maintain
the façade of having [sic] Sweat Equity program, while, in fact, seeking to re-
organize it into something do-able."[53] This letter marked the eventual decline
of alternative management and sweat equity programs for AAB and other
housing groups in Loisaida and beyond.

Number 519 East 11th Street was, as Veronica Anthony states in the magazine *Doing It! Alternatives for Humanizing City Life,* "a beacon—a small
miracle—a hope for the future . . . a model of what community organization, tenant cooperation, and a combination of private and public funds can
accomplish."[54] While AAB and Loisaida residents successfully developed a
program for a tenant-first, sweat equity urbanism, the loss of support from
the city due to lack of profit from these community programs led to the end
of this self-help housing boom in the 1970s. As Ronald Lawson writes, "The
election of Ronald Reagan at the end of 1980 resulted in cuts in the budgets
of the neighborhood organizations engaged in rehabilitation and in the elim-
ination of programs they had come to rely on. Thus, CETA programs were
discontinued, section 8 was phased out, and Community Development funds
were no longer restricted for use by the poor."[55] Being as reliant as it was on
these programs, AAB had to adapt to stay active and continue its work in Loisaida. While President Reagan's cuts certainly affected federal grants, Mayor
Koch's administration was responsible for cutting a range of key pro-tenant
housing laws. In this light, Gliedman's letter must be read as an early sign of

gentrification and how the city administration pushed for pro-developer and anti-tenant policies directly.

This Land Was Theirs

Despite the decline of AAB's model of sweat equity urbanism at the end of the 1970s, AAB continued its work in supporting existing tenant co-ops and participating in a major community campaign against gentrification called "This Land Is Ours." According to an article in *Quality of Life in Loisaida* with comments by Carlos Perkins, who replaced Ruth García and Roberto Nazario as AAB director, AAB was "now concentrating on the issue of Community Management of buildings."[56] This enabled the group to remain relevant to the community. "When CETA flourished, Adopt-a-Building was commonly referred to as the biggest employer in the neighborhood, which Carlos Perkins says was accurate. Now he has no idea who is the biggest employer, but is pretty sure it isn't Adopt-a-Building. 'We don't want the concept of "big" to seep in,' he says."[57] If the first major change in AAB history came when Ibis Marrero and Ruth García refocused AAB's efforts on manageable action in Loisaida, this shift in the early 1980s was the second major change. Even though AAB started small in Loisaida with tenant advocacy and mobilization, thanks to CETA and other programs, AAB quickly became the largest employer in the neighborhood. AAB became a large operation again, working in several dozen buildings, renovating abandoned lots and flats, and getting involved with other communitywide projects such as the windmill and community murals (as discussed in the next chapter). Even though this second shift in AAB's role in the neighborhood was largely forced due to the loss of support from the city, Perkins clearly believed that AAB transformed into an employer that neglected some of the organization's philosophy of people-oriented housing. As Doug Turetsky writes, groups such as AAB "see themselves as more than just landlords and believe that housing management, whether by nature or design, requires a strong dose of social work."[58] Perhaps this mission got lost in the process of designing a model program of sweat equity urbanism, but Perkins saw a chance to return to this philosophy in the early 1980s. Specifically, he saw a chance to work more closely with other neighborhood groups to organize against their new enemy: gentrification.

On May 22, 1982, Lower East Side residents and activist groups marched to City Hall to show their frustration with the loss of community grants and the auctioning of city-owned property. The same issue of *Quality of Life in Loisaida* that discussed AAB's new status as housing managers also featured an article on the May 22 protest. At this rally, "Representatives of all ages, races, and other community groups were represented in a happy and colorful march that included bands of costumed cheerleaders, a Chinese dragon, papier mache figures, and a wealth of different banners and signs."[59] Thousands of people participated in this march that started at Cooper Square and made its way east to Tompkins Square Park to turn south via Pitt Street, Chinatown, and finally City Hall. The march covered not just Loisaida but the entirety of the Lower East Side. "There was a joyful spirit of unity in the parade, combined with the serious purpose of demonstrating the concern of residents over the loss of low-income housing to speculators who wish to convert it to high-income housing."[60] This march was a rallying cry for residents all over the Lower East Side to band together and protest Mayor Koch's actions in the area.

Specifically, HPD and Mayor Koch became "impatient" with the lack of profit and the slow progress of one particular program: the Tenant Interim Lease program (TIL).[61] According to Roland Lawson, this program "was a variation on those early low-income coops where the tenants had taken the initiative without the help of a sponsoring neighborhood organization. In this case, organized tenants could gain experience through managing their building, while rehabilitation . . . was carried out under city auspices; ultimately tenants could purchase the building and form a low-income co-op."[62] AAB had helped many buildings make use of the TIL program to bring the property under its ownership. However, with the city's growing impatience, this took a turn for the worse, and residents' fears were most visibly articulated in the May 1982 protest with the hope of being allowed a "6 month moratorium on all auctions or consolidation of City-owned property on the Lower East Side while the community completes its own comprehensive plan that will truly benefit the people currently living here."[63] This did not deter the city administration because HPD submitted a "proposal to auction *occupied* city-owned buildings" to the Board of Estimate a month later.[64] What Gliedman and Koch had discussed internally two years prior was still not publicly confirmed, as indicated by the confusion Hurwitz articulates in his *City Limits* article: "These actions, along with the lack of clear sales policy, call into question the City's commitment to alternative management."[65] At this point, the commitment was no longer in question but was fully abandoned.

Despite the failure of the city hall protest in 1982 to force the city to stop selling residents' houses and their land, the campaign represented a broader unification of Lower East Side residents and activist groups to work together. As Miranda J. Martínez writes, the slogan "This Land Is Ours" captured "the

popular sentiment. To Lower East Siders, when city administrators abandoned the neighborhood and the upkeep of city-owned property, it morally,
if not legally, *lost the right* to decide unilaterally what would happen to local
land."[66] In other words, Lower East Side residents claimed their right to the
city, which they earned by using their own sweat, time, and money to rehabilitate housing stock across the area and in Loisaida in particular. This land was
theirs, and despite a weak legal grounding to stand on, the city morally lost
the right to claim this land against the wishes of both the larger community
and the individual residents in each property that was auctioned off. The TIL
program was stripped of its sweeping authority to empower tenants to take
control of their own buildings, but even in its reduced form such groups as
AAB continued to help a few select buildings—though nowhere near the full
potential of TIL.

A Legacy of Housing Activism

Even while AAB faded away over the 1980s, its members continued to work
with other community groups such as Charas and Cityarts Workshop (CAW)
to rehabilitate parks, build gardens, and create murals. However, AAB was
only one organization working on housing issues at the time. Cooper Square
Committee had been active in the neighborhood since 1959, Good Old Lower
East Side was founded in 1977, and Pueblo Nuevo was established in 1970.
These groups were not necessarily focused on the Loisaida area as much as
AAB was, but they produced similarly significant work toward tenant-driven,
sweat equity urbanism. These other community groups not purely focused
on housing add to the picture of a highly integrated network of community
groups all working together against the spread of gentrification in the 1980s.
Unlike any other issue plaguing the Lower East Side at the time, it was housing and the fear of private developers and high rents that brought the neighborhood together. Beyond party politics, ethnic background, age, religion,
and educational background, it was the impending loss of residents' homes
and affordable housing in general that resulted in the march on city hall. To
these residents, gentrification represented certain displacement. As a banner
hanging on the wall of 229 East 4th Street in 1982 said: "'*Nosotros No Nos
Mudaremos*' (We Won't Move)."[67] Squatters, homesteaders, and tenant co-
ops still exist in Loisaida because such groups as AAB helped mobilize this
neighborhood in the 1970s.

The end of sweat equity urbanism in Loisaida also marks a much larger
shift representative of similar urban neighborhoods at the end of the 1970s

and the beginning of the 1980s: from anti-disinvestment activism to antigen-trification activism. Whereas these first three chapters focus on the work of activists fighting crime, drugs, housing abandonment, and high unemployment, the next three chapters move into the arena of cultural activism in Loisaida's urban history. The community mural, the focus of the next chapter, represented, in equal measures, a way to fight apathy, drugs, and economic crisis as well as a means to use art and the rich culture of the neighborhood's residents to push back against gentrification. As such it sits in that transitional phase of macropolitical changes from pro-community policies marked by President Johnson's War on Poverty to pro-developer policies representative of President Reagan's neoliberal economic reforms. To keep the community mural movement alive, groups and artists employed all three strategies of sustainable activism: they focused on youth employment and youth education, painted physical objects of the city to claim their right to the city, and worked with larger organizations such as Charas and AAB to integrate murals into communitywide projects.

CHAPTER 4

Loisaida Community Murals as Activism

> We talk about murals as riding this wave of activism and it's not what—so what troubles
> me a little bit about seeing how murals are taught and the mural process is taught in
> more of an academic context is that it's totally devoid of that connection, that really helps
> not only create something that's meaning to the people who live there, but it's so vital,
> it's so critical to the lifespan of a mural.
>
> —Tomie Arai, Interview (2016)

Previous chapters detail the interconnectedness of community groups, projects, and campaigns with regard to housing rehabilitation, alternative youth education, environmentalism, and cleanup campaigns among others. However, there is perhaps nothing as striking as the community mural to vividly encapsulate how collective community work can become embedded in one single object or "cultural 'text.'"[1] The community mural has a multitude of layers of meaning along historic, cultural, and socioeconomic lines. As Elsa B. Cardalda Sánchez and Amílcar Tirado Avilés demonstrate, the mural is "an emblematic montage of the identity of the City:" murals are "social chronicles of the community"; they are "visual voices [that] suggest a symbolic cultural resistance in the face of material poverty and spiritual desolation"; and murals "constitute a historical response of affirmation and resistance both to North American colonialism and, more specifically, to the socioeconomic limitations in which the community is currently immersed."[2] The community mural is also "a collective act, an event," according to Eva Cockroft, John Pittman Weber, and James Cockroft.[3] This is in reference to the *Wall of Respect* (1967)—one of the earliest and certainly most famous murals—which was created in the South Side of Chicago by the Organization of Black American Culture. This mural turned into a collective event of community members and groups that protected its creation. This chapter explores how murals in

Loisaida were inextricably linked to every aspect of community activism from the end of the 1960s to the mid-1980s. As collective acts and local events, as well as through their visual themes and the context of their production, Loisaida murals demonstrated a rich embeddedness within local organizing that made them indispensable as catalysts for community activism and as vehicles to provoke action among residents. Muralists consciously linked the practice of claiming physical space in the neighborhood with a comprehensive artistic education for young people. Muralists were also part of the larger neighborhood network, working with AAB and Charas to paint the walls of Loisaida.

Existing histories of the U.S. mural movement—often written by the muralists themselves—trace the emergence of the exterior community murals in the late 1960s and various influences on muralism in the United States, including the wealth of largely interior Works Progress Administration murals during the New Deal decades of the 1930s and 1940s, the spread of Chicano art in the 1960s, and the tradition of wall writing in Puerto Rico.[4] The many organizations involved in creating murals in Loisaida necessitate a shift of focus away from a single organization to a broader network of community groups that were not primarily concerned with murals in their own right. Yet many of the murals examined in this chapter were cocreated by or included members of CAW. Whereas the chapter in *Toward a People's Art* was written at the height of CAW's activities in the mid-1970s, *On the Wall* presents a much-needed retrospective on the organization's history beyond the 1970s, including its drastic change in vision away from radical and "community-based to a community-service model" concerned with beautification under the new leadership of Tsipi Ben-Haim.[5] *On the Wall* contextualizes the movement with larger events that connect the themes and issues depicted in murals with the AIDS crisis, the fall of the Berlin Wall, South African apartheid, gentrification, urban riots, and 9/11. However, as the authors write, "National and international concerns become subjects of community murals only when issues have local ramifications."[6] This chapter focuses on the creation of Loisaida murals and how they were embedded in a much larger network of community activism—specifically around economic and educational concerns that were present both in mural themes and the process of creation.[7]

Before There Was a Garden, There Was a Mural

The previous chapters highlight several community symbols that were actively promoted to combat widespread apathy among Loisaida residents, including Cuando's solar wall at number 9 2nd Avenue and the windmill at

519 East 11th Street. At the same time, in the mid-1970s, Charas and AAB began work on the community garden La Plaza Cultural at the corner of East 9th Street and Avenue C. This park would serve as a key gathering place for the community and quickly became a catalyst for more community gardens in a neighborhood that is considered the birthplace for the popularization of urban community gardens.[8] Before it was transformed, La Plaza was one of the many abandoned lots full of rubble that were so common in the neighborhood. However, before the lot turned into the community park La Plaza, it was the site of a large mural full of vibrant colors adorning the wall over-shadowing the lot at 137 Avenue C. Painted in 1977 and simply called *La Plaza Cultural Mural*, this was the first of many murals to find its way onto this particular wall. It was painted by a group of neighborhood youth under the direction of CAW muralist Alfredo "Freddy" Hernández in collaboration with Charas—namely Chino García, as evidenced by a written contract between the landlord of 137 Avenue C and the leading coordinators for the mural.[9] Hernández, an artist of Puerto Rican descent, previously worked as lead muralist on *Puerto Rican Heritage* (1975) at 57 Rutgers Place and *Por Los Niños* (1976) at the former Public School 97 on FDR Drive, as well as on other murals in the Lower East Side. As a CAW mural list confirms, the mural was "painted to *complement* local efforts to turn the park into a cultural plaza."[10] The creation of the mural itself was therefore fundamentally embedded in the transformation of La Plaza Cultural from the start. This example shows that "murals can act as a catalyst, and make communities stronger, more visible; but in order to do that they must be a vehicle for the redefinition, or reformulation, of common values."[11] In this case, the community members articulated their common values through a multifunctional park that eventually included a vegetable garden, an amphitheater, and plenty of space to host events, stage protests, and organize community projects. Rather than simply an isolated mural project that celebrated community diversity and the heritage of those who populated the area in the 1970s, it was part and parcel of a much larger grassroots vision of transforming decaying and abandoned urban space into *functional* community space.

To stay with the same space—in fact, the same wall—for a moment, another mural replaced the original *La Plaza Cultural Mural* in 1985, after the first mural had already been tarred over in the early 1980s to repair water leaks in the wall. The new mural project, one of the most famous in the community mural movement in general, comprised twenty-six murals across four buildings surrounding La Plaza Cultural and voiced the concerns of a community that was no longer fighting abandonment and financial disinvestment, but

FIGURE 5. Eva Cockcroft et al., *La Lucha Continua The Struggle Continues,* 1985
Source: Photo by Camille Perrottet, from TDCM. © Camille Perrottet, courtesy of Artmakers Inc.

instead found itself the target of gentrification and reinvestment. Another photo of the La Plaza wall from 1985 spans the entirety of the walls adjacent to La Plaza Cultural and, if one looks closely, shows that the new mural on the large wall included some of the imagery of the original mural in the upper-right corner as an homage (see figure 5). The mural also included other iconic neighborhood symbols of hope and affirmation such as a geodesic dome, a windmill, solar panels, sweat equity housing rehabilitation, a local grocery shop, and an idyllic green space with children playing that recalls the imagery of Charas's dome-building comic book.[12] Beyond visual motifs that reified connections between community projects and a shared vision of self-help and neighborhood improvement, the creation of the mural also demonstrates that this was not merely an isolated art project. As Braun-Reinitz and Weissman write: "Painting over a two-month period, the twenty-nine artists also enlisted the help of family, friends, and neighbors; facilitated community meetings; erected scaffolds; and helped clean up La Plaza. Every morning, the first muralists to arrive on site cleared the park of used drug paraphernalia, and their daily presence sufficiently discomforted the dealers."[13] Just as the first mural was a collaboration between CAW and Charas among other members of AAB, "*La Lucha* united several neighborhood constituencies: Artmakers, Charas and other local organizations, artists, community gardeners, and residents who used the park."[14]

The difference between a humanitarian and a humanist approach to community engagement also comes through in the case of murals, specifically with regard to the relationship between artists and the community. As was the case with many—but not all—community murals of the 1960s, 1970s, and 1980s, artists did not simply descend on a particular wall without at least consulting community members. According to Cockcroft, Weber, and Cockcroft, community murals "have a rationale of working for the local audience around issues that concern the immediate community, using art as a medium of expression of, for, and with the local audience. They involve artists with community issues, community organizing, and community response to their artwork. . . . This thrust toward communal modes of mural creation has led to the development by the community-based mural movement of techniques for working together in cooperative ways, of techniques for helping nonartists to conceive and create in artistic language."[15]

To return to Arnstein's Ladder of Citizen Participation, described in chapter 1, most community murals would fall between degrees of consultation and full citizen control. This meant that community residents and non-artists were usually offered a chance to voice their issues with the proposed design if not also to participate in the visual motifs themselves—especially when the artist was part of the community or when a community group or block association commissioned the mural. This level of participation speaks to the rich embeddedness of community murals in a larger network of community organizations both big and small, not to mention non-activist residents who had to walk by the mural on their way to work. It simply did not matter whether an organization was involved in art programs. Whether it was the educational work of RGS, the environmental activism of Charas, or the housing rehabilitation of AAB, "By refurbishing their own housing, producing some of their food and initiating local industry," according to Barnett, "they were being at least as creative as they were when making an image to express what was happening in their neighborhood."[16] For Barnett, the mural represents "the return of urgent practical purpose to the human propensity to make images," which is why both mural imagery and the act of mural making itself were deeply integrated into Loisaida community activism.

La Lucha Continua promoted a renewed thrust to rehabilitate La Plaza Cultural—a continuation of the first mural's mission—and the garden was designated as a permanent open space, four decades after Hernández's mural helped form the vision of La Plaza Cultural before it became a lively community garden. Although La Plaza Cultural and both mural projects were the most famous examples of how murals were embedded in community activism, the rest of this chapter delves more deeply into areas where this embeddedness served specific purposes: self-help, economic revitalization, and the role of youth in the creation of murals. The first case develops themes around labor and self-help practice touched upon in the previous chapter, while the last part of this chapter returns to Freire and the educational purposes of muralism. Just like the murals of La Plaza Cultural, the following projects demonstrate the ability of community murals to demand action from their audiences—to call upon residents to get involved in community efforts. As such, they provided the same force against neighborhood apathy as community groups did when they built gardens, windmills, geodesic domes, after-school cultural spaces, and functioning housing.

Fictitious Storefronts and Economic Revitalization on Avenue C

In August 1982, CAW sent out a press release titled "A Two Block Long Mural Series Nears Completion on Avenue C."[17] The mural in question, or rather the series of murals, was one of the more creative projects in Loisaida mural history, as the press release explained: "Just as though they actually exist, a series of storefronts complete with customers and items displayed in their windows, will be carefully painted. The fictitious 'Los Niños,' a local children's clothing shop, will stand next to the equally non-existent, 'La Marqueta Tropica,' a grocery store. There will be a fish market, a coffee shop, a pharmacia, a laundromat, and a record store, all reflecting the heritage of Hispanic residents and the type of small service store badly needed on Avenue C."[18]

This series of murals (see figure 6 for one example), coordinated by Artmakers cofounder Joe Stephenson, was part of a large-scale neighborhood project to revitalize commercial activity on the once-thriving shopping street Avenue C—the heart of Loisaida and the designated location for the annual Loisaida Festival. The project that was launched by Charas and AAB in 1979 included a range of other neighborhood groups and municipal agencies such as Artmakers, the Merchants Association of Avenue C, the Federation of Block Associations, the Committee of Concerned LES [Lower East Side] Business People, and the Office of the Manhattan Borough President. A meeting was held on January 10, 1980, at the newly reclaimed Charas/El Bohío building to discuss the revitalization plans. Representatives of the Office of Manhattan Borough President Andrew Stein presented their market analysis and "survey of merchants and shoppers on Avenue C," which the office conducted in 1979.[19] According to this report, the revitalization efforts were supposed to "provide 3,332 square feet of rehabilitated commercial space between East 5th and East 6th Streets in addition to needed housing."[20] The survey concluded, "No one project or program can effect change; however, when targeted into one area and *coordinated with other projects*, revitalization efforts can successfully influence the neighborhood's quality of life."[21] When neighborhood youth under the guidance of Stephenson started painting the murals

FIGURE 6. Records and Tapes (*Ave C Faux Storefronts*), 1982. It appears that this street vendor used the colorful mural as an attractive background to sell bikes and other items. See James T. Rojas's concept of the "enacted environment" in "Los Angeles—The Enacted Environment of East Los Angeles," *Places* 8, no. 3 (1993): 42–53.
Source: Joe Stephenson, *Ave C Faux Storefronts*, 1982, photo by Maria Domínguez, from TDCM.

in 1982, little had changed on Avenue C, which was precisely the motivation behind the murals in the first place: to move things along and promote the project.

The murals directly responded to the city, which kept ahold of many properties until they could be sold for profit. The murals represented early examples of change for a community that had no other avenue to make itself heard and to articulate its concerns with gentrification. As a community and neighborhood that had—alongside many similar urban neighborhoods across the U.S.—"experienced the greatest oppression of their labor," as Barnett writes, it is no wonder that residents and activists "turned to art for the most serious kind of work—their own survival."[22] Just as they turned to self-help housing rehabilitation or self-help education, Loisaida activists embraced and popularized the growing community mural movement because murals represented a "reintegration of art and work—the return of urgent practical purpose to the human propensity to make images, and the recovery of serious expression by labor."[23] This reintegration is at the heart of the embeddedness of murals in community activism. As muralist, long-time community activist, educator, and cofounder of muralist group Artmakers, Maria Domínguez said in an interview with the author: "As a group, as a community, we fused together. We knew each other; we were a family. . . . You weren't just doing art, you weren't just doing poetry, you were trying to survive."[24] The history of Loisaida activism is a history of a struggle to survive and is perhaps most succinctly visualized in the aforementioned *La Lucha Continua The Struggle Continues* mural project that followed Stephenson's *Ave C Faux Storefronts* project. Before gentrification became a key theme for *La Lucha*, the *Faux Storefronts* had already signified the complexities of gentrification through the lens of community-envisioned revitalization. The story of the fake storefronts—as illusions of life—is in large part a story about gentrification on the local level as perceived from the eyes of those most likely to be victims of its worst casualties: dispossession and dislocation.

When Loisaida residents met on January 10, 1980, their call for economic revitalization raised an important question: revitalization for whom? They wanted to support small, local businesses on Avenue C as opposed to chain stores such as Pathmark, which was proposed to be built in the area.[25] In a broader sense, they also wanted to include other aspects of their community work for a more rounded revitalization project: weatherization, homesteading sites, redesign of La Plaza Cultural, recreational spaces and educational facilities, and the Charas recycling center mentioned previously.[26] Indeed, Kathleen Gupta, who had taken over as CAW director from Susan Caruso-Green at the end of the 1970s, was quoted in the *Daily News* as actively opposing gentrification: "There will be . . . no quiche signs, since gentrification, however remote it may seem now, is something that Avenue C also doesn't want."[27] The problem is that gentrification, in all its intangibility, has rarely ever been about what people want, especially not when it comes to the wants of those oppressed and marginalized groups most excluded from the institutions that could articulate and support—or undermine and decline—the wants of these groups. Just a few weeks after the *Daily News* published its article, the *East Villager* promoted a different view of the soon-to-be colorful and imaginative fake storefronts: "We believe the mural project proposed for Avenue C is as much of a sham as the 'storefronts' it will be creating."[28] The article concluded, "Perhaps the City hopes that with the Avenue C façade in place, prospective buyers for those buildings will not be so put off by the prospect of buying into this area, thereby speeding up the gentrification process."[29] This anger and cynicism with regard to gentrification was a growing concern for Loisaida residents, as indicated by an article titled "Gentrification New Trend in Loisaida" in the neighborhood magazine *Quality of Life in Loisaida*, which was published in the same issue as the report on the January 10 meeting.[30] Was the author of the *East Villager* article justified?

Of course, the answer is a mix of yes and no. If one looks at the intention of the community groups engaged in the project, the funding sources used for the mural project reveal a primary concern with youth employment and artistic work. A CAW press release for the dedication ceremony listed the following entities as sponsors: the National Endowment for the Arts (NEA), the New York State Council on the Arts (NYSCA), the New York City Department of Employment—Summer Youth Employment Program, the New York City Office of Neighborhood Economic Development, Dale T. Roberts, American Express Foundation, American Stock Exchange, Citibank, Exxon Corporation, Jobs for Youth, and the Friends of CAW.[31] Though one's eyes might be drawn to American Express, Exxon, or Citibank, large corporations often provided regular small grants to community organizations as part of their charitable work for tax write-offs. They sponsored RGS previously and CAW and AAB in this case. It is highly doubtful whether these corporations requested the monies be spent in particular ways as they tended to be general contributions to organizations and not grants for specific projects. In addition, NEA and NYSCA had always provided funding for murals in the first decade or so since the late 1960s, "through local 'responsible' conduits" such as CAW.[32] However, Barnett points to a shift in funding away from traditional arts institutions such as NEA toward governmental agencies such as the Department of Labor, which, by 1978, "became the leading federal source of funding for artists."[33]

The Department of Employment mentioned in the CAW press release distributed funding on the local level under the oversight of the Human Resources Administration in New York. Before the Department of Employment became its own institution in 1988—and subsequently dissolved in 2003—this subdivision of the Human Resources Administration managed the Summer Youth Employment Program (SYEP), which provided CAW with funds to work with disadvantaged youth.[34] Cockcroft, Weber, and Cockcroft write, "Federal programs geared toward manpower training—such as the Supplemental Training and Employment Program (STEP), the Neighborhood Youth Corps (NYC), and the Comprehensive Employment and Training Act (CETA)—although not intended to support murals, account for the next largest share, say 15 percent, thanks to the imaginative use of these funds at the local levels."[35] Charas and AAB, especially with regard to their environmental projects and housing rehabilitation efforts, were very dependent on CETA. SYEP was established under Title IV, Part C, Sec. 481 of the 1978 amendment to the original 1973 CETA: "Programs shall provide eligible youth with useful work and sufficient basic education and institutional or on-the-job training to assist these youths to develop their maximum occupational potential."[36]

The funding for the mural series, itself part of a larger revitalization project, indicates that there was no meddling through funding sources that could be construed as pro-gentrification policies to intentionally beautify the neighborhood for the purpose of attracting higher-income earners and chain stores such as Pathmark. In fact, most of the funding for the murals was used "for the salaries of the students who will be doing the actual painting."[37] For CAW and AAB, the murals were both a chance to provide artistic education in a community setting to neighborhood youth and a colorful solution to promote a desire for small businesses on Avenue C—businesses for the largely Puerto Rican area run by local residents.

This picture gets more complicated when looking at this issue from the city's perspective because "one-dimensional vilifications of artists as the primary agents of gentrification shift critical attention from the larger economic and political forces at work, as well as from the city officials and political leaders."[38] In an article on the relationship between gentrification and art on the Lower East Side, Anne E. Bowler and Blaine McBurney look at two city initiatives under the Koch administration to turn city-owned property, and most of Avenue C was city-owned, into higher-income housing stock for artists and professionals: the Artists Homeownership Program (AHOP) and the Cross-Subsidy Program.[39] As a supporter of neoliberal city policies, Mayor Koch "employed a new rhetoric of crisis, designed to provide the ideological justification for doling out economic incentives to private development. It is precisely this type of strategy that Mayor Edward Koch put forward in the spring of 1982, when he announced the privately funded AHOP."[40] AHOP would have turned properties on the west side of Loisaida into artist housing, redeveloping properties to raise rents.

This idea for artist housing came about after Anthony Gliedman took over as housing commissioner from Nathan Leventhal in 1979. Chapter 3 briefly mentions the opposing views of Leventhal and Koch—with Leventhal very much in favor of community-led housing reform—and with Gliedman replacing Leventhal, Koch found a ready ally for his pro-business solutions to the housing crisis. The first sign of what was termed "artists housing/shopsteading" came in a letter from Gliedman to Koch on January 15, 1980: "In my sales memorandum to you, I mentioned that I am about to create a new unit within HPD dedicated to the creative reuse of our in rem housing stock."[41] However, the plan was defeated on February 10, 1983, at the official hearing in City Hall due to substantial community resistance that built on the "This Land Is Ours" march from the previous year. Community leaders such as Chino García and Bimbo Rivas spoke at the hearing, but Bonnie Greer—a member of Artists for Social Responsibility—offered perhaps the clearest argument against AHOP: "Housing that displaces people is not artists' housing."[42] It was a much-celebrated victory for a neighborhood that was in its early stages of coming to grips with a sudden interest in its abandoned housing stock by the city and developers after two decades of deterioration. For Loisaida residents and activists, gentrification was simply seen as a continued threat of forced displacement—only this time not through negligence but instead through targeted, private investment.

Of course, Koch would not be remembered as a champion of privatization to developers if he had just given up. One year after the defeat in City Hall, Koch presented a new plan in a press conference on July 24, 1984.[43] According to Bowler and McBurney, "City officials employed a similar rhetoric in the promotion of its Cross Subsidy Program (or "Double-Cross Subsidy" as it became known among neighborhood residents), a deal struck in 1987 between the Department of Housing Preservation and Development and the local Community Board to sell off city-owned properties to private developers for the creation of a thousand units of market-rate housing."[44] The final plan, following three years of tense negotiations, proposed a fifty-fifty split of higher-income housing and affordable housing—a split that started in 1984 with 80 percent higher-income stock. *Quality of Life in Loisaida* dedicated an entire issue to publishing an excerpt of the community's desired plan immediately after Koch presented his version. The community plan emphasized—above all else—the need to ensure "that no current resident of the area will be willfully or illegally displaced."[45] To voice its resistance to a larger audience, the community marched—once again—on City Hall on June 23, 1984. One iconic protest banner exclaimed: "Stop Displacement and Gentrification! Save the Lower East Side!!"[46] What was at stake for protestors, what had always been at stake for them, was their home—their survival as residents of Loisaida. Clearly, the author of the *East Villager* article was right to fear the dawn of gentrification on Avenue C, but the murals that depicted small, imaginary businesses such as La Marqueta Tropica and José's Fish were clearly not intended to attract the kind of tenants, business owners, and artists who would have benefited from AHOP or ended up moving into the area with the help of the "Double Cross-Subsidy" Program.

These battles between Loisaida residents and the Koch administration articulate the struggle over the interpretation of economic revitalization. Marginalized and oppressed groups of migrants, immigrants, and lower-income earners had their eyes set on revitalizing Avenue C to create jobs for local residents—to attract new tenants for the abandoned housing stock on the street. Stephenson's mural project was a creative and, more importantly, necessary aspect to promote the need to return economic activity to Avenue C. After all, "The realities on Avenue C are so depressing—and the prospects for improvement so remote—that some people are looking to art and illusion in an attempt to make the two dead blocks look a little like Main Street."[47] The sociocultural background of Loisaida residents meant that they were often forced to "use 'unconventional' methods such as murals to spark conversation, dialogue, and eventual social action."[48] As muralist Pedro Tirado Vidal explains in a short documentary about *La Lucha*, "murals are like newspapers to educate the people and to inform them . . . because what's the use of putting up a mural that's purely decorative and isn't saying anything to educate the people or to say a message that's important to us."[49] Without the means to participate in city institutions due to economic status and ethnic background, Loisaida residents used murals as activist canvases—to promote action among residents. Avenue C, due to its location on the far east end of the Lower East Side, was relatively safe from gentrification until the early 1990s, according to an analysis by Neil Smith, but nevertheless it still remained a stronghold for the Puerto Rican community—and the growing population of other Latino groups.[50]

Youth Murals and *Conscientização*

While there were some indirect connections between Paulo Freire's work and the efforts of RGS in the late 1960s, it was muralist John Weber, coauthor of *Toward a People's Art* and lead artist for the mural *From One Generation to Another La Lucha Continua* (1984), who took direct inspiration from Freire's ideas for his own work: "Weber acknowledges his debt to Paolo [*sic*] Freire, the Brazilian educator who brought together a variety of ideas about consciousness-raising that had been in the air for decades."[51] Freire's

> use of slides to simulate dialogue and his getting participants to reflect on the language they were learning to read and write are comparable to the chance that is presented when people come together to make a mural. It can become an occasion when the professional muralist can help them develop a critical consciousness of their images and their actual condition to determine whether they, too, are the victims of stereotypes and who profits from them. . . . The mural process thus becomes a means for people to liberate their own thinking and provides them an instrumentality for their self-education so that they can break through the apparent blind alleys of their existence.[52]

While this applies to adults and children alike, it is especially important for young people in the mural projects not just because they participated in one way or another in a majority of them, but because their inclusion in the creation of many murals served three purposes connected to broader efforts of community activism in Loisaida: (1) consciousness-raising, (2) providing a positive alternative to gang life to teach children about responsibility and work ethics, and (3) tapping into various antipoverty and youth employment grants to fund projects. With the youth engagement strategy spreading out from RGS to other organizations, muralists such as Weber, Hernández, Domínguez, Jannuzzi, Arai, and Eva Cockcroft made use of this unique mixture of activist work, consciousness-raising—in the sense of Paulo Freire's *conscientização*—and practical skill training. The emphasis on the educational value of murals for neighborhood youth is a key aspect of precisely why murals were so richly embedded in a larger network—or family, to use Domínguez's word—of community activism.

As explained at the beginning of the chapter, the thrust of community murals in the Lower East Side began with a youth education program at the Alfred E. Smith housing development near the Brooklyn Bridge. CAW founder Susan Shapiro-Kiok began working with black and Latina/o youth that frequented the sports facilities and recreational spaces of the Al Smith. As an outsider coming to the Lower East Side, she was thrown into a "ten-year cold war between the Italian and Afro-Latin communities; the tensions between the Asians and black communities."[53] This was back in 1968 and 1969, so during the peak period of gang activities in the Lower East Side. Shapiro-Kiok hired Susan Caruso-Green (age eighteen) and James Jannuzzi (age fourteen) in 1968 to help her learn about the struggles and the fears of youth in the area of the Al Smith.[54] She learned about gang violence and drug addiction and quickly came to understand that "these burdens did not inspire these young people with self-confidence or optimism for the future."[55] As an artist and educator interested in bringing art to a wider audience, she organized a trip with a group of young people who frequented the Al Smith to one of Boston's most neglected neighborhoods in the late 1960s: Roxbury. As another major community mural city alongside New York, Chicago, and San Francisco, Boston was already creating large exterior murals by 1968. According to an interview with Shapiro-Kiok, they went to see the *Exodus Building Mural* (1968)—a Black Power mural that featured armed black men and black children—which was created by Dana Chandler and Gary Rickson.[56] The mural was painted on the outside of "an alternative school for Black children in the Roxbury ghetto."[57] Children participated in the creation of this

Roxbury mural as well so it made sense for Shapiro-Kiok to talk to Chandler and Rickson about the "mural as a tool for social change."[58]

Her trip to expose the Lower East Side youth to the power of the mural was successful because the young people then "decided to create a mural . . . on the theme of drug abuse."[59] Rather than replicating the theme of the militant Black Power mural, they were inspired to confront one of the problems they encountered in their own environment. The result was a massive installation of plywood panels on the outside of the Al Smith featuring the silhouettes of the young people in powerful stances—it was created in 1970 and called the *Anti-Drug Abuse Mural.* Shapiro-Kiok had realized that her courses on ceramics with the young people she conducted earlier at Al Smith did not find much traction with the children's parents. The mural, on the other hand, "would be seen and it was seen in the midst of this housing project and people, it wasn't something that a parent could throw out or not take notice of because there it was. And not only did it involve their own families, but their neighbors too and in terms of recognition, which I think was something I think was so very important, that I wanted them to be able to experience this sense of recognition— something that they did very well."[60] This supports the notion that murals, unlike other media in youth art education, have the power to instill in young people a sense of pride about their immediate environment and their lives.

These early years explain why CAW built its vision as a muralist organization on the principles of youth education, as an organizational document details:

> Through the creative process, Cityarts Workshop fosters a new set of skills and values, including:
> - Technical training in art and construction techniques
> - An alternative to the problems of drugs, apathy and street life
> - An understanding of responsibility and commitment to a project
> - A knowledge of current issues
> - An understanding of City government and the cooperation of many agencies and groups (block associations, community boards, etc) necessary to achieve a goal to benefit all.
> - A sense of neighborhood history and their own place in the history of New York[61]

All six points follow the tenets of an activist's pedagogy (points 1 to 3) and Freire's ideas of consciousness-raising (points 4 to 6). These community murals were products of their immediate social, spatial, and political contexts— the creation of a community garden, the revitalization of an abandoned street, the struggle against drug addiction. This is an important aspect of critical pedagogy and Freire's work: "People, as beings 'in a situation,' find themselves rooted in temporal-spatial conditions which mark them and which they also mark. They will tend to reflect on their own 'situationality' to the extent that they are challenged by it to act upon it."[62] In the example of the Al Smith youth mural, the young people lived in a neighborhood with substantial drug problems and the mural gave them a vehicle to *act upon it*. To borrow again from Freire, "Thematic investigation [drug abuse] thus becomes a common striving toward awareness of reality and toward self-awareness, which makes this investigation a starting point for the educational process or for cultural action of a liberating character."[63] The trip to Boston, the workshops to create the silhouettes, the actual painting and installation of the mural—all these were part of the educational process, and as such they were key elements for the empowerment of young people who very likely considered themselves helpless on the issue of drug abuse until Shapiro-Kiok offered them a vehicle, a platform to navigate out of the "tormenting blind alley" that was and is youth drug addiction.[64]

Beyond the consciousness-raising ability of murals, muralists often purposefully ensured that they would be able to teach young people, especially those out of school and unemployed, about work ethics and responsibility within the context of their own community. One such example is the 1973 project *Ghetto Ecstasy/Afro-Latin Coalition*—another CAW youth mural directed by nineteen-year-old James Jannuzzi (see figure 7). On the corner of East 4th Street and Avenue C—just a couple blocks from the future imaginary storefronts—Jannuzzi and a group of young people created a colorful mural featuring African and Latin American symbols and motifs such as a tropical jungle, Egyptian pyramids, and a burning sun. This was CAW' first mural in Loisaida proper—East 1st to East 14th Streets and Avenue B to the East River. As was established tradition for CAW by this point, "street kids were brought in during the early stages to plan the mural mock-up depicting their life on this part of the Lower East Side."[65] Specifically, as Braun-Reinitz and Weissman point out, "participating teens wanted to explore both the roots of Afro-Latino culture and the impact of gangs on their neighborhood."[66] The Egyptian symbols represented black heritage, while the portrait of Puerto Rican nationalist and abolitionist Ramón Betances—known as El Padre de la Patria and El Padre de los Pobres (The Father of the Nation and The Father of the Poor)—symbolized the history and culture of Puerto Ricans. The drummer represented the shared influences of both African and Latino cultures, with the African djembe drum as the inspiration for Puerto Rican drums. At the center

FIGURE 7. James Jannuzzi, *Ghetto Ecstasy/Afro-Latin Coalition*, 1973
Source: Photo by Cityarts, from TDCM.

of the mural were seven spears to represent the gangs of the area with each spear painted in the colors of the seven gangs—a gesture that depicted both the reality of gang rivalry and common values shared by all youth gangs.[67]

Just analyzing the motifs and themes of this mural, however, does not present an accurate picture of the work involved by the young people. In one of the key publications among muralists that spread the word of the muralist movement, the authors stress that murals "teach responsibility to others, to the project, and to the public. Students learn about themselves through working with others. They also enjoy the sense of doing something for the people who will see the mural. Students will learn sensitivity to people by seeking a theme that will be meaningful to others. *In the process of doing a mural, the student, perhaps for the first time, will have a role in creating or changing his or her own environment.*"[68] The last sentence is crucial here and is based in the understanding that, as Melvin Delgado points out in his sociological study on memorial murals, "Control over [community place] takes on greater meaning and importance for marginalized youth of color because they are able to exercise control over so few areas of their lives."[69] The mural, then, presented the ideal vehicle for these marginalized young people to both change their own environment in a visibly colorful way—to leave a mark on their neighborhood, to occupy visual and physical space—and learn about teamwork, compromise, and being responsible for one's own decisions. As the mural was being designed in the workshop stage of the project, "local artists heard about the project and began to stop by the workshop, offering critiques of the work and suggestions."[70] Rather than ignoring these artists, "Jannuzzi and the teens recognized the opportunity to learn from professionals and invited them to join the project."[71] All of a sudden, the young people were artists themselves guided by professionals who wanted to help bring to life the young people's message for the mural—through the motifs, the colors, the scale.

It is important to note that the young people *were* in charge of the themes and motifs due to the nature of CAW's aforementioned emphasis on youth education. Caruso-Green says as much in a 2016 interview about her time as CAW director: "The process of creating the images and doing the work largely fell to the group of young people who were recruited, and invited to participate."[72] In the case of *Ghetto Ecstasy*, Jannuzzi mentioned to Braun-Reinitz and Weissman that it was difficult to get all the gangs to agree on the image, but their approval was vital to ensure the mural would represent them accurately.[73] As already mentioned, young people working on murals at this time were often paid through various job training and summer youth employment programs. CAW was an organization that received funding from these federal and city programs to hire young people and muralists. Everyone working on the *Ghetto Ecstasy* mural was employed and paid for his or her work—in fact, CAW used the project to include funding for spontaneous and invited guest artists for future projects. For the young people—and Jannuzzi was certainly no exception at the age of nineteen—the project demonstrated "that painting a mural is hard work, that the job is not glamorous, however chic paint-splattered clothes may be. The same rules that apply in the traditional workplace apply on the wall—reporting on time, cooperating with colleagues, learning new skills, taking on additional responsibilities."[74] Just as RGS used the University of the Streets to train neighborhood youth in vocational and practical skills to increase their chances at earning a job, so did activists and muralists transform the mural into a vehicle for inspiring the same values of community work and work ethics—under the rubric of a pedagogy of activism that pervaded the neighborhood's wealth of activist groups.

Ghetto Ecstasy and *Anti-Drug Abuse* were good examples of the embeddedness of consciousness-raising and the activist pedagogical philosophy within the work that murals symbolized and promoted. Yet failing to understand the funding of mural projects, muralists, youth, and organizations such as CAW or Artmakers would also ignore part of the reason why community murals became a national phenomenon in the first place. The specific use of CETA and SYEP funding was discussed in relation to the *Faux Storefronts*, but the laws that created them were not in effect in the same capacity in the late 1960s and early 1970s. They were continuations, extensions, and replacements of existing programs that go back to one of the key laws of President Johnson's Great Society efforts: the act "to mobilize the human and financial resources of the Nation to combat poverty in the United States"—the Economic Opportunity Act of 1964.[75] This was the legislation that established the Office of Economic Opportunity (OEO) and laid down the foundations for almost two decades of youth employment and skill training programs. Title I, Part A, Section 103, Paragraph (b) authorized the director of the OEO to "arrange for the provision of education and vocational training of enrollees in the Corps: *Provided*, That, where practicable, such programs may be provided through local public educational agencies or by private vocational educational institutions or technical institutes."[76] In more detail on the cooperation between the federal, state, and local agencies, Part B, Section 112 specified "the employment of young people in State and community activities."[77]

Similarly, the Neighborhood Youth Corps (NYC) program was restructured in 1970 to emphasize "education, skill training, and work experience" because the initial phase of the program had not provided adequate support for enrollees after completing the two-year placement.[78] According to the review of the restructured program by the comptroller general of the United States, even the second phase of NYC did not provide an acceptable system for measuring its success. Thus NYC was discontinued after almost a decade only to be replaced by similar programs in CETA. Both the Government Accountability Office, which published the report and presented it to Congress, and the Department of Labor agreed that "NYC-type programs will be carried on under the Comprehensive Employment and Training Act of 1973 for the foreseeable future."[79] This prediction turned out to be correct since local organizations—such as muralist groups—benefited from both NYC as well as the later SYEP, which was tapped for the *Faux Storefronts* murals. This was not just the case in New York, as Maura E. Greany writes: the Philadelphia Museum "provided all materials for the murals and the salaries of the founding artists [of a muralist group]. Many of the teenager painters were paid through the Neighborhood Youth Corps."[80] In Los Angeles, muralist Judy Baca was hired "to teach art to city children" with an initial assignment "to convince twenty teenagers from battling barrios that painting murals was worthwhile public service. The former gang members were paid by the city's Neighborhood Youth Corps program."[81] NYC was especially helpful because it provided jobs and health benefits for young people who "have already abandoned the classroom to make the streets their stage. . . . A mural project, in offering them an infinitely more effective platform, also places them in a role of responsibility to the community, a role daily reinforced by public reaction to their work."[82]

While CAW used NYC and SYEP to pay young people for many murals in the 1970s, there were exceptions, such as Hernández's *Por Los Niños* (1976), which adorned the large wall on the former Public School 97 on FDR Drive. According to a mural list that CAW collected, "Junior High School students and artists painted this mural, which was inspired by recent cutbacks in educational programs in the schools."[83] The mural was a direct response to the city's financial crisis—peaking in 1975—and the creation of the Emergency Financial Control Board, which was a state agency that took over control of New York's budget including "the City's semi-independent agencies which provide elementary and secondary education, higher education, hospitals and other services."[84] Neither the already-replaced NYC nor SYEP were designed for in-school enrollees such as these junior high school students. Instead, school projects like this one were otherwise integrated into the schedule for a specific class or group of pupils under the remit of artistic education or work experience. They would have been too young to receive payment from federal grants, so instead the focus was on the educational aspect of allowing a group of pupils to relate to a financial crisis that affected them through cuts in funding for trips, classroom materials, and teachers. This mural, like most murals that involved young people, became a tool of empowerment, as Shapiro-Kiok says, for "young people to express themselves and to see that they could actually do something quite awesome."[85]

The use of youth employment and skill training programs such as NYC and CETA were never specifically intended for murals or community art projects, but the vagueness of the program goals and their eligibilities left enough space for "imaginative use" by community organizations that were certainly on top of their game with regard to raising funds and applying for grants to keep sustaining their work: to pay activists, to pay young people, to pay artists.[86] For Barnett, the increase of funding from these federal job training programs, which coincided with the decrease in funding from traditional arts foundations such as NEA, indicated "that art is after all a form of ordinary labor."[87] However, these programs were by no means flawless. They tended to "bureaucratize the relationship of the artist and community"; there was a lot of insecurity in receiving funds; and funding for murals "[has] not received anything like the degree of government support that previous programs for public art, such as the Mexican and New Deal mural movements, enjoyed."[88] Eventually, CETA was replaced by President Reagan's 1982 Job Training Partnership Act (JTPA), which tightened restrictions on the use of funding for disadvantaged youth by "*privatizing* training policy and *marketizing* welfare policy" to such a degree that it contributed to a decrease in youth involvement in mural projects.[89] Another contributing factor was the general decrease in funding for community groups, with many key funding bodies that operated in the spirit of President Johnson's Great Society being discontinued or restructured to serve President Reagan's pro-business economic strategy.[90]

The Cityarts Workshop shut down in 1989 for a brief period before being reopened by Tsipi Ben-Haim as CITYarts in the same year with a new mission that critically veered away from radical and community-engaged mural work. Even Artmakers, founded in 1983 to replace the lack of CAW activity and return to the political aesthetics of the early mural movement, was not as focused on youth involvement despite strongly emphasizing the radical and political nature of community murals. Nevertheless, young people played a critical role in the community mural movement in Loisaida and elsewhere for almost two decades. There were occasional exceptions, such as a mural project on the wall of El Bohío in 1988 entitled *Art Meets Life*. This was a Charas project, organized by Maria Domínguez, and it included collaborating artists Eva Cockcroft (*Pou and Frade: Art Meets Life*) William Acevado (*El Altar*), Roland Vega, Pedro Tirado Vidal, and an unnamed artist who painted the mural *Paz*. Maria Domínguez herself painted the mural *Festival Loisaida* and worked with Charas at this time to provide art education to children. Similarly, Domínguez remembers one project of plywood murals that was also done by children:

> *Yo hice como 8 [murales] en el bajo Manhattan, no queda uno; queda uno adentro de Charas en plywood, que fue con niños y no sé qué va a suceder. Está todavía intact.* [I did 8 murals in the borough Manhattan, not one remains, one still remains inside Charas on plywood, which was made by children and I don't know what will happen. It is still intact.] We should reclaim it, because this building it was closed—for so long it was cold so the climate was perfect it was on plywood and it stayed there intact, it looks like as if I painted it yesterday and this was with little kids.[91]

Community muralism in Loisaida was clearly tied to an engagement with gang members, neighborhood youth, and school children in fundamental ways as tools of consciousness-raising, vehicles to teach responsibility and work ethics, and projects to tap into federal funding.

The Power of Community Murals

As publicly visible cultural texts, the colors of Loisaida murals—the green of palm trees, the red and blue of Puerto Rican flags, the yellow of a bright sun—were not purely artistic representations. Indeed, these colors catalyzed and amplified ongoing and projected community activism. They were clearly "fulfilling important social, political, and economic motives within an urban community."[92] Whether it was the creation of a significant community park and garden, the promotion of a grassroots economic revitalization project, or the ability to play a meaningful role in youth education and job training, murals were deeply embedded in these community efforts. This aspect of community muralism explains why murals were never meant to be permanent objects; murals have always been and continue to be ephemeral in nature. In a short documentary on *La Lucha*, Canadian artist and photographer Philip Pocock says, "Murals are done for the moment and they're allowed to die."[93] While Pocock is talking about private art versus public art—commercial art versus street art—this takes on another meaning in the context of the murals' embeddedness in community organizing: they were created for the moment to catalyze specific projects and often were allowed to die once they served their purpose—only to be replaced by new murals if necessary. Murals also depended on collaboration between various community groups because they required artists to design and paint them, gain access to scaffolding and other equipment for large walls along with people to set it all up, groups and schools to reach out to young people, and a broad organizational portfolio to raise funds. Muralism was and is intrinsically collaborative, which means that Loisaida murals *had to be* collective events. How else would they have been able to truly capture the diversity—the colors—of Loisaida community activism?

CHAPTER 5

The Battle against Gentrification

The strength and spirit of Charas is the synergy that is created on a daily basis by the continuous intersection of cultural expression and community development activities that contribute to a collective vision of community that is characterized by creativity, respect and common humanity.

—Charas, Charas History flyer

"Picture if you will, a sturdy, old former school building given new life."[1] That is how Charas members began an undated document on their vision for the future of Loisaida activism. Following their adventures with geodesic domes, windmills, solar walls, and housing revitalization, Charas leaders claimed the abandoned Public School 64 at 605 East 9th Street as their new headquarters. They renamed this damaged and largely vandalized building El Bohío, which aptly translates to "shack" or "hut." The dream was to turn the rundown former public school into "a mecca for the visual and performing arts . . . bursting with activity from morning to night." When Charas activists began renovating the building with the help of AAB in 1978, they clearly envisioned the imposing five-floor, H-style architectural giant as the future "focal point and activity anchor for Manhattan's Lower East Side." These clairvoyant activists, always anticipating what their community would need, imagined the many art exhibitions that would be held at La Galería en El Bohío, the experimental and independent plays that would be performed at La Terraza, the inner courtyard that would come alive with concerts and dance events, the protest films that would be screened and discussed in the basement's cinema, the big plays that would find a home in the theater, and all the people who would breathe life into this shack for the next twenty-five years. Although their dream was cut short when the city auctioned off the property on July 20, 1998, it remained alive for almost a quarter of a century, during a time when Puerto Ricans and low-income residents were being pushed out of Loisaida due to rising rents.[2]

While the second chapter details the organization's initial phase of building a community network through pioneering urban projects, this chapter unearths the crucial role El Bohío played in allowing Charas to not just expand its network and become a community hub, but also to shift its activist strategy away from environmental and housing projects toward cultural activism. This shift was necessary because funding and support from city and national agencies died off in favor of a burgeoning neoliberal governance model. As important as El Bohío became for Charas, the strong ties of community activism to a physical space ended Charas's mission too soon.

In the 1979 Loisaida special issue of *WIN Magazine*, Chino García made it very clear that Charas was "people-oriented," claiming the organization prioritized "working together, sharing ideas and trying to make them come true . . . developing a strong *foundation for the future*."[3] One key example was a conference that resulted from its relationship with Goddard College in Vermont: "Urban Alternatives: Towards a New Urbanism." It took place at Charas's new community center El Bohío on May 8 and 9, 1983, and was co-organized by Charas and the Institute for Social Ecology. It brought together esteemed academics such as Murray Bookchin and faculty from Columbia University, New York University, and the Pratt Institute as well as community organizations such as the Green Guerillas, Cuando, and Charas.[4] This conference turned out to be an amalgam of creative and progressive panels that highlighted the activist spirit in Loisaida. Some sessions focused on basic, neighborhood topics such as urban gardens; neighborhood governance; or personal safety, while other sessions such as "Women Claiming Space," "Non-Nuclear N.Y.," and "Education Alternatives" highlighted Charas's political leanings and socially progressive thinking at a time of strong national conservative backlash against the liberal years of John F. Kennedy and Lyndon B. Johnson.[5] Moreover, the event touched on the majority of issues that defined the 1960s and 1970s countercultural movement in the United States: nuclear weapons and energy, the Vietnam War, women's rights, civil rights, education reform, and environmentalism.

The integral nature of community murals in Loisaida activism already exemplified the increasing importance of art for an urban neighborhood and how artistic and cultural activity became part and parcel of the gentrification debate in the 1980s.[6] The conference in 1983, at a time when El Bohío was still in dire need of repair, symbolized a new direction for Charas, which began offering cultural programs almost as soon as it moved into the new headquarters in early 1980. Interestingly, García did not present at the "Energy Alternatives" or "Housing" sessions but instead offered a panel on "Culture, Arts, and the Media" alongside his friend playwright Bimbo Rivas.[7] In an interview for the *WIN Magazine* article with Charas member Josie Rolon, four years prior to the conference, García said that through his work at Charas and with the Loisaida community, he "learned to be an artist—for the arts flourish here *like a flower growing in between fence wire*—beauty amongst the beast. It's become a way of life—to be an artist is the ultimate goal, for in the back of our minds we know what it means. It's an attempt to love, communicate, feel the spirit of the movement."[8] García did not just feel the spirit of the burgeoning Nuyorican arts and culture movement: through Charas he helped *shape* it. Though Charas never stopped engaging in housing and environmental projects, El Bohío brought along a new phase in the group's history, one that catapulted the Charas Cultural Community Center—as El Bohío was also known—to the forefront of Loisaida cultural activism. It was during its El Bohío years that Charas saw the return of its investment into sustainable strategies in the form of community leadership.

The Shack

Before Charas members started renovating their future community center, the building had served the Lower East Side since the early twentieth century as a progressive reform school in the spirit of educators such as John Dewey. A report by the Landmarks Preservation Commission, which designated the building as a landmark in 2006, explains how John Dewey and other school reformers "believed that schools could help society's problems and saw them as community centers, offering recreation, adult education and health care during the hours that classes were not in session."[9] The famous school architect Charles B. J. Snyder originally designed the building to serve its direct community, evidenced by a large auditorium that can be accessed from the street for large events.[10] Due to financial difficulties, the school board closed P.S. 64 in 1977, but it did not stand empty for long:

> in the spirit of Snyder's original vision, the building continued to function as a busy community center. Just as it had served as a center of education and acculturation for European immigrants of the early twentieth century, this building was adapted to the needs of a new generation of immigrants. It was taken over by CHARAS/El Bohío a group formed in the 1960s to meet

the needs of the Latino community. They used the former school for classes, meeting rooms, performances, rehearsal space, art studios and galleries to foster and promote local culture and community. As El Bohío, this building served as an area focal point for the broad-based, citizen's movement to preserve the buildings and the community of a poor and minority neighborhood despite its deterioration and the city's fiscal crisis of the late 1970s and 80s. During a period when the Lower East Side was beset by owner disinvestment and abandonment, this building served as a physical and symbolic center of local efforts to restore and invest in the buildings and community of the Lower East Side, or Loisaida, neighborhood.[11]

When the Landmarks Preservation Commission mentions "Snyder's original vision," the authors refer specifically to Charas's cultural programming, which they developed at El Bohío based on their experiences with the University of the Streets in the 1960s. This included, for example, performances by local groups and artists in El Teatro La Terraza and the auditorium.[12] Charas also featured exhibition space at La Galeria en El Bohío and provided artist-in-residence programs for both local and national talent. Lastly, Charas "provided an audience to such (then) unknown film makers as John Sayles, Todd Haynes and Spike Lee."[13] Overall, the report that designated this building a landmark traces how various aspects of Charas's work was consistent with a long tradition of activism and progressive reform in the Lower East Side: (1) community-centered cultural programs, (2) after-class youth programs, (3) "linking environmental and ecological issues to that of neighborhood revival," and (4) organizing protests and marches.

However, as much as it was concerned with the needs of Loisaida residents, Charas was engaged in a long and tense struggle with the city to keep the building. Initially, when it moved into the building, it did so without any formal agreement with the city, which still owned the property. For a few years there were no issues as the city was still recovering from the financial crisis and was too distracted by much larger problems designed to get New York back on track. A letter from Carlos Perkins, director of AAB at the time, to the Department of General Services shows there was some agreement to renovate the building, but Perkins noted that for him "everything seems rather vague" and that he wanted a meeting with the city "to discuss in detail the future of the school building."[14] It seems the city was not interested in any such meeting because the Department of General Services responded later in 1984 with a notice to vacate the premises of 605 East 9th Street. According to the notice, addressed simply to John and Jane Doe, Charas and any other organization occupying the building "intruded into or squatted upon said real property without the permission of the undersigned."[15] García protested this notice to vacate the premises in his response to the letter: "We feel that this type of notice is a very negative action, it makes local community groups like us very uncomfortable with a sense of insecurity in our relationship with the Administration of your Dept. of the City Of New York, and it affects our positive planning and development of our center."[16] Charas had worked with a law firm since 1982 to sort out a long-term solution between El Bohío Public Development Corporation—the umbrella collective of Charas, AAB, and Seven Loaves that managed El Bohío—and the city. The Department of General Services backed off from forcing Charas and other groups to vacate the building by the June 30, 1984, deadline and agreed to a month-to-month lease of the property.

At a pivotal moment in 1989, during a Charas retreat to formulate a new strategy for the future of Charas, all participants identified various problems with their current situation, and the list of bullet points included the following items: "Feeling of treading water by staying in the building," "Frustration at not being able to move ahead with building," "Month to month lease," and "No long term financial plan."[17] Clearly, Charas members agreed that their relationship with the city was tense and they knew that the city could decide to evict them at any moment. Of course, this is exactly what happened in 1996. Yet despite their struggle with the city to keep hold of El Bohío, Charas managed to bring together a collection of community groups to occupy El Bohío and turn it into a true community center, largely because Charas was by no means the only organization that "intruded into or squatted upon said real property."[18]

Besides Charas and AAB, which were mainly involved in the renovations and acquisition of El Bohío, the Lower East Side arts collective Seven Loaves, founded in 1972, was invited to work with El Bohío early on in 1979.[19] Seven Loaves had existed for several years, strongly tied to the work and events of Charas and AAB. In fact, Charas was one of its members alongside CAW and El Teatro Ambulante. Fred Good, who worked with Charas members when they were still RGS, worked with Seven Loaves at this point and was therefore involved in many organizational aspects such as applying for a tax-exempt status in 1983.[20] Seven Loaves was founded specifically as a collective "to serve as a center for pooled resources, to encourage communication among the groups, and to provide administrative training for programs that had existed independently."[21] Seven Loaves essentially took care of the administrative and financial side for several smaller community groups. According to its records, it coordinated "festivals, exhibits, block parties and other community projects in which the arts can play a part."[22]

When Seven Loaves moved into El Bohío in 1980, the art collective's membership included Tylis Photo and Documentation, the *Quality of Life in Loisaida*, Tu Casa, and Plaza Cultural, among others. Seven Loaves' influence in helping create a network of artists and art groups cannot be understated because its fund-raising efforts and administrative training resulted in increased funds for all member organizations: "By the time the coalition was in its second year, grants to the members were four times what they had been before Seven Loaves was formed."[23] In this light, it is no wonder that El Bohío housed, almost exclusively, arts and culture groups until 1992: the Puerto Rican Traveling Theater, Tompkins Square Artists, Scavenger Theater, 9th Street Theater, Marlis Tylis Photo, and, of course, Charas.[24] With AAB moving out of El Bohío in 1981 and the building still in a state of disrepair, it was only due to Charas and Seven Loaves that any form of cultural programming took place in the early 1980s. According to one of the earliest pamphlets on El Bohío, in this time of crisis, "a lot of the people involved in the day to day operations of the building and the major negotiations still were able to provide the community with music concerts, poetry readings, theatre, film screenings, martial arts workshops, and many other activities including the on-going community organizing."[25]

Bringing all these smaller community groups together under one house was a key goal for Charas. As Charas began to take shape as a professional organization, it formulated a set of responsibilities in its bylaws:

- To provide space in the Loisaida and the Lower East Side Community (hereafter referred to as Loisaida) where a wide variety of artists can work at their art, rehearse, store their materials, and present their products. The space is only available to non-profit groups and artists sponsored under El Bohío's Special Program for Individual Artists, and there is a special emphasis on its use for minority groups whose members are in the lower and moderate income brackets.
- To promote a strong sense of fellowship, networking, and harmonious cooperation among El Bohío Tenants.
- To encourage El Bohío tenants to serve the children of Loisaida on an ongoing basis.[26]

In essence, Charas and El Bohío used arts and cultural programs to serve minority groups, Loisaida residents, young people, and artists. Taking into account some key funding bodies, including the National Endowment for the

Arts, the New York State Council of the Arts, the New York City Department of Cultural Affairs, the Lower Manhattan Art Council, and the Association of Hispanic Arts, makes it clearer why Charas shifted its activism from housing and environmental projects to cultural programs. Funding for housing and community projects declined, and the cultural grants required an emphasis on arts and culture. Unlike mural organizations such as CAW and Artmakers, described in the previous chapter, Charas was able to tap traditional arts sponsors for funding due to its more traditional portfolio of cultural programs that emphasized film, theater, and art exhibitions—murals were only supported by these arts foundations for some time in the 1970s. While the shift was somewhat forced because pro-community housing grants were reformed at city, state, and federal levels at the end of the 1970s, this did not in any way deter Charas from staying true to its original vision of serving Loisaida Puerto Ricans and youth. The organization specifically encouraged El Bohío tenants and other community groups occupying space in the building to serve children first and foremost. Equally, its programs over the next two decades emphasized support for noncommercial artists. Lastly, it had to start charging for some of its events as well as rental space, but it always had special lower-income price brackets as well as in-residence programs and volunteer programs to ensure that it did not outprice its primary audience. Charas was keenly aware of the changing demographics in Loisaida: it was "one of the few forces in the community to provide interface and dialogue between the earlier low-income, predominantly Puerto Rican groups and the most recent low-to-moderate income Anglos, many of them artists."[27] As friendly host-residents, Charas members reached out to the new wave of more affluent artists and residents—a sign of Charas's long-term commitment to inclusionary community work for all of Loisaida.

This change in demographics and the slow gentrification of the area during Charas's time at El Bohío go hand in hand with Charas's turn to cultural activism. The need to renovate properties became less important because developers returned to do renovation work themselves—increasing rents in the process. Of course, these changes drove out the neighborhood's lower-income earners, many of whom were Puerto Rican. The nearby Greenwich Village had already become an expensive, hip downtown neighborhood in the 1960s and 1970s, and it was clear to Loisaida residents that their neighborhood was next. In an article on art and activism, Brian Maxwell explains the dilemma Charas struggled with as a cultural organization in downtown New York in the 1980s and 1990s: "The catch is that the more work Charas does on the space to prove itself worthy, the more attractive the space becomes to city and other organizations—not to mention developers—who all see it as a prime location in a rapidly gentrifying neighborhood."[28] When interviewed for this article, García expressed his and Charas's thoughts on gentrification quite bluntly: "We have to put up a fight against those trying to commit genocide against the lower classes of this city."[29] The word "genocide" might seem too strong to describe gentrification, but this is exactly how it felt to García at the time when loosened rent regulation enabled developers to cheaply acquire the rundown properties in Loisaida, bring them up to code, refurbish them, and hike up the rent.[30] This rapidly displaced Loisaida residents, who had to move out to Brooklyn or the Bronx. Thus the focus of activism had to shift from housing and environmentalism to culture. After all, this was a community organization that required financial support from sponsors and governmental agencies. Charas had previously tapped into programs that AAB also used for housing renovation and homesteading programs. When these programs were replaced by new pro-privatization policies, Charas had to find other funding sources.

The renovation and repair of El Bohío was initially supported by the city, as one letter to the Department of General Services shows: "In discussion with Chino García I am told the design money originally allocated in the amount of approximately $40,000 is still in abeyance."[31] The lack of communication with the city made it clear to Charas that it could no longer rely on these community grants. Instead, it rebranded itself as a cultural organization, which was a good fit for Charas "because a lot of people who got involved with Charas [were] artists," according to García.[32] The shift toward the cultural and artistic arena—working on plays, films, exhibitions—was as much forced by external circumstances as it was part of Charas's direction since the University of the Streets and its emphasis on classes in photography, arts, and crafts to engage and educate Loisaida youth. Using its new expanded cultural programs, especially its film series, Charas began to broaden its organizing activity in Loisaida.

The Survival Show

In 1981, while still working on emergency repairs and having barely moved into El Bohío, Charas and Seven Loaves presented their first major arts event: the Survival Show. An article about this show in *Quality of Life in Loisaida* hardly gives the impression that the building was still in a state of disrepair:

"Walking into old PS64 during June was like walking into an explosion of art. From the minute you stepped through the doors you were bombarded with forceful murals (painted directly on the walls), sculptures, pipes that sang, photographs, stairwells full of neon lights, song, theatre, paintings, imaginative environments, and so on."[33] Charas had always taken its motto—"Doing more with less"—to heart, and this was no exception. As spring came around and the weather got warmer, Charas was finally able to open El Bohío for the summer. For many years, El Bohío was only able to open its doors for events during the warm months as there was no central heating, and its temporary gas-fired heating solution was not good enough to fight the New York winter.[34] On May 31, the show opened with a full day of celebratory performances. The event made use of all available space in El Bohío, including the gym, the courtyard, and the lobby, and the day was packed with local artists displaying the breadth of Loisaida talent. Performances ran simultaneously in different rooms so that at any given time, between 1:00 p.m. and late into the night, some part of the building was making audible noise. In general, dance performances by artists such as Susan Sugar took place in the gym, the lobby and its hallway were used for slide projections and films such as *You Say You Want a Revolution/a Meditation*, and the outside courtyard was largely reserved for inviting music by groups such as Avant Squares.[35] Seven Loaves and Charas wrote an introduction not just for the show but also to introduce El Bohío and Loisaida to newcomers. This text likely greeted visitors in the form of a flyer or poster when they entered the building for the exhibition and opening performances on May 31:

> Welcome to Loisaida and to "El Bohío" which is the name we have given to old PS64, a former New York City public school which was abandoned by the Board of Education several years ago. We hope that you will enjoy and learn from the exhibit taking place on the first and third floors of this building during the month of June. . . . Entirely a volunteer effort, the exhibit involves the cooperation of many people. Its aim is to bring attention to the struggle of local community groups and individuals to keep old PS64 from falling into the hands of real estate speculators. Rather, these people and organizations want to create a community center which involves and serves residents of the Lower East Side.[36]

From the beginning, Charas and Seven Loaves wasted no time in organizing a big event framed as a protest show to support local and independent talent during a period "when art [had] become big business."[37]

The Survival Show was by no means an isolated event. In 1980, two other protest shows debuted: the Times Square Show at Times Square and the Real Estate Show in the Lower East Side. The Times Square Show featured, most notably, the work of Jean-Michel Basquiat and was overall a mix of pop art and graffiti.[38] The Real Estate Show took place, illegally, in a vacant city-owned building at 123 Delancey Street. This art and performance show "had its roots in the anger many Tribeca artists felt in being gentrified out of their neighborhood."[39] In this sense, the Survival Show at El Bohío was part of a "three-year run of exhibitions that embodied both the politicized spirit and commercial growth of [an] alternative art community in the early 1980s."[40] Back in 1981 it was not widely understood yet that these kinds of alternative art projects— actively protesting gentrification and commercial art—developed an attractive culture that played into the hands of developers, who were able to sell their expensive properties in this hip neighborhood. Nevertheless, the Survival Show was in many ways symbolic for Charas's consequent work: using art and cultural events as a tool for its activism. Its was a drawn-out battle of survival against the commercialization of art, real estate developers, city agencies, and an onslaught of young and naive tenants inadvertently displacing an entire generation of Puerto Ricans who were desperate to hang onto their home—a home they built and maintained with their own sweat.

According to Fred Good, "The Survival Show was emblematic of a trend which would characterize Charas for the next two decades."[41] Through its after-school classes for children, its training programs for teenagers, its protest organizing, and its cultural programming, Charas's work at El Bohío was a two-decade-long survival show itself. In remembering El Bohío, Loisaida activist and *Quality of Life in Loisaida* editor Alfredo Irizarry wrote: "Saving the abandoned PS64 School building on East Ninth Street and creating a community center to address the issues [gentrification and displacement], became our Alamo. It became our last stand to fight the city and the developers, to prevent them from bull dozing our LES neighborhood."[42] Early on in this show of survival, Films Charas—a community films initiative—emerged as a vital part of Charas's annual summer programming and activist space. It ran its first season in 1982 with "programs which do favour independent work, and cultivate close relationships among filmmakers, local audience and subject matter."[43] Over the years, it supported community filmmakers as well as other independent talent by providing a space to exhibit their work in Loisaida's new community hub. El Bohío's basement featured a large auditorium that was converted into a film and performance space with 340 "plush theatre seats in decent repair even if a bit shabby."[44] This space was known as the New Assembly Theatre and was accessible directly from East 10th Street, at the back of El Bohío.

Community Cinema as Protest Space

The former auditorium was aptly named New Assembly Theatre, as this was the primary space within the large building to gather for large events. Films Charas was no exception to this. This community film initiative was not simply dedicated to screening movies and sending people home after the credits rolled. Films Charas combined "subjects and filmmakers of minority interest/background with avante [sic] garde films. In many cases the artists [were] present to discuss their films."[45] In an interview with the Village Voice, Films Charas director Doris Kornish emphasized this aspect of the group's film events in relation to a series of films on prisons and police violence: "There was very heated dialogue after we showed those films . . . People came with a lot of hostility against the police. They had flyers and buttons, and they wanted a place where they could talk about their problems."[46] If El Bohío represented the neighborhood's last line of defense, this performance space became its strategy room—built around a carefully selected program of protest films to frame and spark discussions.

The person responsible for turning a largely passive activity of silently staring at a screen into an activist platform was Doris Kornish, the director of Film Charas. Kornish founded the initiative alongside filmmaker Matthew Seig in 1981—they were both amateur filmmakers. Soon after, Seig left the program and was replaced by Kevin Duggan, also an amateur filmmaker. Neither Kornish nor Duggan went to film school; however, Kornish exhibited movies "at a college in West Virginia," while Duggan showed his movies "at Long Island's New Community Cinema."[47] Kornish was married to Philip Hartman at the time and produced her husband's feature film about the East Village, No Picnic (1986), starring Steve Buscemi and Charas activist and actor Luis Guzmán. She joined Charas with the acquisition of El Bohío because she "always wanted to have a movie theater or a space that could accommodate different kinds of people . . . it's important that we represent all the people in the community and give them a neighborhood meeting place."[48]

Creating this meeting place, this strategy room, was always part of the plan for Films Charas, and it was equally important for the codirectors to engage with social issues such as the 1988 Tompkins Square Park riot, the occupation of the Puerto Rican island Vieques by the United States Navy, and gentrification. For Duggan, Films Charas always had "a commitment to what you might call 'social-issue' filmmaking."[49] To turn the screenings into proper social events first, to draw a crowd and present a more engaging program, film screenings were—whenever possible—both coupled with a discussion with the filmmakers and other types of performances. One example of this was a series of Lower East Side movies throughout September 1984. Films Charas screened all manner of short and long movies related to its neighborhood: "Tompkins Square Park" (1967) is a celebration of the community park adjacent to El Bohío; *Pull My Daisy* (1959) is a Beat Generation film; and *The Heart of Loisaida* (1979) is AAB's documentary on sweat equity housing in Loisaida. There were fourteen films altogether, and each night included at least one speaker, usually the filmmaker, and some form of performance such as poetry by Bimbo Rivas or salsa dancing with Joe and Luis Ortiz—apparently the "hottest conga players on the Lower East Side." In a continuing commitment to support Loisaida youth, six of the fourteen films "were made by teen-age film students at the Film Club of the Young Filmmakers Foundation, a Lower East Side public access center."[50] It was, as always, important for Charas to turn its events into a mix of social, creative, and political outings.

The myriad of film schedules over the years indicates that films and ensuing discussions covered a broad range of political topics: immigration, gentrification, housing, police violence, colonization, the Three Mile Island incident, nuclear warfare, women's rights, workers' rights, solar power, communism, the Algerian War, and Puerto Rican independence. Beyond these, and many more, two specific events stand out: the occupation of Vieques and the Tompkins Square Park riot of 1988. Both of these developments had a significant impact on Charas and showcase its broad concerns for justice and its use of films in the New Assembly Space as a means to discuss and mobilize around important threats to the community.

The United States Navy acquired two thirds of the Puerto Rican island Vieques in the 1940s to store ammunition and conduct live training exercises, including a Live Impact Area (LIA) used to test explosives. The island gained international attention following an incident in which civilian employee David Sanes Rodríguez was killed when ordnance was dropped too close to his post on April 19, 1999. According to a congressional report, "the pilot of a Marine Corps F-18 on a training mission mistakenly identified an observation post located just to the west of the LIA (but still well within the overall range perimeter) as its intended target."[51] As the report explains, the death of Rodríguez galvanized Puerto Rican opposition to DON's [Department of the Navy] activities on the island. Puerto Rican political leaders and overwhelming segments of Puerto Rican public opinion soon declared their firm opposition to any further military training operations on the island and called for DON to withdraw from the island immediately and return the land to Puerto Rico. At the same time, dozens of demonstrators entered the range (most of which was off-limits to the civilian population) and established several protest camps, preventing DON from easily resuming training activities there.[52]

While the protests broke out on a large scale following the 1999 incident, forcing the navy to close the facilities in 2003, the occupation had been an issue for Puerto Ricans since the navy decided to occupy a large portion of the island and displace the farm workers who relied on the land. In his important study of property ownership and the social and economic structure of Vieques during the transfer of land to the navy, César J. Ayala explains how the navy's occupation of the island led to "a transition from a plantation economy, based on sugar *centrales* before the war, to an economy geared to providing services for the U.S. troops stationed on the island. One can also observe the proliferation of bars, restaurants, hostels, and their exact locations, and the closure of rural stores where *viequenses* had previously purchased their food."[53] In short, the occupation of Vieques played a key role in the collapse of the agricultural economy of Puerto Rico.

As a politically engaged community center, Charas hosted an event on the issue of land occupation back in 1987.[54] Rather than focusing on Vieques alone with the documentary *The Battle of Vieques* (1986), Films Charas screened alongside it *The Contrary Warrior: A Film of the Crow Tribe* (1985) because the film examines the fight for Crow tribal lands. (The Crow Tribe, or Apsáalooke in the Siouan language, has historically lived in the Yellowstone River valley.) Both films showcase the struggles of a group of people, Puerto Ricans and Native Americans, in the face of United States occupation and land expropriation. In the case of Puerto Rico, the film not only highlights the specific issue of this military base on a smaller island near the Puerto Rican mainland; it also is representative of the larger history of U.S. occupation of Puerto Rican land—and it should be remembered that Puerto Ricans are descendants of the indigenous Taínos.[55] It is also important that both films feature oral accounts from people directly affected by the struggles over land: *Contrary Warrior* is largely told by the ninety-seven-year-old tribe leader Robert Yellow-tail, who lived through a century of poverty and mistreatment of his tribe. *The Battle of Vieques*, on the other hand, is a story "told by Vieques' people—fishermen, merchants, workers, students and local officials—and by U.S. military offi-cials."[56] Over a decade prior to the death of Rodríguez, Charas was already discussing the occupation in its community center in New York.

Charas was also involved in organizing protests and support for peace in Vieques after April 1999; in fact, Charas was the main organizing hub in the city. After the annual 2000 Puerto Rican Parade featured the bombing on Vieques, Mayor Rudolph Giuliani tried to ban political issues in the 2001 parade, citing violent outbursts against a group of women during the 2000 parade.[57] In response, Charas scheduled an emergency meeting at El Bohío on June 4, 2001. For Puerto Ricans in New York, this proposed ban was not just about lessening protest against the occupation on Vieques; it represented an occupation of a cornerstone Puerto Rican cultural festival and an infringe-ment of free speech. Promoting the emergency meeting online, one anony-mous person wrote: "There is enough reason to believe the attempts to silence the pro-Vieques movement at the annual Puerto Rican Day Parade is ulti-mately aimed at doing away with the freedoms of speech and assembly, not only for Puerto Ricans but for all peoples' struggles everywhere. . . . What bet-ter way of eliminating the Puerto Rican Day Parade than to begin the process with the exclusion of the political movement which supports the struggle to get the U.S. Navy out of Vieques and which is opposed to the general oppres-sion of the Puerto Rican people?"[58]

Despite the proposed ban by authorities, Puerto Ricans marched against Navy occupation during the 2001 parade on June 10. Leading the protest for peace in Vieques, Charas produced a large banner that was carried during the parade, featuring the Puerto Rican flag and the peace dove. During its thirty-fifth anniversary celebrations in 2000, Charas received a message of gratitude from VSC: "For us who are directly involved in the present day struggle to get the U.S. Navy out of the Puerto Rican island municipality of Vieques, do not extend this salute to you lightly. We view the deeds of those forces trying to take this valuable institution away from the community, as being ultimately rooted in government-corporate policy and behaviours that once expelled the native population of Vieques from three quarters of that island."[59]

This simple message of thanks to Charas explains a fundamental reason why Charas persisted in its support for Vieques: at the same time Charas was marching with banners demanding peace in Vieques, it was involved in marches to save El Bohío and its community work in Loisaida. The struggles that Viequenses had been facing since the early 1940s were, at their core, the same struggles Loisaida Puerto Ricans had encountered since the 1940s. The radical economic shift in Puerto Rico, caused in great parts by the destruction of the sugar industry that "had produced the highest degree of land concentration" in Vieques, resulted in the migration of over six hundred thousand Puerto Ricans to New York alone between 1940 and 1960.[60] In this context, the struggles Puerto Ricans faced in Loisaida, a key arrival destination for poor migrants, were also a direct result of the occupation of Vieques. Charas's support for Vieques was not just born out of pure solidarity for Puerto Rico; this was Loisaida's history and its fight too. Vieques was a fight over space and territory. The original film screenings in 1987 on the struggle over land for marginalized groups were not just a mere happenstance because both films had come out recently; rather, this event was a chance for this community to discuss its own fight to maintain ownership of El Bohío—against the desire of the city authorities who refused to grant Charas a long-term lease. It demonstrates the potential of social and cultural events to create political space in both intellectual (discussion) and practical (organizing) terms.

Just a year after the Vieques film screening in 1987, a large-scale police riot terrorized the Loisaida neighborhood on August 6, 1988. The riot was the consequence of attempts by the city and Mayor Ed Koch to "clean up the park" (forcibly remove its homeless inhabitants), which had been home to Loisaida youth and homeless people as well as a whole range of radical and marginalized subcultures such as punks, drug addicts, anarchists, communists, and squatters. The dramatic showdown between protestors and police on the night of August 6 was both the result of an ongoing fight to keep the park free of curfews and other restrictions and the start of a much larger wave of protests and riots that lasted until the city authorities arrested key activists in 1991. Why would Loisaida activists and residents fight so hard for this park? As with the Vieques movement, this was entirely a battle over space—in this case public, urban, and community space. Not simply a park, Tompkins Square Park was known as Tent City (see figure 8) due to a vast number of tents occupying the space, providing homes for groups displaced by the gentrification of their neighborhood. Whereas the U.S. military force was responsible for the land grab on Vieques, urban renewal and gentrification were the driving forces behind the Tompkins Square Park expropriation.

Chronicling the history of the protests around the park, A. Kronstadt writes that he "will not put an exact date upon the beginning of the Revolt because, in a sense, the rebellion began when the first bohemian artist set foot in downtown Manhattan."[61] Here, Kronstadt is referring to the early signs of gentrification, such as the battles over artist housing mentioned in the previous chapter. While simplifying the issue somewhat, Kronstadt goes on to

explain the causality between artists and wealthier professionals moving in
and current residents being forced out of their proper homes:

> Yuppies poured in and filled the apartments that the neighborhood folk, be
> they Puerto Rican, Slavic, Jewish, beatnik, hippie, punk, or conceptual art-
> ist, had been priced out of. In the bohemian/ethnic vs. yuppie/mainstream
> dichotomy, one can see the central conflict of our story. The word "yuppie"
> would play a prominent part in the discourse of the Tompkins Square Neigh-
> borhood Revolt because we perceived the young upper middle class and rich
> boys and girls moving into the neighborhood in an adversarial manner. Many
> of us had been through co-op conversions in which groups of yuppies bought
> into a building and put the apartments up for sale at prices that we could
> never hope to come up with, and in which the threat of eviction and displace-
> ment from the neighborhood was ever present.[62]

Although some residents moved to other neighborhoods, others wanted to
stay, and so gentrification gave birth to Tent City—poor New Yorkers finding
a way to survive a desperate situation not unlike the Hooverville shanty towns
that were created during the Great Depression. While academics, activists,

and residents have written about various aspects of this infamous event, no one has highlighted the role of Charas as a hub for the community to come together and organize.[63]

With El Bohío located not even forty meters away from the park, Charas was bound to be affected and get involved. Following the clashes on August 6, Charas sent out a press release to promote an upcoming film event on November 16 in its well-established strategy and meeting space: the New Assembly Theater. The press release states: "Films Charas is screening Garrin's 'Free Society' and the 'Tompkins Square Park Riot' FREE to keep everyone informed about the continuing struggle over the park (an ACLU press conference is scheduled at St. Brigid's, Nov. 19); the police investigation that just creeps along; and to remind everyone that it's OUR COMMUNITY, OUR PARK!"[64] Documentarian and filmmaker Paul Garrin made both videos, and while only the latter was recorded on the night of August 6, it is important that Charas decided to screen these two films together. "Free Society" (1988) is a four-minute, experimental collection of video scenes that juxtapose images of police violence in the United States with images of military parades and action in South Africa, Northern Ireland, and the West Bank. As such it highlights the militarization of U.S. law enforcement, a key issue with Tompkins Square Park, as a *New York Times* article shows: "What occurred was indeed the 'police riot' some have charged. As the confrontation began to escalate, a panicky captain, finding himself in command because his deputy chief had left the scene, issued a '10–85 forthwith' radio call for help. 'This call is widely interpreted as being of an extreme emergency nature,' the report says. Hundreds of police flooded into the area, though they 'had not been briefed about the event . . . were not equipped for such an encounter . . . were not under the direct supervision of a superior officer.'"[65]

The more important film was the second one, however, a recording of the clashes between police and protestors. Although a few people recorded footage of the events, such as Lower East Side historian Clayton Patterson, it was Garrin's "riot tapes that ignited the police department investigation" mentioned in the *New York Times* piece.[66] As Garrin explains in a retrospective on the events, the tape "served as a tool, a weapon, and a witness," being used by the district attorney as evidence.[67] No doubt Garrin, a local resident, chose Charas to screen his videos because he knew how important it was to spread the word about what was happening with the park and why it mattered. Examining guerilla video and Tompkins Square Park, Richard Porton calls videos such as Garrin's community video, which for him was "neither mass culture not 'bohemianism' (to use Habermas' rather simplistic term for twentieth century avant-garde tendencies), but it certainly promotes a type of documentary practice that marks a sharp divergence from the ideologies of the 'political and economic systems.'"[68] As a guerilla video documentarian, Garrin presented his footage at the longest-standing guerilla activist organization in Loisaida, known for its passion to serve the community. Charas, once again, became a hub for protests, offering its space—the neighborhood's space—for ongoing organizing activity. As Amy Starecheski writes, El Bohío "became a vital space for local organizing, from the squatters and homesteaders of the 1980s to the antiglobalization Direct Action Network in the late nineties."[69] Unlike the Vieques movement, the movement to save Tompkins Square Park eventually failed, as grassroots campaigns against the symptoms of gentrification often do, but it was nevertheless a battle Charas needed to fight.

For Loisaida activists, every single battle over urban space, whether it was housing or public space, was important because every defeat would directly result in the erosion of this neighborhood: their housing, their gardens, their parks, their families. While Vieques and Tompkins Square Park represented only a small percentage of the overall battles Charas had fought for forty years between the early 1960s and the early 2000s, they provide a glimpse into the importance of Films Charas and Charas's newfound emphasis on cultural activism to stay financially afloat and continue serving Loisaida. Not every single film event turned into direct, community action, of course. And the film screenings were not free either; Charas charged a small amount to finance the operational and utility costs. Yet, Charas never strayed from its community-focused vision. The struggles with gentrification and its real effects on an urban community ran through Charas's entire stay at El Bohío. While some might argue that its cultural and artistic activity in Loisaida only furthered gentrification by presenting the area as an attractive and unique selling point, its relentless attacks on developers, the city, commercial artists, the U.S. government, and the U.S. Navy suggest that Charas did not represent bohemianism or a hip counterculture. Throughout its history, Charas had proven that its members cared about people—and not just in the abstract and general sense. Charas started out as RGS, a social service and educational group, then morphed into an environmental and housing organization, and finally became Loisaida's foremost cultural community center with a strong activist core. It sustained its work for nearly four decades based on its ability to change its activist strategies. García was there from the very beginning and made it his job to serve his community in whatever capacity he could. And it is important to understand that Charas considered itself as always acting on behalf of its community: those who attended events, those who participated in protests, and those who complained about rising rents and displacement. As García explained in an interview: "If we don't involve community people and keep the spirit, we lose their support."[70] Charas's last protest to save itself shows that it never lost this support.

Save Charas

In 1996, the fears that members of Charas expressed about their lease with the city and its fragility became reality. Out of the blue, "the City scheduled the building for auction on October 2, 1996."[71] As always, Charas responded swiftly by mobilizing its family of community organizations, which initially worked to cancel the auction as an article in the *Villager* shows: "In balancing what the city could gain by auctioning off the two properties, and comparing that to the artistic and social and community programs that they support, the Deputy Mayor (Randy Mastro) decided that they are obviously important to the community, to cultural groups, and to individual artists. So we're going to work with them to get them on sounder financial standing."[72] Feeling victorious, Charas drafted two plans for the financing and development of El Bohío and sent these out to Mastro on November 14, 1996. However, a letter by García from January 29, 1997, shows that the city did not care about Charas's proposals:

> it has been clear for some time now that the City is not keeping its word or dealing with us in good faith, as shown in the meetings between ourselves and the representatives assigned from your office. In the last two meetings that we had—November 20, 1996 and January 13, 1997—we found that your staff was not prepared and had not even studied the plans that we had presented on November 14th. We therefore question the seriousness of the City and of your office in "trying to reach an honorable settlement" with us, as you expressed in your statement to the press.[73]

A second letter to Mastro indicates that Mastro's associates promised to work out a deal by March 1, which did not take place.[74] Finally, real estate developer Gregg Singer secured the property in a 1998 auction for 3.15 million dollars with plans to turn it into a dormitory for students.[75] The city finally sent its order of eviction out on August 24, 2001, at which point Charas was forced to leave the premises for good.[76] And so it did.

Before Charas members vacated the premises, they had mounted their last defense beginning with a large community march on August 2, 1997.[77]

A flyer for the march shows the route within Loisaida starting at 10th Street Garden and ending at Chico Mendez Mural Garden. Rather than staging a march to save El Bohío, this was fashioned as a Loisaida unity march, which is why the march had nine stops on its path to protest very specific activities of displacement in the neighborhood. They stopped at the Riis, Wald, and Baruch public housing complexes, which represented "the last bastion of sane and reasonable rents . . . to provide decent, affordable housing and stabilize communities!" The march also stopped at the home of a local developer who was trying to destroy 10th and 11th Street Gardens. Their message: "You will be held accountable by the community!" At 5th Street Squat, which was demolished a year earlier, the marchers exclaimed solidarity with the squatters in Loisaida: "The squatters must be respected and defended because they represent those who took *direct, effective and exemplary action* while a corrupt and criminal government created mass homelessness and double rents for everyone else!"[78] This march demonstrates how Charas was not a singular, isolated organization but saw itself as part of a whole network of community groups and organizations. The flyer for the march had a hopeful and empowering message for its community: "If we think for ourselves and respect the work of others, we can unite our efforts. The result can only be the beginning of the end of error and oppression."

As with all of Charas's previous protests, this march was full of joy: a second flyer told people to "bring drums, banners, musical instruments, costumes," a sign of the importance of creativity and socializing even at a time of crisis.[79] As such, a political cry for justice turned into a family event complete with entertainment, refreshments, and snacks. Despite its best efforts, the defense by this community did little to stop the powerful forces of real estate developers and New York authorities. However, even while this flower wilted away, short of its lifespan, other flowers grew in its place. The organization Loisaida Center continued the mission of Charas, passing on the torch to a new generation of activists and artists who had grown up with Charas and were in an ideal position to transform Charas's spirit and vision for young Loisaida residents. Loisaida Center was founded in the 1970s to battle poverty and drug addiction and eventually grew into a social hub supporting families in particular. It created the Loisaida Festival and continues to host this annual festival to this day. Loisaida Center itself faced eviction in 2008 but was able to keep its center at 709 East 9th Street, just steps from El Bohío. Charas handed over the baton to another community center that had been a great partner in the past and whose mission is to celebrate "the urban surroundings, grassroots invention and immigrant spirit of the Loisaida neighborhood in its dedication to celebrate Latino cultural vitality and their contributions to NYC."[80] El Bohío might be gone, despite ongoing protests to return the landmark building to the community, but its legacy is deeply woven into the fabric of Loisaida and its history of community activism.[81]

The story of El Bohío's acquisitions and loss also exemplifies a major issue when it comes to sustaining community activism: the need for physical space. RGS, AAB, Cityarts, Charas, and the majority of community organizations in Loisaida frequently had to deal with the issue of keeping ahold of a center of operations or office space. AAB and Charas moved from street to street, their headquarters always in flux due to lack of funding, discriminatory landlords, or a lack of space required for a growing organization. The fact that Charas's mission was cut short by simply being evicted from the property demonstrates the importance of ownership over physical neighborhood space for the vitality of community activism. If youth engagement, network building, and claiming a right to the city can help sustain community activism, the loss of an organization's headquarters can put an end to it far too easily.

CHAPTER 6

The Resident Dissidents of El Spirit Republic de Puerto Rico

In 1994, Rev. Pedro and I re-established El Puerto Rican Embassy—conceptualized by Eduardo Eddie Figueroa—as a conceptual territory where audience/participants were confronted with Puerto Rico's colonial status and urged to decolonize their psyches and encouraged to empower themselves through their own creative expression. While El Puerto Rican Embassy is a form of popular political theatre the performances we staged were unique since El Puerto Rican Embassy included the issuing of passports that identify the bearers as members of El Spirit Republic de Puerto Rico. These passports were created and signed by me, and imprinted with a manifesto by Pietri.

—Adál Maldonado, e-mail message to author (2017)

At the dawn of the new millennium in 2001, the famous Nuyorican Poets Cafe in Loisaida hosted a strange event. A key hub for Puerto Rican and Latino culture alongside El Bohío, the Nuyorican Poets Cafe hosted a benefit event for Dylcia Noemi Pagan, a member of the former paramilitary organization Fuerzas Armadas de Liberación Nacional or FALN. This Marxist-Leninist group, which used direct action to advocate for Puerto Rican independence, was responsible for over 120 bombings in the United States from 1974 to 1983.[1] Pagan was sentenced to federal prison in 1981 for fifty-five years, but she was released early on September 10, 1999, as part of a clemency offer by President Bill Clinton.[2] According to the *New York Times*, "Mr. Clinton demanded as one of the conditions of their release that the jailed Puerto Ricans renounce the use of terrorism to achieve their aim of independence for the Caribbean commonwealth."[3] President Clinton's decision did not sit well with New York law enforcement, New York Democratic senator Daniel Patrick Moynihan, Mayor Rudolph W. Giuliani, or with his own wife, First Lady Hillary R. Clinton.[4] Mayor Giuliani declared, "You can emotionally be on one side or the other of this issue . . . but to say that it doesn't raise some very serious and legitimate questions and now to see his own political allies and close associates abandoning him like a sinking ship, you wonder what's going on here."[5] At the benefit event, former executive director of the Nuyorican Poets Cafe Carmen M. Pietri-Díaz, sister of poet Pedro Pietri and friend of Pagan's, welcomed Pagan to a new cultural movement that would allow her to continue the fight for Puerto Rican independence via slightly different means.

To celebrate her release two years earlier, Pagan was baptized with a poem by Pedro Pietri, who wrote his famous poem "Puerto Rican Obituary" in Pagan's apartment in the 1970s.[6] Afterward, Pagan was "issued her Baptism Certificate and Puerto Rican Passport [and] All others who wish to be baptized [were] asked to step forward and Rev. Pedro [said] a few words and [threw] some water on them."[7] Of course, there is no such thing as a Puerto Rican passport as Puerto Ricans were granted U.S. citizenship with the Jones-Shafroth Act in 1917. However, Puerto Ricans on both the island and mainland have contested Puerto Rico's limbo status as a commonwealth ever since the United States invaded the former Spanish colony in 1898 and seized control. As Carmen T. Whalen points out, the Jones Act provided de jure citizenship, but de facto: "Puerto Rico's political status was not changed. Puerto Ricans were now U.S. citizens living in an 'unincorporated territory.'"[8] Like the strange passport Pagan received, the baptism certificate was issued by La Santa Church de La Madre of Los Tomates with its supposed spiritual leader Reverend Pedro Pietri. Still more curious, the event was co-organized by El Puerto Rican Embassy when there has never been such an entity as a Puerto Rican embassy. If the handing out of baptism certificates by the Holy Church of the Mother of Tomatoes and the issuing of Puerto Rican passports by a nonexistent Puerto Rican embassy sound somewhat surreal, this is because it was designed this way.

El Embassy was a multimedia, interactive performance and art project created mainly by visual artist Adál Maldonado and poet Pedro Pietri in 1994 to form "a new Puerto Rican Art and Cultural movement."[9] This final chapter traces how El Embassy envisioned an imaginary nation whose members hold an imaginary citizenship that protects how Puerto Ricans identify their nationality beyond the century-old political battle over Puerto Rico's status as a commonwealth territory. Through the lens of El Embassy, which is based on the earlier concept of El Spirit Republic de Puerto Rico by former Young Lords member Eduardo "Eddie" Figueroa, artists and supporters actively promoted a claim to cultural citizenship through a process of decolonizing the imaginary.[10] This surrealist project existed both in the shared and individual imaginary of people and in the physical world they inhabited. This approach to activism, the quest to decolonize the imaginary and claim cultural citizenship, deserves attention not only for its unique reimagining of Puerto Rican citizenship but also for its broader ideas about citizenship, identity, and nationhood. The guiding question for this final chapter was articulated by Maldonado: "Is it possible to assume a national identity which has no citizenship privileges, as the country (El Spirit Republic de Puerto Rico) has no territories other than conceptual ones?"[11] El Embassy artists needed to complicate the concept of citizenship and national identity because that was the only way to capture and confront the paradox that Pietri so eloquently captured in El Spanglish National Anthem, which was performed at many El Embassy events in the 1990s and 2000s:

> I'm still in Puerto Rico
> Only my body came
> My strong spirit remains[12]

Following the more traditional community organizing work described in the previous chapters, this surrealist art project in the 1990s marks a clear shift in the activist methods employed as part of a larger tradition of Loisaida Puerto Ricans claiming the human right to the city or a right to citizenship. Just as Charas turned increasingly to film, theater, and art in this decade, so did Maldonado and his network of Puerto Rican artists contribute significantly to a new wave of Puerto Rican cultural activism commonly called the Nuyorican Movement—even when many artists and activists also operated on the periphery of this movement.

The Path to Cultural Citizenship

In his seminal work *Imagined Communities* (1983), Benedict Anderson advanced our understanding of nationhood and nationalism by arguing that "all communities larger than primordial villages of face-to-face contact (and perhaps even these) are imagined."[13] Anderson speaks of an "imagined political community" within the framework of nationhood, but as Renato Rosaldo and William V. Flores point out, Anderson "makes national communities appear static and independent from relations of inequality within the society in question. Second, he conceives of the national community as if there were a universal consensus among all citizens. He does not recognize the contestation and conflicts that animate a hegemonic process."[14] Jorge Duany also complicates Anderson's argument by pointing out that "the subjective sense of a separate nationality can thrive without the formal recognition of citizenship."[15] This applies to Puerto Ricans too, despite the de jure recognition of citizenship—especially for those living on the U.S. mainland. The task of analyzing, nuancing, and conceptualizing Puerto Rican citizenship and national identity has been at the forefront of scholarship in Puerto Rican studies for decades.

Duany reminds us that "none of the traditional criteria for nationhood—a shared territory, language, economy, citizenship, or sovereignty—are fixed and immutable in Puerto Rico and its diaspora but are subject to constant fluctuation and intense debate."[16] Instead, he postulates the nation "as a translocal community based on a collective consciousness of a shared history, language, and culture."[17] This translocality allows Duany to complicate questions of "citizenship, migration, and identity [which] acquire a sense of urgency seldom found in well-established nation-states that do not have to justify their existence or fight for their survival."[18]

As the 2005 case of *Gregorio Igartúa-de la Rosa, et al. v. United States of America* confirmed, Puerto Ricans are not able to vote in U.S. national elections, and the Puerto Rico Federal Relations Act of 1950, while enabling local government on the island, disqualified Puerto Rico's representation in the U.S. Congress.[19] Clearly, citizenship status for Puerto Ricans is limited, which is why the island's population voted in a referendum in 2012 on the question of their future political status. Two-thirds of those who voted in the referendum favored full statehood within the United States, while the rest favored sovereign free association.[20] For Juan Flores, the question of Puerto Rico's political status is less about the specific form (sovereignty, statehood, increased autonomy), but rather about the overarching goal that all possible programs have in common: "decolonization—that is, the recognition of an ongoing condition of subordination and external tutelage and the need to put an end to it."[21] Whether the United States will finally grant full statehood in the wake of the referendum results remains to be seen. Yet it is unlikely to radically change how Puerto Ricans, especially those with permanent residence on the mainland, will continue to challenge and complicate neatly defined notions of citizenship and belonging that have been imposed upon them from outside forces including academia, the media, and the government.

In the first half of the twentieth century, "U.S. citizenship facilitated a migration freed from immigration barriers, which sparked both labor recruitment and social networks."[22] However, the usefulness of U.S. citizenship, second class or not, declined dramatically in the second half of the century. Against the displacing forces of deindustrialization, gentrification, and neoliberalism, Puerto Ricans could no longer rely on labor from the largely industrial sector that had employed them earlier. This lack of economic opportunity shifted Puerto Ricans' claims to citizenship increasingly toward the cultural and social arenas of community life; namely, social practices and artistic expression. As Rina Benmayor, Rosa M. Torruellas, and Ana L. Juarbe point out: "Historically, culture has been the site of strongest resistance and the indelible mark of nationhood. Cultural commitments become even stronger in the context of a migration that has been disenfranchising and has imposed de-facto second-class status on a colonial people. Thus, the claim to cultural citizenship is an affirmation of a historical identity, a claim for social dignity, and a challenge to the exclusionary practices upon which legal and political citizenship have so long been based."[23]

This is not to say that community life and cultural celebrations had been unimportant before, quite the opposite. Still, as unemployment began to rise on both the mainland and the island, Puerto Ricans turned to cultural activism to resist their ongoing status as lesser citizens.[24] Rosaldo coined the term "cultural citizenship" to recognize how "culture interprets and constructs citizenship, just as the activity of being citizens, in the broad sense of claiming membership in the society, affects how we view ourselves, even in communities that have been branded as second-class or 'illegal.'"[25] Going beyond legal questions of citizenship status, cultural citizenship describes an empowerment process "of constructing, establishing, and asserting human, social and cultural rights [to the city]."[26]

What seems quite broad simply refers to the basic right "to be different (in terms of race, ethnicity, or native language) with respect to the norms of the dominant national community, without compromising one's right to belong," as Rosaldo and William Flores write.[27] This right to belong, to be different, is played out chiefly in the daily life of isolated and dispersed communities and neighborhoods across the United States, such as Loisaida. Wherever Puerto Ricans settled, they have tried to adjust to their new surroundings as well as attempting to adjust their environments to their own needs.[28] This has historically been the catalyst for the involvement and creation of various community organizations to improve the lives of themselves and others. However, Puerto Rican communities "increasingly fail to fit the 'barrio' model of a bounded ethnically homogeneous space . . . broken up by freeways, and dispersed in pockets throughout the city or even among cities."[29] So while communities are "essential foci for solidarity and for the struggle to claim and expand existing rights," the very definition of "community becomes a central research problem as one explores the networks of social relations that connect a series of dispersed points."[30] In this light, it is understandable why activists, residents, and artists needed to find alternative ways of building communities that supported the ongoing fight for the right to be different, to belong. El Embassy, like more traditional efforts to build a community by Puerto Ricans, focused on "creatively blending cultural icons and symbolic repertoires of various origins."[31] However, by blending the material with the spiritual, the real and the imaginary, El Embassy strove for something more lasting than the fragility of community groups with their temporary headquarters and campaigns—to varying degrees of success.

El Embassy's Mission to Decolonize the Imaginary

On June 10, 1994, just a short walk from the Nuyorican Poets Cafe, the art gallery space Kenkeleba House—appropriately named for a West African plant that is believed to possess spiritual powers—issued a press release for an upcoming exhibition entitled "El Puerto Rican Embassy Show."[32] This was the inaugural exhibition for Maldonado's and Pietri's amalgam of ideas and projects that would reintroduce the concept of El Republic and El Embassy after former Young Lords member Figueroa first conceptualized this "counterinstitutional and counterpolitical space . . . a translocal and non-juridical utopian space that cut across the upheavals of colonialism and diaspora."[33] From June 26 to July 30, thirty-one Puerto Rican artists, including Papo Colo, Marcos Dimas, Maria Domínguez, Pepón Osorio, and Juan Sánchez, exhibited their work at this Lower East Side location. Apart from the work of these artists, El Embassy appointed "Ambassadors of the Arts": Miguel Algarín (poetry), Miriam Colón (theater), Willie Colón (music), Raúl Julia (film), Antonio Martorell (visual arts), Ed Morales (journalism), Marta Moreno Vega (culture), and Piri Thomas (letters).[34]

Honoring those who had gone before them as artists, activists, and heroes, Maldonado and Pietri conceived of the "Hall of Fame of Deceased Diplomacy," which was presented in honor of Julia de Burgos, Eddie Figueroa, Antonia López, José Ferrer, Miguel Piñero, and Bimbo Rivas. Of particular note are de Burgos, Figueroa, Piñero, and Rivas: Rivas was a Loisaida playwright who coined the term "Loisaida" in the 1970s; Piñero was a poet and cofounder of the Nuyorican Poets Cafe; Figueroa was the founder of the New Rican Village (1976) and El Republic; and de Burgos was a beloved Puerto Rican poet who served as secretary general of the Daughters of Freedom (*Hijas de la Libertad*), the women's branch of the Puerto Rican Nationalist Party (Partido Nacionalista de Puerto Rico or PNPR).[35] The memorialization of these figures symbolized the philosophy of El Republic as a space that cut across the geo-

graphical distance of Loisaida and Puerto Rico. As with many future events
of El Embassy, Pietri read out the manifesto while Maldonado issued his passports. This inaugural exhibition was only the first in a series of events and
projects over the next decade that would reconceptualize and expand upon El
Republic as an active process of decolonizing Puerto Ricans' imaginaries in an
effort to claim cultural citizenship—a citizenship marked by a symbolic repertoire of cultural artefacts: the passport, the anthem, the baptism certificate,
and the use of Spanglish as the official language of El Republic.

In Maldonado's own words, this repertoire was "an attempt to reconstruct
the memory of a lost tradition merged with elements found in a new environment."[36] To understand the need for this artistic approach to decolonizing
one's imaginary, it is important to first trace Maldonado's conceptualization
of the colonizing process that he and El Republic attempted to counteract:

> The idea is that we are fixed to a particular place in physical reality due to an
> assemblage point located somewhere on our bodies. This point where the
> cosmic energy cross each other is the Assemblage Point (According to indig-
> enous peoples of New Mexico). Very much in the same way when taking a
> photograph an object or subject is in focus when the rays of light that bounce
> off the object being photographed cross each other when these light rays pass
> through the camera lens. This point where the light crosses each other in the
> camera lens is called the Focal Point. It is believed that when the Assemblage
> Point is moved or shifted from its place, either accidently or by trauma, that
> the person is no longer in the present. That person may experience a psycho-
> logical deconstruction that may appear to make him crazy to people in the
> physical reality when all that's happened is that his assemblage point has been
> shifted and he now may be experiencing life in another mental dimension.
> The account continues that men of knowledge or brujos of these New Mexico
> tribes were able to figure out how to purposely shift the Assemblage Point for
> the purpose of form changing and astral projecting empowering themselves
> in the process.[37]

Maldonado likely learned about the idea of an assemblage point from the
book *The Fire from Within* (1984) by author Carlos Castaneda, who published
over twenty-eight million books in seventeen languages on his experiences
with shamanism, which critics consider to be works of fiction rather than
firsthand experiences.[38] No matter the legitimacy of Castaneda's work, Maldonado used the idea of the assemblage point to relate how colonizing forces
"on the island caused a great psychological and emotional trauma that caused
the Puerto Rican's assemblage point to shift."[39] Like the indigenous people of

New Mexico, Maldonado was keenly aware that Puerto Ricans and the Puerto Rican diaspora "embraced their (out of focus) condition, and empowered themselves through their own creative intentions."[40] This psychological and emotional trauma is essentially the colonization of the imaginary—the effects that conquest, subordination, and colonization have on Puerto Ricans. It is exactly this trauma that the imaginary nation El Republic worked to visibilize and confront. All the artefacts and events were key to enabling citizens to rethink their own identities and decolonize their minds—to untangle oneself from the authoritarian power of the United States.

The insistence on the spirit, or the spiritual, in El Embassy's rhetoric—what Maldonado terms a "cosmic Assemblage Point"—had already been present in the rhetoric of Charas and AAB projects described in previous chapters. It goes back to Figueroa and the founding of the New Rican Village, which an attendee described as "a different conception of who we are as beings on this planet—beings that are part of nature, that are creators, that are *spiritual*."[41] As Ed Morales, the ambassador of journalism, recalls in a piece on El Republic, Figueroa "found a way to spark an eternal flame of *spiritual resistance*."[42] Figueroa himself said to Morales, the spiritual refers to "the belief in magic, the belief in a multidimensional universe, the belief in simultaneous eternal time, that what we're seeing is only part of what it is, and that this is inside of something else, and that the real mystery, the real point of all of this is the investigation, the navigation of the self, of the heart, the spirit, because that is where the truth is.[43] Figueroa was concerned with identity, "Puerto Rican spiritual identity" to be precise.[44] For Figueroa, a second-generation Puerto Rican who grew up in the United States, this simply meant "learning about mother and father and people being born again."[45] The idea of being born again is, of course, spiritual in nature and tied to encountering Puerto Rico and one's own roots—both familial and ancestral. Pietri writes about this spiritual rebirth in *Out of Focus Nuyoricans* in which he conceives of Puerto Rico as "an island where eternal life and reincarnation is possible and multiple personalities aren't considered mental illness but a gift from the gods who will never allow us to cease speaking in tongues to get a message across the centuries."[46] As the imaginative poetics of Figueroa and Pietri demonstrate, spirituality for these artists was far from an easily identifiable belief system that could be appropriated by outside forces—as was the case with physical spaces and the infiltration of the Young Lords by the FBI. On the contrary, (Puerto Rican) spirituality was conceived of as a metaphysical philosophy that allowed for multiple identities, a complicating of national identity, and a lasting resistance to the dragging question of independence.

Both Figueroa and Pietri were members of the Young Lords until they realized that it quickly "became impossible for the YLP [Young Lords Party] to deliver on the revolutionary issues put forth on its platform."[47] They started channeling their revolutionary spirit through cultural activism infused with clear political messages in the forms of poetry, music, and theater. Within the experimental atmosphere of the early incarnations of the New Rican Village and the Nuyorican Poets Cafe, Figueroa and Pietri "would use the Embassy as a means to produce and present Pedro's plays and poetry events where they would invite the other Nuyorican poets to perform their poetry."[48] However, Figueroa passed away before they had a chance to flesh out the project. When no one assumed responsibility for continuing the work on El Republic and El Embassy, Maldonado "approached Pedro and said to him that the Embassy project was too important to drop and that as [his] work as an artist dealt with the creation of imaginary worlds and alternative realities that [he] knew how to take the Embassy to its next level."[49] While Maldonado and Pietri had previously collaborated on a musical entitled *Mondo Mambo: A Mambo Rap Sodi* (1990), this marked the beginning of their collaboration on El Republic and El Embassy. Together they set out to "create the artefacts that would define a citizen of this imaginary country and in the process bring it to the world of hard objects."[50] Early on, the connection between the imaginary and the "world of hard objects" was a clear priority for Maldonado and Pietri, who, according to Maldonado, shared "a kind of Dada Rican" sensibility, with Pietri being the "Nuyorican satirist" and Maldonado the "jíbaro existentialist."[51]

Unlike Figueroa's idea of El Republic as a purely imaginary space, Maldonado, Pietri, and other artists shaped El Republic's vision to sporadically tap in and out of the physical world of exhibitions, events, and material objects and actively promote the importance of decolonizing one's imaginary as a means to claim cultural citizenship (see figure 9). Initially, though, Figueroa and later Maldonado and Pietri tried to find physical spaces to permanently house the project, according to a letter by Maldonado: "Pedro and I envisioned securing a building which would serve as our Embassy and within this structure we could house a gallery, performance space, television broadcasting facilities, offices for the Embassy and a residence for visiting artists."[52] Maldonado wanted to revive the New Rican Village and create a fully fledged community center such as El Bohío. Failing to find a physical location—a paradoxical idea that arguably works against the concept of an imaginary space—Maldonado and Pietri instead built a website at ElPuertoRicanEmbassy.org (1994) to serve "as a multimedia installation and archive of Maldonado and Pietri's daring works."[53] Unfortunately, a website requires maintenance; virtual space is not

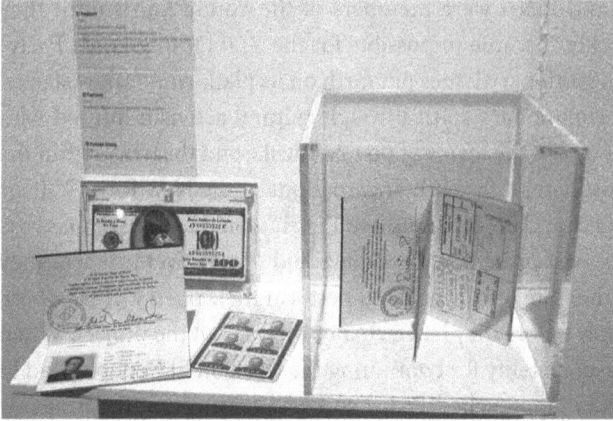

FIGURE 9. El Passport
exhibition at CEPA
Gallery
Source: Adál Maldonado,
"Installation view of El
Passport stamped on
entering Colombia, Curacau,
Paris and Milano," 2000,
Los Blueprints for a Nation,
CEPA Gallery, Boston, N.Y.

safe from being lost to obscurity when the domain rights are not continuously upheld or fees are not paid.[54] The website occasionally gets hacked and disabled as well, and Maldonado has to manually restore the site that he still looks after for the sake of archiving remnants of the overall project.[55] Neither the failure to find a permanent physical location nor the instability of a website undermines the core concept of El Republic as a community space that lived, lives, and hopefully will continue to live in the minds of individuals who represent a collective that has been scattered geographically, yet united in a spirit of resistance. Making use of their symbolic repertoire to connect this world with El Republic was the ideal way to avoid losing the essence of El Republic through either obscure abstractedness or fragile physicality—Maldonado uses the term "material space" to describe the representation of El Republic through material objects.[56]

Artefacts of Resistance

Rather than anchoring El Embassy in a physical location, which could be subject to external forces restricting that physical space, Maldonado and Pietri amassed a collection of material objects that traveled from location to location, wherever they hosted an event or exhibition. The events and exhibitions that Maldonado and Pietri organized as well as their work and the work of other artists were crucial to the expansion of El Republic from an idea into an interactive process that promoted cultural citizenship just as much as the work of the Young Lords, Charas, and AAB. As Urayoán Noel points out, "With its (mock) passports and anthem and blueprints, the Embassy project offers the paraphernalia of the nation-state seemingly as a parody of its hollowness, as if to underscore that it is *spirit* and not the accoutrements that vouchsafe the nation-state that animates this republic."[57] El Republic was brought to audiences through multimedia performance events at famous Loisaida and other New York venues such as the Nuyorican Poets Cafe, Kenkeleba Gallery, Village Gate, Club Broadway, and El Museo del Barrio as well as excursions into galleries across the country—including the Austin Arts Center and Harvard University.[58] The nature and content of these events changed depending on which artists were in attendance and what Pietri and Maldonado were working on at the time because they continually reimagined their own work within El Republic and El Embassy frameworks, which in turn reconceptualized what El Republic meant to them. Consequently, they started with a peculiar object such as El Passport at their inaugural event and eventually exhibited Out of Focus Nuyoricans at Harvard University in 2004 and 2005.

While passports were initially issued to Puerto Rican artists and ambassadors, over time El Republic evolved into a much more inclusive space that was "not limited to people of Puerto Rican descent. Anyone could participate. Anyone could become Nuyorican through a 'baptism' performed by Mr. Pietri who represented his own sect La Iglesia de la Madre de Los Tomatoes."[59] In an interview with the author, Maldonado recounts the moment when he realized that citizenship in El Republic should be broadened out to anyone who wanted to be baptized as a born-again-Nuyorican:

After one of our events an older Jewish lady (must have been in her 70s) approached Rev. Pedro and I and remarked how wonderful she felt in this creative environment where identity issues were reaffirmed. She felt that our project transcended ethnicity and could be appreciated by all open-minded races and cultures. At that moment I recalled one day when I stopped by Pedro's place and found him baptizing people in his bathtub into the Church of Our Mother of Tomatoes. Many people don't know that Rev. Pedro was indeed an ordained minister. He took a correspondence course and on completing he had to have a flock to minister to so he founded La Santa Iglesia de la Madre de los Tomates / The Church of Our Mother of Tomatoes. One of the more brilliant consequences of his ministry was that he was able to legally and officially marry couples that were in the States illegally and therefore they were able to file for citizenship of the U.S. So remembering this unorthodox baptism ritual I turned to Rev. Pedro and said, *Hey Pedro why don't you baptize her a born-again-Nuyorican and I'll issue her El Puerto Rican Passport.* That day El Embassy became an all-inclusive project and as Pedro's manifesto says, *we welcome everyone regardless of race, religion, or color.* From that day forward there was always a moment in our events where we would take time out to do a collective baptism ritual for anyone who wanted to be a citizen of our imaginary country and I'd issue each person a passport for a small donation of $10.[60]

Pietri's actual work as an ordained minister and his ability to marry non-U.S. citizens and grant them the right to file for citizenship in the United States is just one aspect of the work of the entire El Republic project to blur the lines between the real world and their imaginary world. The printed passport served multiple functions: its design resembles that of an actual passport, it is written in Spanglish, and its humorous tone parodies the legal rhetoric of a government-issued passport. However, the passport was more than just a witty and nicely designed material object. It was created to be used, to be handed out, and to be filled out. That is why it includes a section that was intended to be stamped at various cultural institutions associated with El Embassy events. The passport itself represented the most striking symbol of blurring the lines between the real and the imaginary, because some passport bearers "went further and were able to have their passports stamped going at customs while entering Italy, Paris, Cuba, Venezuela, Colombia and Curasao."[61] Finally, the personal information section allows passport holders to choose their own *nacionalidad*, including Boricua, Nuyorican, Mexijentirican, and Puertorriqueño (see figure 10).

Beyond the materiality of the object itself—and its functionality as an object to be *actively* used—the very act of issuing the passport as part of an event or exhibition helped spread the word about El Republic and welcome new citizens to its imaginary territory. The passport was one of many important artefacts that yanks the imaginary republic into the physical world for a moment without endangering it in any way. As Jose Luis Falconi points out in *Out of Focus Nuyoricans*, a booklet based on the 2004/2005 Harvard exhibition, the galleries and events where Pietri and Maldonado exhibited their artefacts did not function as exact re-creations "of the imaginary territory, but as [places] where imperfect memories of it are gathered."[62] The passport was ultimately a creative artefact that allowed each passport bearer to proclaim independence on his or her own terms; this was not a claim to political independence but rather an attempt to decolonize one's imaginary by becoming part of what Urayoán Noel calls "a new kind of affective, deterritorialized, self-created community."[63] Pietri alludes to this in the manifesto printed in the actual passport: "the imagination has always been an independent country

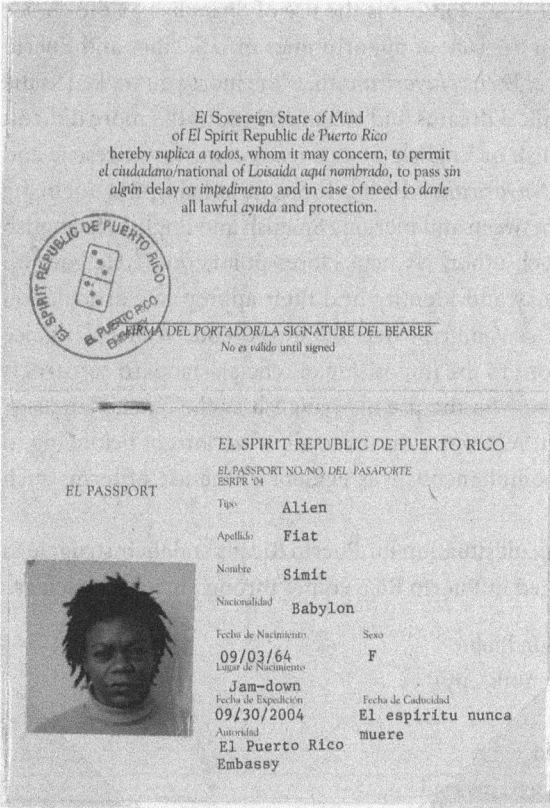

FIGURE 10. El Passport: Adál Maldonado

Source: Adál Maldonado, *The Passport*, from the series The Spirit Republic of Puerto Rico, 1995, ink on paper, 29.2 × 50.8 cm, Harvard Art Museums/Fogg Museum/ Transfer from the David Rockefeller Center for Latin American Studies Harvard University, Gift of the artist, © President and Fellows of Harvard College.

with a spontaneous sense of survival!"[64] In an interview, Maldonado says that the passport bestows a kind of "schizophrenic citizenship" upon the passport holder, referring to the "condition created by being on two islands at the same time."[65] Most importantly, unlike the U.S. passport, the loss of this schizophrenic passport would in no way remove one's status as citizen of this affective, self-proclaimed community. It is simply a representation, a material object that stands in for something much larger.

Among the collection of artefacts that Maldonado, Pietri, and other artists created in the 1990s and 2000s, El Anthem is best suited to explain how an imaginary space—promoting the project of a decolonized imaginary through real-life gatherings—can sustain the idea that Puerto Ricans "can be in two Islands at the same time," as Pietri notes in the manifesto of the passport.[66] Based on and to the tune of the Puerto Rican love hymn to San Juan, "En mi Viejo San Juan," El Anthem was performed by Pietri from the very beginning of the resurrection of El Republic in 1994 to the last years leading up to Pietri's death in 2004.[67] The first thing to note is the use of Spanglish as the choice for El Anthem. Riffing on the lack of opportunities in U.S. cities and Puerto Rico, Pietri writes in *Out of Focus Nuyoricans* that "the more you walked in the opposite direction of tropical dreams and urban ambitions the more difficult it became to talk in Spanish or English. So *Spanglish* came to the rescue and we became *Out of Focus Nuyoricans* which is the same as being and not being lost."[68] Fluently moving between and merging Spanish and English, Spanglish is a "'breaking' (into) each other," as Juan Flores points out.[69] He goes on to say, "Collective memory and identity find their appropriate articulation in this lively, 'macaronic' sensibility, where the mixed-code vernacular voice responds in both directions to the imposition of official, standard constructs of 'the' national language."[70] So the use of Spanglish as the official language of El Republic and El Anthem was a means to allow notions of belonging to flow in both directions simultaneously as evident in the use of terms such as "Nuyorican."

In El Anthem, the difficult situation for Puerto Ricans and their struggle to keep one foot firmly rooted in Puerto Rico comes through in verses such as:

> We have been in limbo
> (We're in New York City)
> And so
> And so And so
> Almost misplaced my soul
> (Somewhere in New Jersey).[71]

Here, New York is considered a temporary station, a limbo space, where Puerto Ricans struggle economically and never really left Puerto Rico in their hearts:

> If I can't fly I'll swim
> Straight from El Barrio
> Back to Puerto Rico
> (Island by the sun blessed
> Island I never left).

The entire anthem serves to underpin the importance of not losing one's Puerto Rican and Borinquen roots, urging one to resist assimilation so as not to lose one's identity:

> Some did assimilate
> In de United States

> They got rid of de accent
> Tho whenever they spoke
> That will always unmask them!
> But de majority
> Kept their identity
> Never did lose their accent!
> They were proud not ashamed
> Of their Boricua names.

As video recordings of the performances prove, El Anthem was designed to be sung with an audience in mind. Pietri created this social performance to engage audience members who more often than not experienced the situations El Anthem describes and criticizes, such as the necessity for higher educational degrees to get jobs in a new service economy:

> Many dropped out of school
> Others went to college
> Trying hard to get somewhere.
> In the land of da free
> Where without a degree
> You cannot collect welfare.

El Anthem drew on the experiences of Puerto Ricans in the United States—especially those living in big cities—and in doing so highlighted the importance of retaining and celebrating Puerto Rican tradition and culture off the island, including urban community gardens, the plena, and the mambo:

> Las botanicas saved
> Us from an early grave
> All aspirin did wass kill joo!
> Muchas gracias Chango
> La Plena y el Mambo
> For coming to the rescue!

In Puerto Rico, *chango* refers to someone who does nonsense, a joker. The anthem makes fun of Western medicine when the real medicine was spiritual in nature: Puerto Rican music and dance. The significance of spiritual health through social and cultural interaction with friends, family, and community is emphasized in another verse as well:

> De hard time were plenty
> De pockets stayed empty

But the soul nunca dyyyyyed
And junto we survived
And danced after we cried
Defending nuestro pride.

El Anthem was not simply a song that was performed for an audience; it was an important gesture in El Embassy's symbolic repertoire. Its purpose was to solidify the use of Spanglish as a language of resistance for Puerto Ricans who speak "two languages simultaneously."[72]

The examples of El Anthem and El Passport, as well as rituals such as the baptism and the recital of poetry, are indicative of another key element of the overarching project that Maldonado, Pietri, and a network of Puerto Rican artists were building: political theater. Maldonado refers to El Embassy's staged and interactive rituals as "political theatre."[73] As Diana Taylor notes in her work on performance and cultural memory, "Performances function as vital acts of transfer, transmitting social knowledge, memory, and a sense of identity."[74] The political theater of El Embassy events was clearly absurdist in a satirist and Dadaist fashion. Yet it was marked by acts of defiance against the colonial legacy of Puerto Rico and its enduring presence in the minds and lives of Puerto Ricans. What I've referred to as "symbolic repertoire" in this chapter, following Duany, is a conflation of what Taylor calls archival memory and embodied memory, or "the *archive* of supposedly enduring materials (i.e., texts, documents, buildings, bones) and the so-called ephemeral *repertoire* of embodied practice/knowledge (i.e., spoken language, dance, sports, ritual)."[75] However, Taylor notes that "the archive and the repertoire exist in a constant state of interaction, [so] the tendency has been to banish the repertoire to the past."[76] This emphasis on the archives of conquest, subordination, and colonial rule has created an artificial hierarchy of archival memory over embodied memory. In order to create a history for their imaginary nation, Maldonado and Pietri had to create archival and embodied memories, as well as digital and visual memories, which Taylor mentions as existing alongside the archive and the repertoire. In addition to the website, the passport, the anthem, and the church, this included a supposed pre-NASA moon landing and a map of El Republic.

The meshing together of imaginary maps, moon landings, baptism certificates, anthems, and passports is also a deliberate meshing together of archival, digital, visual, and embodied forms of memory that make up a nation and its citizens. As a whole, they interact in various ways to complicate the notion that any one form of memory stands above the rest. While the passport can be considered a written document that could survive the test of time if properly preserved, it was handed out in a very ritualistic and embodied way at specific times and locations. In addition, the digital archive of El Embassy projects and artworks has existed for over two decades. The performative nature of El Embassy events and its symbolic repertoire are inherently decolonizing in their methodological aim to transmit a form of cultural resistance to imposed ideas of national identity and memory. Taylor says, "The repertoire requires presence: people participate in the production and reproduction of knowledge by 'being there,' being part of the transmission."[77] Superficially, people participated by attending El Embassy events, but more importantly, they participated through affirming the imaginary reality of El Republic when they had their passports stamped or recognized El Anthem.

A Shift in Loisaida Community Activism

This chapter begins with Dylcia Pagan and her release from prison in September 1999 on the condition that she would renounce terrorist activities in her pursuit for Puerto Rican independence. Just a few weeks after Pagan left federal prison, Giuliani began a vicious battle with the Brooklyn Museum of Art "over an exhibition that includes a painting of the Virgin Mary on a canvas adorned with elephant dung," according to the *New York Times*.[78] Playing the role of amateur art critic, Giuliani asked for offensive works to be removed and declined weekly payments to the institutions when the museum refused to censor their exhibition. Within just two months, Giuliani started and lost his battle over free expression. As Judge Nina Gershon of the United States District Court in Brooklyn declared in her decision: "There is no federal constitutional issue more grave . . . than the effort by government officials to censor works of expression and to threaten the vitality of a major cultural institution as punishment for failing to abide by governmental demands for orthodoxy."[79] This was only the beginning for Giuliani, however, as he clearly disagreed with the judge's decision and announced a "'decency' committee" or "art police" in 2001.[80] The committee's mission was simple: "To follow Giuliani's ideas on what is acceptable artwork at city-supported institutions. No more exhibitions like 'Sensation' or 'Yo Mama's Last Supper,' both of which offended Giuliani's sensibilities and made him rant and rave against the Brooklyn Museum of Art."[81]

The Pagan benefit in 2001 was partially a response to the art police, as notes on the evening's program show: Maldonado screened his short film *Delito Cha Cha Cha* at the benefit "because it deals with the arrest of a woman for the crime of dancing the cha cha cha in a totalitarian state where any form of entertainments is forbidden."[82] The film connected Pagan's imprisonment for fighting her war against the imperial United States with Pagan's new direction in art as her weapon of choice in the struggle for Puerto Rican independence. Giuliani's coincidental intersections with Pagan's causes—symbolically represented through this particular benefit—exemplify the larger story of how the United States has treated Puerto Rico and Puerto Rican independence movements in the past and how Puerto Ricans have continued to innovate ways to keep on fighting.

Just like Pagan's approach, Maldonado's resistance took the form of art—performance art to be precise. He asked whether it was possible to assume a national identity without citizenship privileges and, as this chapter shows, a largely conceptual El Republic in conjunction with an activist El Embassy provided the ideas and tools to claim a cultural citizenship that defies and disables the legal limits of U.S. citizenship in the minds and hearts of Puerto Ricans. Rather than being an isolated art project at the end of the twentieth century, El Embassy promoted this claim to cultural citizenship as a culmination of the decades-long community activism by Puerto Rican organizations in Loisaida. Throughout the decades, community groups have relied heavily upon occupying physical space to meet, strategize, or hold events. However, few groups managed to maintain the costs for buildings, made even more difficult in the 1980s era of advancing gentrification. Most groups either moved, disbanded, or were forced out of their headquarters, as the case of El Bohío shows. El Republic was different. Figueroa thought of El Republic as "a concept, it's an idea, it's not a physical location."[83] On a very pragmatic level, imagining El Republic as a nonphysical space was a creative way to ensure its existence beyond the fragility of physical community institutions, which "have seen some of their most significant accomplishments undermined by federal and local government policies," according to Félix V. Matos Rodríguez.[84]

El Passport and El Anthem were just two artefacts of a much larger collection of objects, artworks, events, and exhibitions that served to manifest the imaginary space of El Republic as reality for Puerto Ricans, Latinos, and anyone else who chose to become a citizen of this nation. The use of this repertoire allowed them to actively push for a decolonization of the imaginary—a decolonization of the brain as one particular exhibition artwork demonstrates with terms and phrases such as "jump without moving an inch," "create dissent," and "make non-sense." Ultimately, El Embassy—brought to life again by Maldonado and Pietri—was a temporary project for a collective of Puerto Rican artists, all of whom have since moved on to other ventures or passed away into the spiritual world of El Republic. Nevertheless, its physical and material representations in the form of passports and other objects ensured that a new generation would hear and learn about El Republic's vision to "make non-sense" of Puerto Rico's ongoing struggles.[85] If "a key element of cultural citizenship is the process of 'affirmation,' as the community itself defines its interests, its binding solidarities, its boundaries, its own space, and its membership," then El Republic was only able to claim this right for its citizenry by building and nurturing an affective community of resident dissidents—as Maldonado calls himself in the booklet *Out of Focus Nuyoricans*.[86] While not engaging with youth in any significant way as did the organizations of the previous five chapters, El Embassy did emphasize building a broad network of artists and activists while at the same time expanding the idea of the human right to the city to a right to citizenship for Puerto Ricans. For Maldonado and all the artists who contributed to this short-lived multimedia performance project, sustainable activism was rooted in the efforts to spread a message of resistance in the form of a made-up nation.

Of course, El Republic's focus on decolonizing the imaginary had always been at the heart of earlier and more traditional community groups. One example was Charas's community recycling center, which was praised as a place "where not only our garbage, but our spirit is recycled."[87] As part of a documentary on Loisaida, a resident said that a "dirty, unclean community is not only a physical condition, but it is a mental condition also because anything physical has to start first as a thought."[88] Decades-long community leader Chino García put it most succinctly when he wrote that he "learned to be an artist—for the arts flourish here like a flower growing in between fence wire—beauty amongst the beast. It's become a way of life—to be an artist is the ultimate goal, for in the back of our minds we know what it means. It's an attempt to love, communicate, feel the spirit of the movement."[89] Whether they worked with gangs to provide them with a way to channel their work for the good of the community, painted murals across Loisaida walls to activate apathetic residents to participate, or created gardens out of dirty lots, Puerto Rican activists always had their eyes set on decolonizing people's minds in all their efforts. In essence, El Republic was the next step in what was already a three-decades-long process of claiming cultural citizenship in this neighborhood, a process that stretches back to the first wave of Puerto Ricans who settled in El Barrio at the beginning of the twentieth century and struggled to claim their rights as citizens. El Embassy recognized and deputized all the Puerto Ricans who still lived in Loisaida and those who had already moved away due to gentrification: they became a citizenry made up of resident dissidents who faced a myriad of problems and yet never gave up *la lucha*.

CONCLUSION

The Joys of Activism

> Brujas is a free-form, autonomous, and creative organization that seeks to build radical-
> political coalition through youth culture. . . . It's that one or it's: Brujas is I don't know.
> —Member of Brujas, 2017

In October 2016, the young activist group Brujas—Spanish for "witches"—
launched a crowdsourcing campaign to raise money for a legal fund that
would support people affected by policing and incarceration. As a "free-form
autonomous, and creative organization that seeks to build radical-political
coalition through youth culture," Brujas was born from a female skater group,
cofounded by Sheyla Grullon and Arianna Gil in the Bronx.[1] Brujas came
up with the idea to create its own fashion line inspired by the 1971 incident
at Attica prison in New York in which mostly African American and Latino
inmates started a riot after failing to negotiate better medical treatments and
fairer visitation rights. Brujas's campaign came in the wake of a national pris-
oner work strike on the fortieth-fifth anniversary of the Attica riots, and the
proposed legal fund would contribute to a bond fund toward paying bail and
lawyer fees and provide people with cash upon their release from prison.[2]
This campaign, aptly titled "1971," might come across as a charity event at first,
but a member of Brujas disputed that notion in an interview with the popular WNYC podcast *United States of Anxiety*: "We all have people in our lives
and some of us have been in jail so I mean mostly we're all anti state like we
think that prisons are basically a nexus of domination and control. . . . It's not
charity. This is a solidarity project that is very focused on bringing material
resources to people who are affected by the issue."[3] It was a deeply personal
cause for these young New York women, and they outlined clearly how a
portion of the funds from the campaign would be used for members of the
Brujas community. The remainder of the funds were given to Freedom2Live,

an organization that supports queer and transgender people of color facing time in prison in New York. How did Brujas promote its campaign? Naturally, it created a video in which Brujas members play a game of capture the flag wearing prototypes of the clothing line, which also included a poem referencing Angela Davis's book *Are Prisons Obsolete?* (2003):

> Prisons are obsolete
> Give em hell
> Negotiations from the
> Door of a cell.[4]

Capture the flag, Angela Davis, skateboard fashion, antiprison activism, and a group of girls shut out from the male-dominated culture of skateboarding amount to an odd campaign indeed—one that could not be more reminiscent of the work of Loisaida activists discussed in this book.

In an interview with *GQ Magazine*, Brujas member Isabelle "Izzy" Nastasia describes the "1971" campaign "as a combination of both the political DIY cultures that [they] were radicalized in in the Lower East Side, anarchist organizing where people sell T-shirts and throw parties to get their friends out of prison, and the really brash street and skate wear aesthetics that have been developing for ages."[5] Though Brujas members were born decades after gentrification started eroding the Lower East Side and driving out most of the activists and residents discussed in the previous chapters, a statement like this exemplifies their conscious understanding of the radical history of that neighborhood—one Brujas member even has a tattoo on her arm that simply reads "LES" (Lower East Side). Sophia Carre, who interviewed Brujas members, mentions the Black Panthers and the Young Lords as influences on the group and sees the group's rapid growth as reminiscent of these earlier movements, which also became marginalized spaces for kindred souls to be a part of something positive for their communities. Brujas's work is part of the legacy of earlier grassroots organizers such as AAB and Charas, which fought to reclaim urban space for their needs rather than the needs of the city or private developers. As member Antonia Pérez says in a video interview on *BBC*: "Brujas to me is part of that reconquering of the spaces that we live in."[6] Brujas might have started out as a female-only skater group, but it has evolved into a cohort of radical young activists who constantly redefine their mission as the epigraph above shows—carrying on in the spirit of groups like Charas.

Hopefully this book has broadened our current imaginary of this radical history of the Lower East Side. This area is synonymous with anarchists, Beatniks, punks, and hippies, but alongside all these rebellious subcultures was a dense and resilient network of Loisaida residents, muralists, and artists fighting for their human right to the city through organizations such as the Real Great Society, Charas, and AAB. While the groups examined here were by no means the only significant ones—several dozen smaller groups were part of the overall network of activist organizations—they certainly were leading the charge to improve the neighborhood. From the early years of a group of young gang members uncertain about their future to the eventual loss of El Bohío, Loisaida residents developed their own strategies to sustain their collective mission as an ethnically diverse community: to improve the neighborhood and not (be forced to) move away. RGS established the groundwork of engaging young people with its University of the Streets, which most groups in the following decades included as a necessity in their community development efforts. This became a core strategy for activists because it served to give children and teenagers a purpose as well as provide them with skills for the job market. Once RGS transitioned into Charas, these young activists began to create administrative structures to professionalize their work and mobilize a larger part of the neighborhood. They established lasting partnerships with such groups as Cuando, Seven Loaves, AAB, and Cityarts to consciously build a strong network of community organizations addressing all manner of issues ranging from childcare and medical services to housing rehabilitation and educational programs. They implemented the very solutions set out by Manuel Díaz Jr. at the 1967 conference discussed in the beginning of this book. The conference title was "Puerto Ricans Confront Problems of the Complex Urban Society: A Design for Change," and as this book demonstrates, Loisaida activists *did* confront the problems of a complex urban New York environment by producing a set of ideas and strategies to claim their human right to the city. Their design for change emphasized not profit but people—those pushed out of the school system, harassed by landlords, discriminated against for their skin color, and those who did not make enough money to adjust to rapidly increasing rent hikes due to gentrification.

Youth engagement, network building, and the human right to the city, the three strategies that Loisaida activists developed in their urban laboratory over almost half a century, are not meant to be comprehensive. If one were to do the intensive work of digging out the stories of other smaller groups that operated alongside Charas, new strategies would emerge that are distinct from the three highlighted here. One of these would be joy. Social movements expert James M. Jasper identifies a whole range of emotions that can lead someone to become an activist and fight for a cause—anger and frustration being the obvious ones.[7] Among them is joy, which Jasper explains as follows:

"One can be attracted by the joys of empowerment, a sense of 'flow' in protest and politics, or the anticipation of a better state of affairs in the future."[8] The joy that Jasper refers to is the motivation to get into protests and activism; however, he does not detail how joy can become an important tool throughout the work to keep activists motivated while they sacrifice their time and resources. However, the myriad of flyers, letters, and other ephemera make it clear that Loisaida groups considered joyous moments and social interactions as integral parts of their day-to-day efforts. Primarily, Loisaida activists became involved out of frustration with issues that eroded their neighborhood, but they enjoyed their work as they renovated buildings or cleaned up community parks in the fight against apathy. Jasper argues that scholars should pay more attention to the "careers of protest, the personalities of protestors, and the pleasures of protest," to give credence to the activists' lives and not just the overall cause—no matter how big or small the cause may be.[9] For many Loisaida activists, organizing turned into a full-time job, and finding time to enjoy themselves in a state of being perpetually underfunded and marginalized served an important role in their activist arsenal.

Joy is also a key component of Brujas's work. In reference to a youth summit held at the New Museum in New York on the theme of "Scamming the Patriarchy," assistant curator Sara O'Keeffe says, "While the seriousness and importance of this work is never lost on them [Brujas] ... they are *having fun* dislodging the patriarchy."[10] These witches are *having fun,* and this is not because they do not take their work seriously—quite the opposite. One Brujas member says: "Tonight we're like let's play Bingo, we're Brujas. Last week: let's go have a [sic] ice cream social, Brujas. Last summer: let's play capture the flag, Brujas. It's just, there is [sic] long-term ideas about how this can develop and then there's also in order for this to continue to be a space for ourselves not just for the world, we have to be able to do what we feel like doing."[11] While all strands of sustainable activism explain some key aspects of maintaining grassroots campaigns, the ability to find joy in one's activist work, no matter how grim the situation is, emerges as an integral aspect of community activism that keeps activists and residents motivated as they fight for justice. This is certainly true of Brujas, whose members cherish the ice cream socials, anti-proms, skate parks, bingo nights, and capture the flag games to ensure that Brujas continues to be a space for its members as well as for the world. Joy in activism sustains their cause.

Of course, joy also helped sustain the cause of Loisaida activists. From the road trip that RGS organized on its national tour, the afterwork drinks Charas hosted during its dome project, the amphitheater AAB helped build in La Plaza Cultural, the mural workshops CAW conducted with children, and all the way to the Dadaist El Passport events held by Maldonado, all these projects were accompanied or driven by social interaction, joy, and a generous amount of creativity. The social interaction provided by working on community projects such as the domes, the windmill, the gardens, the murals, and the solar wall was as important as the more obvious joy when attending events at El Bohío, the New Rican Village, La Plaza Cultural, the Nuyorican Poets Cafe, and the annual Loisaida Festival. These cultural spaces represented invaluable sites where political ideas and joy intertwined on a regular basis, as was the case with the Films Charas program. The amalgam of flyers, oral histories, newspaper articles, neighborhood magazines, documentaries, poetry, and multimedia performances demonstrates that these Loisaida activists were serious about their work *and* serious about connecting their work to brief moments of relief and joy. They lived in an urban neighborhood that was, and this cannot be understated, a cement wasteland at first and then a playground for a new class of wealthy urban professionals and artists who were buying into a marketable radical culture—a culture that residents, whether they wanted to or not, shaped when they danced, recited poetry, and organized.

The case study of Loisaida activists is in many ways exceptional and in many ways an all-too-familiar story. It is familiar because these groups' overarching mission to make a home in Loisaida was eventually thwarted by gentrification and a range of anticommunity, anti-tenant, and antipoor policies that reverted the progress of the 1960s and 1970s. Sweat equity housing rehabilitation was quickly defunded under Mayor Koch, rent prices displaced residents and families, green spaces such as Tompkins Square Park were "cleaned up" and policed, funding for community murals ran out, and community hubs such as El Bohío were auctioned off. These are the consequences of a move from the height of pro-community efforts under President Johnson to the neoliberal policies enacted under the eyes of President Reagan. However, the Loisaida story is also exceptional because of what it tells us about the response of an urban neighborhood in transition toward gentrification and because of the legacy it left behind. The Brujas of the Bronx are part of that legacy, but so is the Loisaida Center, only minutes away from El Bohío. While navigating a very different Loisaida terrain than Charas did decades ago, the Loisaida Center is clearly indebted to the work of previous activists and artists who operated—and still operate—in the area. Similarly, recording artist Alynda Segarra's Nosotros Fest has merged performance, joy, and activism both in 2016 and 2017 with Young Lords legend Felipe Luciano speaking at the 2017 event at Lincoln Center. Segarra saw an exhibition on the Young Lords at the Bronx Museum in 2015—part of a series of Young Lords exhibits, one of which was organized by the Loisaida Center—and connected the line between the work of the Young Lords and her own activism: "This is where my radicalism comes from; this is where my feminism comes from."[12] Loisaida's past is deeply embedded in Loisaida's—and indeed New York's—present.

On a macro level, the activities of organizers between the 1960s and the late 1990s make up a key part of the much longer history of radical activism in the Lower East Side, which goes back to the turn of the twentieth century, as Christopher Mele shows.[13] The Loisaida story illuminates what happens to grassroots organizing when deregulation, landlord abandonment, and developer disinvestment shift to city control, rent decontrol, and large-scale redevelopment. Neither phase benefited the Loisaida activists and residents. At least the pro-community policies such as youth employment, manpower training, and community housing management allowed such groups as RGS, Charas, AAB, and CAW to find their own solutions as the city was incapacitated or unwilling to fix the housing crisis itself. The investment phase, characterized by gentrification, was much more consciously malicious in its oppression of the Puerto Rican and lower-income residents of Loisaida. Nevertheless, both abandonment and gentrification displaced and marginalized a host of hard-working New Yorkers.

As an urban laboratory that experimented with grassroots strategies around such basic issues as housing, education, and culture, Loisaida activists experienced successes and failures. As with any laboratory, the failures are just as important as the successes. However, the laboratory metaphor ends here because Loisaida is and was home to people, not scientific experiments. Their homes and their survival were at stake. Their desperate situation led these activists to mobilize an entire community by emphasizing their human right to the city, engaging with young people, building a network of community organizations, and injecting a strong dose of (often Puerto Rican) joy into their mission against the odds. What historians can do is shine a light on these stories that might otherwise be left in the shadow of grand narrative histories about the United States. The history of Puerto Ricans in the Lower East Side reverberates into present-day developments as well. Battles over gentrification are being fought in the Bronx and in Brooklyn today. Puerto Rico's crisis in the 1950s led to the migration of many islanders to such cities as New York—Puerto Ricans whose children would become Loisaida activists—and just in 2017, Puerto Rico had to file for bankruptcy to sustain public services, which might have a myriad of implications for new migration shifts or calls for independence.[14] The cycle of migration to the mainland in response to island economic crises is continuing, and the new arrivals coming to such places as Miami are "hitting the same barriers most migrants face: language difficulties, costly certification, confusing requirements and cultural clashes."[15] As well, with the devastation caused by hurricane Maria in 2017, it is projected that many Puerto Ricans will migrate to the U.S. mainland and many already have—temporarily or permanently.[16] Loisaida Puerto Ricans faced almost the exact same issues half a century ago, and this new generation, fleeing the environmental and economic devastation on the island, will face challenges both old and new as they attempt to find a home in such places as Miami and Orlando.

In Loisaida itself, a new wave of largely young and relatively affluent activists is learning about the richness of their neighborhood's radical history while trying to find their place in this tradition.[17] Time will tell how new organizations such as the Museum of Reclaimed Urban Space and the newly launched Loisaida Center fit into the radical history of the Lower East Side. Future scholarship will have to wrestle with the fact that unlike Charas, CAW, and AAB, these younger organizations have not experienced the drug-ridden and abandoned Loisaida of the 1960s and 1970s or the battle against developers in the 1980s and 1990s. Loisaida—or the East Village as it is now called—is gentrified and therefore expensive. What does radical activism and grassroots organizing look like when the organizers themselves are educated and affluent? For now, these are questions for ethnographers and social scientists, but what historians and books such as this one can do is evaluate the legacies of previous organizers and find a framework for the new activists. As Puerto Rico continues to push against United States oppression, the story of Loisaida activism provides a useful guide for future activists and a cautionary tale for any grassroots organization attempting to work with the federal government or the city administration. Building more diverse and more intersectional coalitions will have to pay a crucial part in combating the ills facing Puerto Ricans moving to and settling in the U.S. mainland.

NOTES

INTRODUCTION. VIVA LOISAIDA

1. "Resolution Adopted at Final Session, Sunday, April 16, 1967," *Puerto Ricans Confront Problems of the Complex Urban Society: A Design for Change, April 15–16, 1967* (New York: Human Resources Administration, 1967), 1.

2. John V. Lindsay, "Presentation by the Hon. John V. Lindsay, Mayor, City of New York," *Puerto Ricans Confront Problems*, 3.

3. Peter Kihss, "Lindsay Promises Aid for Programs of Puerto Ricans," *New York Times*, April 16, 1967.

4. The driving force behind the conference was second-generation Puerto Ricans who grew up or were born in the United States and had a much stronger bond with the continental environment—this being New York for most.

5. Alfredo Nazario, "Presentation by the Hon. Alfredo Nazario, Secretary of Labor of the Commonwealth of Puerto Rico," *Puerto Ricans Confront Problems*, 26.

6. Badillo has had quite an odd political history following his role as Borough president from 1966 to 1970. From 1971 to 1977 he represented New York's twenty-second and then twenty-first districts in the U.S. House of Representatives, both of which are districts in upstate New York as of 2018 but which encompassed the whole of the Bronx in the 1970s. He unsuccessfully ran for mayor of New York every election cycle from 1969 to 1985 and was for two years one of the deputy mayors under the highly controversial mayor Edward I. Koch, before resigning in 1979 because Koch would not support his programs to revitalize the Bronx. He then held various other positions in New York and lost in the 2001 mayor campaign against Michael Bloomberg, this time as a Republican candidate. He established the Congressional Hispanic Caucus, worked to include non-English-speaking people in the Comprehensive Manpower Act of 1973, and gave Hispanic minorities a voice on the Committee on Education and Labor.

7. Herman Badillo, "Presentation by the Hon. Herman Badillo, President of the Borough of the Bronx of the City of New York," *Puerto Ricans Confront Problems*, 14–15.

8. Lisa W. Foderaro, "Will It Be Loisaida or Alphabet City? Two Visions Vie in the East Village," *New York Times*, May 17, 1987.

9. Jack J. Olivero, Esq., "Recommendations. Presented by Mr. Jack John Olivero, Esq.," *Puerto Ricans Confront Problems*, 112.

10. Stephanie Lewthwaite, *Race, Place, and Reform in Mexican Los Angeles: A Transnational Perspective, 1890–1940* (Tucson: University of Arizona Press, 2009), 1.

11. Howard Brick and Christopher Phelps, *Radicals in America: The U.S. Left since the Second World War* (New York: Cambridge University Press, 2015), 6, emphasis added.

12. Díaz held prominent, leading positions in some of the most influential and active community organizations. He was a board member of the Puerto Rican Forum, a community outreach director for Mobilization for Youth, the executive director of the Puerto Rican Community Development Project, and the Northeast regional director of the Equal Employment Opportunity Commission.

13. Manuel Díaz Jr., "Paper Presented for Discussion by Audience. Prepared by Mr. Manuel Díaz," *Puerto Ricans Confront Problems*, 167, emphasis added.

14. Paul Goodman made similar comments in his November 20, 1965, open letter to Mayor Lindsay in the *New York Review of Books*: "the only way to remedy powerlessness is to give power: in their neighborhood City Halls, the local citizens must exercise initiative and make decisions, including making trouble and/or mistakes. Change the present districting of municipal functions—schools, police, etc.—which was designed for the convenience of various central departments."

15. Díaz, "Paper Presented for Discussion," 167.

16. Ibid., 169.

17. John Emmeus Davis, *Contested Ground: Collective Action and the Urban Neighborhood* (Ithaca, N.Y.: Cornell University Press, 1991), 12.

18. Ibid., emphasis added.

19. Ira Katznelson, *City Trenches: Urban Politics and the Patterning of Class in the United States* (Chicago: University of Chicago Press, 1981), 26.

20. Liz Ševčenko, "Making Loisaida: Placing Puertorriqueñidad in Lower Manhattan," in *Mambo Montage: The Latinization of New York*, ed. Augustín Laó-Montes and Arlene Dávila (New York: Columbia University Press, 2001), 295.

21. Arlene Dávila, *Barrio Dreams: Puerto Ricans, Latinos, and the Neoliberal City* (Berkeley: University of California Press, 2004), 14.

22. Ibid., 38, emphasis added.

23. Christopher Mele, *Selling the Lower East Side: Culture, Real Estate, and Resistance in New York City* (Minneapolis: University of Minnesota Press, 2000), 196.

24. For example, the Nuyorican Poets Cafe's early phase from 1974 to 1982 at 505 East 6th Street, the New Rican Village from 1976 to 1979 at 101 Avenue A, or the umbrella organization Seven Loaves at 177 East 3rd Street.

25. Mele, *Selling the Lower*, 197.

26. Census data shows that the projects along the Hudson River were the first hubs for the emerging Puerto Rican demographic in the 1950s and 1960s and in 2010 still remain significantly Latino, which include Puerto Ricans as the biggest Latino group. Just like disinvestment and abandonment forced them back to the public housing projects in the 1970s, gentrification has been pushing them once again out of the areas to the West beyond Avenue B. White non-Hispanics are now the dominant group in all census tracts in Loisaida with the exception of 20, 24, 26.01, and 28. Of course, 20, 24, and 28 encompass the housing projects, which are difficult to gentrify, meaning that the only census tract without a significant number of housing projects is 26.01.

27. William K. Tabb, *The Long Default: New York City and the Urban Fiscal Crisis* (New York: Monthly Review Press, 1982), 12.

28. Ibid., 30–31. As Tabb points out, the percentage of black and Spanish-surnamed teachers fell from 11 percent to 3 percent, the city lost half of all its Spanish-surnamed workers, and overall these minority groups who made up 31 percent of the city payroll suffered 44 percent of the cuts in the austerity measures of the Koch administration.

29. Neil Smith, *The New Frontier: Gentrification and the Revanchist City* (London: Routledge, 1996), 18.

30. Dávila, *Barrio Dreams*, 31.

31. Smith, *New Frontier*, 21.

32. Neil Smith uses the much more eloquent term "locational seesaw" to describe "the successive development, underdevelopment, and redevelopment of given areas as capital jumps from one place to another, then back again, both creating and destroying its own opportunities for development"; see Smith, "Gentrification and Uneven Development," *Economic Geography* 58, no. 2 (April 1982): 151.

33. Dávila, *Barrio Dreams*, 87.

34. Ibid., 86.

35. U.S. Bureau of the Census, "The Hispanic Population: 2010," Table 1, Hispanic or Latino Origin Population by Type: 2000 and 2010, http://www.census.gov/prod /cen2010/briefs/c2010br-04.pdf. Historically, the Puerto Rican population has been part of a rapidly growing Spanish-speaking minority in the United States—a "minority" that grew by 43 percent from 2000 to 2010 while the total population in the United States only grew by 10 percent. The introduction in the 2010 Census on the Hispanic population shows that, in raw numbers, the Hispanic and Latino population increased by 15.2 million in this decade, making up more than half of the entire population increase of 27.3 million.

36. This includes works such as María E. Pérez y González's *Puerto Ricans in the United States* (2000) and Edna Acosta-Belén's and Carlos E. Santiago's *Puerto Ricans in the United States: A Contemporary Portrait* (2006).

37. Andrés Torres's *Between Melting Pot and Mosaic: African Americans and Puerto Ricans in the New York Political Economy* (1995) demonstrates the systemic patterns of inequality and injustice that affected the two largest minority groups in the city, while Sonia Song-Ha Lee's *Building a Latino Civil Rights Movement: Puerto Ricans, African Americans and the Pursuit of Racial Justice in New York City* (2014), provides more detail on political power and dissent among both groups and their spaces of collaboration and conflict. On casitas specifically, see Luis Aponte-Parés, "What's Yellow and White and Has Land All Around It? Appropriating Place in Puerto Rican Barrios," *CENTRO Journal of the Center for Puerto Rican Studies* 7, no. 1 (1995): 8–19. For the significance of community gardens, often the space where casitas were built, see Barbara D. Lynch and Rima Brusi's article "Nature, Memory, and Nation: New York's Latino Gardens and Casitas," in Peggy F. Bartlett's edited collection *Urban Place: Reconnecting with the Natural World* (2005), as well as Karen Schmelzkopf's article "Urban Community Gardens as Contested Space" in *Geographical Review* 7, no. 1 (1995): 364–381. On murals, there is a great article in *Mambo Montage: The Latinization of New York* (2001) by Elsa B. Cardalda Sánchez and Amílcar Tirado Avilés called "Ambiguous Identities! The

Affirmation of Puertorriqueñidad in the Community Murals of New York City." For a broader insight into New York community murals beyond those created by Puerto Ricans, see two excellent books with plenty of images by Alan W. Barnett, who wrote *Community Murals: The People's Art* (1984), and Janet Braun-Reinitz and Jane Weissman, who wrote *On the Wall: Four Decades of Community Murals in New York City* (2009). Looking beyond New York, Andrés Torres and José E. Velázquez's edited collection *The Puerto Rican Movement: Voices from the Diaspora* (1998) provides a wealth of articles detailing the involvement of Puerto Ricans in radical political movements, which historically have often focused on advocating for Puerto Rican independence or voting rights.

38. Mele, *Selling the Lower*, 22.

39. "The Charter of the New Urbanism," *Congress for the New Urbanism*, https://www.cnu.org/who-we-are/charter-new-urbanism, accessed August 22, 2018.

40. Jill Grant, *Planning the Good Community: New Urbanism in Theory and Practice* (London: Routledge, 2006), 177. For similar criticisms see Kenneth Till, "Neotraditional Towns and Urban Villages: The Cultural Production of a Geography of 'Otherness,'" *Environment and Planning D: Society and Space* 11 (1993): 709–732; and Karen F. Al-Hindi and Caedmon Staddon, "The Hidden Histories and Geographies of Neotraditional Town Planning: The Case of Seaside, Florida," *Environment and Planning D: Society and Space* 15 (1997): 349–372.

41. Andrew M. Busch, "Crossing Over: Sustainability, New Urbanism, and Gentrification in Austin, Texas," *Southern Spaces*, August 19, 2015, https://southernspaces.org/2015/crossing-over-sustainability-new-urbanism-and-gentrification-austin-texas, accessed August 22, 2018.

42. James T. Rojas, "The Enacted Environment: The Creation of 'Place' by Mexicans and Mexican Americans in East Los Angeles" (MSc diss., Massachusetts Institute of Technology, 1991).

43. Mike Davis, *Magical Urbanism: Latinos Reinvent the U.S. City* (London: Verso, 2000). Mike Davis examines urban inequality and argues that Latino urbanism could offer a productive alternative to Anglo-American models of urban living. Similarly, David R. Diaz wrote the first major study of Latino urban planning policies in the twentieth century called *Barrio Urbanism: Chicanos, Planning and American Cities* (New York: Routledge, 2005). This book exposes the failures of planners and developers to address the needs of the rapidly growing Latino population, which accounts for one fifth of the total U.S. population today and accounted for more than half of the total population growth between 2000 and 2010.

44. David R. Diaz and Rodolfo D. Torres, *Latino Urbanism: The Politics of Planning, Policy, and Redevelopment* (New York: New York University Press, 2012).

45. See, for example, Jonna McKone, "Cities in Flux: Latino New Urbanism," *TheCityFix*, November 2, 2010, https://thecityfix.com/blog/cities-in-flux-latino-new-urbanism/, accessed August 22, 2018; and Josh Stephens, "Out of the Enclave: Latinos Adapt, and Adapt to, the City," *Planetizen*, September 22, 2008, http://www.planetizen.com/node/35091, accessed August 22, 2018.

46. Manuel Castells, *The City and the Grassroots: A Cross-Cultural Theory of Urban Social Movements* (Berkeley: University of California Press, 1983), xviii.

47. Ibid., 58.

48. John Mollenkopf, "Community Organization and City Politics" (PhD diss., Harvard University, 1973).

49. Mele, *Selling the Lower*, 7.

50. Tabb, *Long Default*, 93–94.

51. Mele, *Selling the Lower*, 196.

52. Ibid.

53. Smith, *New Frontier*, 203–205.

54. Ibid., 211.

55. Ann E. Cudd, *Analyzing Oppression* (Oxford: Oxford University Press, 2006), 121.

56. For details on the discriminatory practices see Timothy Bates, "Commercial Bank Financing of White- and Black-Owned Small Business Start Ups," *Quarterly Review of Business and Economics* 31, no. 1 (1991): 64–80; and George H. Brown et al., *The Condition of Education for Hispanic Americans* (Washington, D.C.: U.S. Government Printing Office, 1980), 112.

57. The data is derived from tables 6 and 7 in the 1960 U.S. Census of Population, *Subject Reports: Puerto Ricans in the United States* and tables 5 and 6 in the 1970 U.S. Census of Population, *Subject Reports: Puerto Ricans in the United States*. These tables show only the overall numbers for New York.

58. U.S. Bureau of the Census, "Table 4. Social Characteristics of Puerto Ricans: 1970," Census of Population, *Subject Reports: Puerto Ricans in the United States* (Washington D.C.,: U.S. Government Printing Office, 1973).

59. Minimum wages for New York are based on statistical data from the New York State Department of Labor, which is available only for the state and not the city— historically more expensive than rural or suburban areas. "History of the General Hourly Minimum Wage in New York State," https://www.labor.ny.gov/stats/minimum _wage.asp, accessed August 22, 2018.

60. U.S. Bureau of the Census, "Table 3. Per Capita Income by Metropolitan Statistical Areas (MSA): 1959, 1969, 1979, and 1989," https://www2.census.gov/programs -surveys/decennial/tables/time-series/historical-income-metro/msa3.csv, accessed August 22, 2018.

61. Emmanuel Tobier, *The Changing Face of Poverty: Trends in New York City's Population in Poverty: 1960–1990* (New York: Community Service Society, 1984), 93–94.

62. On Puerto Ricans and gang affiliation see Philippe Bourgois, *In Search of Respect: Selling Crack in El Barrio* (Cambridge: Cambridge University Press, 1995); and Martin Sánchez Jankowski, *Islands in the Street: Gangs and American Urban Society* (Berkeley: University of California Press, 1991).

63. Federico Aquino, "Recommendations on Education—Presented by Mr. Federico Aquino," *Puerto Ricans Confront Problems*, 29–33.

64. Jose Aguayo, "Recommendations Regarding Manpower and Career Development. Presented by Mr. Jose Aguayo," *Puerto Ricans Confront Problems*, 434–438.

65. Brown et al., *Condition of Education*, 37.

66. Vincent J. Cannato, *The Ungovernable City: John Lindsay and His Struggle to Save New York* (New York: Basic Books, 2001), 268.

67. Nilda Koenig, "Recommendations Regarding Cultural Affairs. Presented by Mrs. Nilda Koenig," *Puerto Ricans Confront Problems*, 188–189.

68. Humberto Aponte, "Better Utilization of School Facilities in New York City—Prepared by: Humberto Aponte, Anibal Asencio, Nicolas Delgado and Mrs. Esther Gollobin. Presented by: Humberto Aponte," *Puerto Ricans Confront Problems*, 47.

69. Wilson Valentín-Escobar, "Bodega Surrealism: The Emergence of Latin@ Artivists in New York City, 1976–Present" (PhD diss., University of Michigan, 2011).

70. David Harvey, "The Right to the City," *New Left Review* 53 (2008): 23–40, emphasis added.

71. Maria Domínguez, interview by author, April 28, 2016.

72. See the following books for a broader understanding of civil rights activism during the War on Poverty: Allen J. Matusow, *The Unraveling of America: A History of Liberalism in the 1960s* (Athens: University of Georgia Press, 2009); John Dittmer, *Local People: The Struggle for Civil Rights in Mississippi* (Urbana: University of Illinois Press, 1995); and Emilye Crosby, *Civil Rights History from the Ground Up: Local Struggles, a National Movement* (Athens: University of Georgia Press, 2011).

73. Eileen J. Suárez Findlay, *We Are Left without a Father Here: Masculinity, Domesticity, and Migration in Postwar Puerto Rico* (Durham, N.C.: Duke University Press, 2014), 20.

74. Ann Laura Stoler, *Along the Archival Grain: Epistemic Anxieties and Colonial Common Sense* (Princeton: Princeton University Press, 2009), 107, 138.

CHAPTER 1. FROM DRAGONS TO THE REAL GREAT SOCIETY

A version of this chapter originally appeared in the *Journal for the Study or Radicalism* 12, no. 1 (Spring 2018), 123–159.

1. See the website of the United Nations for the full text of the UDHR: http://www.un.org/en/universal-declaration-human-rights, accessed August 22, 2018.

2. Unlike the valid critique of human rights values as Western values, posed by postcolonial theorists such as Samuel Huntingdon and Antony Anghie, RGS approached human rights from the bottom up by establishing their own framework tied to community activism as a space and praxis.

3. Angelo González, quoted in Roger Vaughan, "The REAL Great Society," *Life* magazine, September 15, 1967, 80.

4. Angelo González, "An Open Letter from The Real Great Society," CP.

5. Joshua B. Freeman, *Working-Class New York: Life and Labor since World War II* (New York: New Press, 2000), 143. Also see Rebecca Morales and Frank Bonilla, "Restructuring and the New Inequality," in *Latinos in a Changing U.S. Economy: Comparative Perspectives on Growing Inequality*, ed. Rebecca Morales and Frank Bonilla (Beverly Hills: Sage, 1993). While most scholars present the 1970s as the most pronounced period of deindustrialization for New York, manufacturing jobs had already declined by around 273,000 between 1950 and 1970, according to Samuel M. Ehrenhalt, "Some Perspectives on the New York City Economy in a Time of Change," in *New York City's Changing Economic Base*, ed. Benjamin J. Klebaner (New York: Pica Press, 1981), 17. In a 1984 report on poverty levels in New York, Emanuel Tobier found that from 1950

to 1969 213,000 manufacturing jobs were lost—a slightly different number due to the reliance on census data but nevertheless a strong indication of significant decline prior to the 1970s; see *The Changing Face of Poverty: Trends in New York City's Population in Poverty: 1960–1990* (New York: Community Service Society, 1984), 67.

6. See Norma B. Tarrow, *Human Rights and Education* (Oxford: Pergamon Press, 1987); Winifred Tate, *Counting the Dead: The Culture and Politics of Human Rights Activism in Colombia* (Berkeley: University of California Press, 2007); and Jim Ife, *Human Rights from Below: Achieving Rights through Community Development* (Cambridge: Cambridge University Press, 2009).

7. For an in-depth discussion of Freire and Guevara, see Peter McLaren's *Che Guevara, Paulo Freire, and the Pedagogy of Revolution* (Lanham, Md.: Rowman and Littlefield, 2000). Besides Freire, whose work became known in the neighborhood later on, RGS's pedagogical philosophy and their University of the Streets predate the emerging Black Panther liberation schools in Oakland, California, and McComb, Mississippi, as documented by Russel Rickford, *We Are an African People: Independent Education, Black Power, and the Radical Imagination* (Oxford: Oxford University Press, 2016).

8. For an excellent collection of studies on grassroots action during the War on Poverty, see Annelise Orleck and Lisa Gayle Hazirjian, *The War on Poverty: A New Grassroots History, 1964–1980* (Athens: University of Georgia Press, 2011).

9. Freire's efforts in Brazil were officially commended by the government in 1961 before a military coup against the left-wing president João Goulart, backed by the United States, implemented the military leader Humberto de Alencar Castelo Branco, who imprisoned Freire and later forced him into exile. In the United States, of course, the Great Society programs and the efforts of Presidents John F. Kennedy and Lyndon B. Johnson were proposed with the best intentions in mind but ultimately failed to provide substantial, lasting improvements for poor, young, racial, and ethnic minorities in the United States—particularly in urban settings.

10. Paulo Freire, *Pedagogy of the Oppressed* (New York: Seabury Press, 1968), 62.

11. David R. Diaz, *Barrio Urbanism: Chicanos, Planning, and American Cities* (New York: Routledge, 2005), 93. Herman Badillo detailed the manipulation of antipoverty programs by local elites: "the concept was a noble concept but it became a concept for stealing money, because those people who got elected in the poverty programs in housing and education and hospitals and health and drug addiction programs would take the money for themselves and for the people who campaigned for them, and it never really filtered down to the poor." See Herman Badillo, interviewed by John Metzger, Reminiscences of Herman Badillo: Oral history, 1994, Columbia Center for Oral History, Columbia University, New York.

12. See Howard Gillette Jr., *Between Justice and Beauty: Race, Planning, and the Failure of Urban Policy in Washington, D.C.* (Philadelphia: University of Pennsylvania Press, 2006) for an in-depth analysis of the failures of federal antipoverty programs.

13. Paul Goodman, *Compulsory Miseducation* (Harmondsworth, U.K.: Penguin Education, 1971), 21, emphasis added.

14. Ibid., 22, emphasis in original.

15. Andrea Tone, *The Business of Benevolence: Industrial Paternalism in Progressive America* (Ithaca, N.Y.: Cornell University Press, 1997), 160. Vicki L. Ruiz, *From Out*

of the Shadows: Mexican Women in Twentieth-Century America (New York: Oxford University Press, 1998), has highlighted how the Americanization programs sought to force an American identity onto (im)migrants and Latino workers.

16. Paul Goodman, *Growing Up Absurd: Problems of Youth in the Organized Society* (New York: Vintage Books, 1960), 87, emphasis added. Goodman's book focuses on boys and men only due to Goodman's own conservative view on gender roles. He writes that, at the time, women were not expected to "make something" of themselves since a woman's career "does not have to be self-justifying, for she will have children, which is absolutely self-justifying" (22).

17. Paul Goodman, *Paul Goodman Changed My Life*, dir. Jonathan Lee (New York: Zeitgeist Films, 2011).

18. Freire, *Pedagogy of the Oppressed*, 53, emphasis added.

19. For example, John Dewey, in *Democracy and Education: An Introduction to the Philosophy of Education* (1916), argues for education as a communal and democratic process, while Alexander S. Neill argues for anti-authoritarian education in *Summerhill: A Radical Approach to Child Rearing* (1960).

20. Harvard Education, "Pedagogy of the Oppressed: Noam Chomsky, Howard Gardner, and Bruno della Chiesa Askwith Forum," *YouTube* video, 1:31:04, May 24, 2013, https://www.youtube.com/watch?v=2Ll6M0cXV54, accessed August 22, 2018.

21. Goodman, *Compulsory Miseducation*, 23, emphasis in original.

22. Taylor Stoehr, interview by Elizabeth Murphy, "Unfinished Revolutions: Revising Goodman's *Growing Up Absurd*; Taylor Stoehr in conversation with *The Straddler*," *Straddler*, June 2013, http://www.thestraddler.com/201412/piece7.php, accessed August 22, 2018.

23. Goodman, *Compulsory Miseducation*, 33.

24. George Dennison, *The Lives of Children: The Story of the First Street School* (New York: Vintage Books, 1969), 6.

25. Stoehr, "Unfinished Revolutions."

26. Dennison, *Lives of Children*, 29–30.

27. Alfredo Irizarry, *Lower East Side Biography Project*, full video interview provided by project creator Steve Zehentner. Excerpt available online at https://vimeo.com/62523847, accessed August 22, 2018.

28. Dennison, *Lives of Children*, 31.

29. Freire, *Pedagogy of the Oppressed*, 76–77.

30. Goodman, *Compulsory Miseducation*, 32. Decades later in the 1990s, Goodman's ideas found fruition in so-called place-based education (PBE), a pedagogical model that emphasizes place- and community-based learning as well as environmental sustainability.

31. Dennison, *Lives of Children*, 114, emphasis in original.

32. Paul Goodman, *First Street School*, February 1965, 4, Paul Goodman Papers, 1925–1983, Houghton Library, Harvard University, Cambridge, Mass.

33. Dennison, *Lives of Children*, 218–225.

34. Ibid., 247.

35. Goodman, *Compulsory Miseducation*, 264.

36. Freire, *Pedagogy of the Oppressed*, 36.

37. Sherry R. Arnstein, "A Ladder of Citizen Participation," *JAIP* 35, no. 4 (1969): 216–224, http://lithgow-schmidt.dk/sherry-arnstein/ladder-of-citizen-participation .html, accessed August 22, 2018.

38. Arnstein, "Ladder of Citizen Participation."

39. Tone, *Business of Benevolence*, 158.

40. Freire, *Pedagogy of the Oppressed*, 53, emphasis in original.

41. McLaren, *Che Guevara*, 35.

42. Dennison, *Lives of Children*, 260–261.

43. Eric C. Schneider, *Vampires, Dragons, and Egyptian Kings: Youth Gangs in Postwar New York* (Princeton: Princeton University Press, 1999).

44. Angelo González, quoted in Richard W. Poston, *The Gang and the Establishment* (New York: Harper & Row, 1971), 6.

45. Poston, *Gang and the Establishment*, 6.

46. González, quoted in Poston, *Gang and the Establishment*, 7.

47. Moacir Gadotti, *Reading Paulo Freire: His Life and Work* (Albany: State University of New York Press, 1994), 37.

48. Poston, *Gang and the Establishment*, 9.

49. George H. Brown et al., *The Condition of Education for Hispanic Americans* (Washington, D.C.: U.S. Government Printing Office, 1980), 112. According to Brown et al., less than one percent of all public elementary and secondary school employees in New York were Hispanic or Latino.

50. Ibid., 37.

51. Chris Chapman et al., *Trends in High School Dropout Rates in the United States: 1972–2009* (Washington, D.C.: National Center for Education Statistics, 2011), 21. This reports shows that around 35 percent of Hispanics between the ages of sixteen and twenty-four were either not enrolled in high school or lacked a high school credential in 1972. While the report does not distinguish between Hispanic groups, Puerto Ricans represented a significant number in 1972 alongside persons of Mexican descent (birth or parentage).

52. Chino García, quoted in Poston, *Gang and the Establishment*, 13.

53. Poston, *Gang and the Establishment*, 14.

54. García, quoted in Poston, *Gang and the Establishment*, 15.

55. Ibid.

56. Ibid.

57. James L. Dietz, *Puerto Rico: Negotiating Development and Change* (Boulder, Colo.: Lynne Rienner, 2003), 172.

58. García, quoted in Poston, *Gang and the Establishment*, 21.

59. Frederic Good, quoted in Poston, *Gang and the Establishment*, 29.

60. Charles W. Slack, "My History of Drug Abuse and Recovery," *Christian Network*, April 4, 2015, http://www.thechristiannetwork.com/my-history-of-drug-abuse -and-recovery, accessed August 22, 2018.

61. Charles W. Slack, quoted in Poston, *Gang and the Establishment*, 36.

62. García, quoted in Poston, *Gang and the Establishment*, 37, emphasis in original.

63. Marc Landy, "The Real Great Society," *Oberlin Review*, September 27, 1966, Grant Files 1966, Box 11, VAFR.

64. Frederic Good, "The Early History of the Real Great Society," Grant Files 1966, Box 11, VAFR.

65. "Former Street Fighters Urge Respect for Law," *Fauquier Democrat*, September 1, 1966, CP.

66. Good, "Early History."

67. Vaughan, "REAL Great Society," 80.

68. Poston, *Gang and the Establishment*, 39. Teaching machines were mechanical devices that presented programs of instructional material—essentially progenitors of the modern computer.

69. Good, "Early History."

70. Jack P. Robbins, "Now, Meet the Other Great Society," *New York Post*, May 1, 1967, Grant Files 1967, Box 11, VAFR.

71. Good, "Early History."

72. Ibid.

73. "Former Street Fighters."

74. Ibid.

75. Vaughan, "REAL Great Society," 82.

76. Poston, *Gang and the Establishment*, 41.

77. Frederic Good, quoted in Poston, *Gang and the Establishment*, 52–53.

78. Ibid., emphasis added.

79. A. W. Betts to Frederic Good, January 5, 1967, Box 11, VAFR.

80. Pauline Lipman, *The New Political Economy of Urban Education: Neoliberalism, Race, and the Right to the City* (New York: Routledge, 2011), 165.

81. David Harvey, *Rebel Cities: From the Right to the City to the Urban Revolution* (London: Verso, 2013), 73.

82. "A 'University' Is Opened by Former Street-Fighters," *New York Times*, June 27, 1967.

83. Various grant receipts, Box 13, Box 15, Box 19, VAFR. Adjusted for inflation, $200,000 in 1967 corresponds to roughly $1,420,000 in 2015.

84. Angelo González, quoted in Syeus Mottel, *Charas: The Improbable Dome Builders* (New York: Drake, 1973), 149.

85. "'University' Is Opened."

86. Frederic Good, quoted in Peter Kihss, "Ex-Gang Leaders Obtain U.S. Funds: Antipoverty Grant Is Made to the 'Real Great Society,'" *New York Times*, February 27, 1968.

87. Good, "Ex-Gang Leaders."

88. Tom Rosario, quoted in "The Real Great Society and Its University of the Streets," *Scope*, January 18, 1968.

89. Eve Tuck, *Urban Youth and School Pushout: Gateways, Get-aways, and the GED* (New York: Routledge, 2012), 96.

90. Caroline Porter, "High-School Equivalency Degree Loses Its Dominant Position," *Wall Street Journal*, February 9, 2015.

91. Kihss, "Ex-Gang Leaders."

92. McLaren, *Che Guevara*, 103.

93. Bob Rivera, quoted in "Real Great Society and Its University," emphasis in original.

94. McLaren, *Che Guevara*, 103, emphasis added.

95. Arnstein, "Ladder of Citizen Participation."

96. Ibid.

97. Edward C. Burks, "45 Teachers Get a Message from Slum Youths," *New York Times*, May 4, 1968.

98. Arnstein, "Ladder of Citizen Participation."

99. Real Great Society, "Report to Astor Foundation," 15, Box 15, VAFR.

100. "Harlem Youths Buy 2 Buildings: Structures to Be Converted to Community Center," *New York Times*, March 19, 1968.

101. For a detailed analysis of the East Harlem branch see Luis Aponte-Parés, "Lessons from El Barrio—the East Harlem Real Great Society/Urban Planning Studio: A Puerto Rican Chapter in the Fight for Urban Self-Determination," *New Political Science* 20, no. 4 (1998): 399–420.

102. Poston, *Gang and the Establishment*, 107.

103. Receipt of $25,000 grant to RGS, Grant Files 1968, Box 15, VAFR.

104. González, quoted in Mottel, *Charas*, 151.

105. David Harvey, *Social Justice and the City* (Oxford: Blackwell, 1993), 314.

106. Harvey, "Right to the City," emphasis added.

107. Lipman, *New Political Economy*, 165.

108. Chino García, quoted in Josie Rolon, "Doing More with Less," *WIN Magazine*, December 20, 1979, 12.

CHAPTER 2. CHARAS AS PIONEERS OF URBAN ENVIRONMENTAL ACTIVISM

1. Angelo González, quoted in Syeus Mottel, *Charas: The Improbable Dome Builders* (New York: Drake, 1973), 150.

2. Ibid.

3. "Charas" stands for the initials of the six founding members: Chino García, Humberto Crespo, Angelo González, Roy Battiste, Anthony Figueroa, and Sal Becker. Crespo died in 1970, and Battiste vanished despite the fact that he was the major force behind the dome project.

4. Mottel, *Charas*, 21.

5. Richard Buckminster Fuller, foreword to Mottel, *Charas*, 14, emphasis added.

6. Luis Antonio Lopez, quoted in Mottel, *Charas*, 81–82.

7. "25th Anniversary Celebration," CP. The slogan was likely inspired by R. Buckminster Fuller's idea of "ephemeralization," explained in his 1938 book *Nine Chains to the Moon* (Philadelphia: Lippincott, 1938; rpt., New York: Anchor, 1973) as the ability to use technology to do "more and more with less and less" (252–259).

8. Mottel, *Charas*, 21.

9. Ibid.

10. Richard Buckminster Fuller, *Education Automation: Freeing the Scholar to Return to His Studies* (London: Jonathan Cape, 1973), 5–6, emphasis in original.

11. While the first project between 1970 and 1973 took a lot of time and resources, Charas eventually streamlined the process of both building domes and sharing knowledge of building domes, discussed later in this chapter.

12. Mottel, *Charas*, 24.

13. Ibid.

14. González, quoted in Mottel, *Charas*, 152, emphasis added.

15. David Lorenzano, quoted in Mottel *Charas*, 90.

16. Paulo Freire, *Pedagogy of the Oppressed* (New York: Seabury Press, 1968), 54.

17. Roy Battiste, quoted in Mottel, *Charas*, 162.

18. García, quoted in Mottel, *Charas*, 125.

19. Chino García to Wilbur H. Ferry and Carol Bernstein Ferry, December 20, 1974, FP, emphasis added.

20. "Building Geodesic Dome Tests Skills of Students," *New York Times*, November 4, 1972.

21. Mottel, *Charas*, 25.

22. Ibid., 35.

23. Ibid., 25.

24. Ibid., 29.

25. Ibid., 59.

26. Ibid., 44–45.

27. Ibid., 61.

28. Richard Buckminster Fuller, "Cosmic Plurality," *The Quality of Life in Loisaida*, January–February 1982, 10, emphasis in original.

29. Chino García, quoted in Daniel Chodorkoff, "Un Milagro de Loisaida: Alternative Technology and Grassroots Efforts for Neighborhood Reconstruction on New York's Lower East Side" (PhD diss., New School for Social Research, 1980), 150.

30. García to W. H. Ferry and C. B. Ferry, December 20, 1974, FP, emphasis added.

31. John Holmstrom and Charas, Inc., *Dome Land* (1974), 8, Box 4, FP, emphasis added.

32. Edgar Rivera, quoted in ibid., 17.

33. Chino García to W. H. Ferry and C. B. Ferry, December 20, 1974, FP.

34. Arthur A. Tucker Jr. to Chino García, November 14, 1975, CP.

35. Chino García to Eileen Fox, July 18, 1974, CP.

36. García to W. H. Ferry and C. B. Ferry, December 20, 1974, FP.

37. Ibid.

38. Ibid.

39. Ibid.

40. Chino García to Hugo A. Ruiz, June 11, 1974, CP.

41. García W. H. Ferry and C. B. Ferry, December 20, 1974, FP.

42. Ibid.

43. Chino García to Wilbur H. Ferry and Carol Bernstein Ferry, May 11, 1978, FP. The Plaza Cultural Area Development in particular was important because this group was responsible for creating La Plaza Cultural on the corner of East 9th Street and Avenue B, later renamed La Plaza Cultural de Armando Perez. There is no space here to discuss this community garden project, which was spearheaded by Charas, but other scholars have discussed this project in detail, such as Miranda J. Martinez, whose excellent book *Power at the Roots: Gentrification, Community Gardens, and the Puerto*

Ricans of the Lower East Side (2010) contextualizes the community garden movement on the Lower East Side against the growing gentrification of the area.

44. In the same issue as the announcement article, *Quality of Life in Loisaida* printed a page on instructions for recycling various materials.

45. "Don't Waste Waste," *Quality of Life in Loisaida*, June–July 1978, 10.

46. "Editorial," *Quality of Life in Loisaida*, March–April 1979, 6.

47. Note to a photograph, CP.

48. James Quinn and James M. Ohi, "Decentralized Energy Studies: Compendium of U.S. Studies and Projects" (Golden, Colo.: U.S. Department of Energy, 1980), 31.

49. Ibid. This is the first report of the Energy Task Force engaging with this neighborhood. The organization worked with urban lower-income communities on environmental projects such as this one and was located at AAB's headquarters, 519 East 11th Street.

50. Graciela Olivarez to Rick Hutcheson, November 3, 1978, Records of the Office of Staff Secretary, Presidential Files, Folder 11/8/78, Container 97, Jimmy Carter Presidential Library, Atlanta.

51. Ray Reece, *The Sun Betrayed: A Report on the Corporate Seizure of U.S. Solar Energy Development* (Boston: South End Press, 1979), 220.

52. Alfredo Irizarry, "Solar Wall," *Quality of Life in Loisaida*, November–December 1978, 5.

53. Ibid.

54. Murray Bookchin, *Social Ecology and Communalism*, ed. Eirik Eiglad (Oakland, Calif.: AK Press, 2007), 19.

55. Ibid., 20.

56. Ibid., 46.

57. Bookchin, "What Is Social Ecology?," in Bookchin, *Social Ecology and Communalism*, 47.

58. Murray Bookchin, *The Ecology of Freedom: The Emergence and Dissolution of Hierarchy*, rev. ed. (Montreal: Black Rose Books, 1991), xix, emphasis added.

59. Edward O. Wilson, *The Future of Life* (London: Little, Brown, 2002), 155–56, emphasis added.

60. Bookchin, "What Is Social Ecology?," 24.

61. "Outline for an Economic Development and Job Creating Program," November 25, 1983, CP.

62. Eric Goldstein, "Part 1: New York City's History-Making Recycling Law Turns 25 Years Old (Part I)," *New York Environment Report*, August 19, 2014, www .nyenvironmentreport.com/new-york-citys-history-making-recycling-law-turns-25 -years-old-part-I, accessed August 22, 2018. As the article notes, the majority of residents still did not recycle in 2014, so the fact that LEAC ran such a successful center in their neighborhood is even more astounding.

63. Edgard Rivera to Department of Health, Education, and Welfare, April 13, 1979, CP.

64. Ibid.

65. Ibid.

66. Charas, "Proposal for an Environmental Education Program," April 10, 1979, CP.

67. Ibid.

68. Although Charas never published a neighborhood directory for environmental organization in Loisaida, *Quality of Life in Loisaida* did publish a directory in their holiday issue, which listed at least some of the major environmental organizations such as Charas, Cuando, and AAB. See *Quality of Life in Loisaida*, December 1980–January 1981, 5–9.

69. Chino García to Linda L. Gillies, March 13, 1979, CP. The Institute for Social Ecology had worked with Charas before, providing technical assistance on Charas projects as well as sending two of their students for a summer program (likely for the dome project, the windmill project, or the solar wall).

70. García, "Proposal for an Environmental Internship Program for the Summer of '79," CP, emphasis added.

71. Ibid. This covered pretty much the work of Cuando, AAB, Charas, and the Northeast Neighborhood Association (NENA). NENA emerged as a community health care and nutrition center for the neighborhood and cooperated with Charas on various projects such as a cultural exchange trip to Canada for a dome exhibition.

72. Ibid.

73. Ibid.

CHAPTER 3. ADOPT A BUILDING AND SWEAT EQUITY URBANISM

The epigraph is from Roberto Nazario, cover of *Communities: Journal of Cooperative Living*, May 1977, Box 15, RLRF.

1. "Miracle on Avenue C," *Quality of Life in Loisaida*, August–September 1980, 7.

2. *The Heart of Loisaida*, dir. Bienvenida Matias and Marci Reaven (New York: Unifilm, 1979).

3. Ibid.

4. Ibid.

5. Manuel Castells, *The City and the Grassroots: A Cross-Cultural Theory of Urban Social Movements* (Berkeley: University of California Press, 1983), 27.

6. Ibid., 32.

7. See Julia Rabig, "Fixers for the 1970s? The Stella Wright Rent Strike and the Transformation of Public Housing," in *The Fixers: Devolution, Development, and Civil Society in Newark, 1960–1990* (Chicago: University of Chicago Press, 2016); and Rhonda Y. Williams, "'We're Tired of Being Treated like Dogs': Poor Women and Power Politics in Black Baltimore," *Black Scholar* 31, no. 3/4 (2001): 31–41.

8. William "Bill" Eddy, "Speech on the Interfaith Adopt-a-Building Program," congregation of Temple Shaaray Tefila, January 22, 1971, Grant Files, 1971, VAFR.

9. Reuben B. Johnson III field notes, October 11, 1973, Box 15, RLRF.

10. Reuben B. Johnson III field notes, November 8, 1973, Box 15, RLRF.

11. Ibid.

12. Ibid.

13. Reuben B. Johnson III field notes, December 13, 1973, Box 15, RLRF.

14. Reuben B. Johnson III field notes, January 3, 1974, Box 15, RLRF.

15. Adopt a Building, "Proposal for 1974," 1, Box 15, RLRF.

16. Ibid., 2.

17. Adopt a Building, "The Interfaith Adopt a Building Programs," Grant Files, 1973, 6, VAFR.

18. Adopt a Building, "Interfaith Adopt a Building," Grant Files, 1971, VAFR.

19. Steven Katz and Margit Mayer, "Gimme Shelter: Self-Help Housing Struggles within and against the State in New York City and West Berlin," *International Journal of Urban and Regional Research* 9, no. 1 (March 1985): 19.

20. Ibid.

21. Brent Sharman, "Rent Strikers," *Quality of Life in Loisaida*, August–October 1978, 6.

22. Roberta Gold, *When Tenants Claimed the City: The Struggle for Citizenship in New York City Housing* (Urbana: University of Illinois Press, 2014), 251.

23. Brent Sharman, "Tenant Self-Management," *Quality of Life in Loisaida*, November–December 1978, 11.

24. Gold, *When Tenants*, 2, emphasis added.

25. Ibid.

26. Ibid., 6.

27. Adopt a Building, "Case Studies for the Preparation of the International Study Day for a Society Overcoming Domination," June 1977, Box 15, RLRF.

28. Adopt a Building, "Case Studies."

29. Adopt a Building, "Irving Dankner Report," Box 15, RLRF.

30. Susan Baldwin, "City Paves Busy Road to Realty Redemption," *City Limits*, January 1979, 1.

31. Adopt a Building, "Irving Dankner."

32. Reuben B. Johnson III field notes, February 4, 1974, Box 15, RLRF. A lot of properties were being taken into city ownership after landlords couldn't pay the taxes anymore, including many of Dankner's buildings.

33. Baldwin, "City Paves Busy Road," 4.

34. Department of Housing and Urban Development to Honorable Abraham D. Beame, January 19, 1977, Box 15, RLRF.

35. Urban Homesteading Assistance Board, "The Urban Homesteading Assistance Board Third Annual Progress Report," April 1977, 2, Box 15, RLRF.

36. Malve von Hassell, *Homesteading in New York City, 1978–1993* (Westport, Conn.: Bergin and Garvey, 1996), 2.

37. Ibid., 7.

38. Sari Bodi, "From Block Burning to Block Building," *Our Town*, February 11, 1977, Box 15, RLRF.

39. "Windmills in the City," *Suburban News*, May 11, 1977, 6.

40. Sarah Ferguson, "The Struggle for Space: 10 Years of Turf Battling on the Lower East Side," in *Resistance: A Radical Political and Social History of the Lower East Side*, ed. Clayton Patterson et al. (New York: Seven Stories Press, 2007), 146.

41. Chino García, quoted in Josie Rolon, "Doing More with Less," *WIN Magazine*, December 20, 1979, 12.

42. A great article at the *Gothamist* on this project explains that Ted Finch "located

an old, inoperable wind machine" in the Midwest and left New York to retrieve it and use it for the project. The article, "The Almost Forgotten Story of the 1970s East Village Windmill," from September 29, 2014, can be found on the *Gothamist* website, www .gothamist.com/2014/09/29/east_village_windmill_nyc.php, accessed August 22, 2018.

43. "Windmills in the City," 6.

44. *Viva Loisaida*, dir. Marlis Momber (New York: Gruppe Dokumentation, 1978).

45. Ibid.

46. "Windmills in the City," 6, emphasis added.

47. "Adopt-a-Building," *Quality of Life in Loisaida*, March–April 1988, 13.

48. Nathan Leventhal, interviewed by Sharon Zane, Reminiscences of Nathan Leventhal: Oral history, 1992, Columbia Center for Oral History, Columbia University, New York.

49. Ibid.

50. Jonathan Soffer, *Ed Koch and the Rebuilding of New York City* (New York: Columbia University Press, 2010), 187.

51. Ibid.

52. Nathan Leventhal to Mayor Edward Koch, August 1, 1979, 3, Edward Koch Mayoral Records, Box 174, Folder 3, Municipal Archives, New York City Department of Records, New York City.

53. Anthony Gliedman to Mayor Edward Koch, May 16, 1980, 5, Edward Koch Mayoral Records, Box 174, Folder 3, Municipal Archives, New York City Department of Records, New York City.

54. Veronica Anthony, "Solar Power, People Power," *Doing It! Practical Alternatives for Humanizing City Life*, December 1976, 7–10, Box 15, RLRF.

55. Ronald Lawson et al., *The Tenant Movement in New York City, 1904–1984* (New Brunswick, N.J.: Rutgers University Press, 1986), https://libcom.org/history/tenant -movement-new-york-city-1904–1984, accessed August 22, 2018.

56. "Getting Down to Basics," *Quality of Life in Loisaida*, July–August 1982, 5.

57. Ibid.

58. Doug Turetsky et al., "We Are the Landlords Now: A Report on Community-Based Housing Management" (New York: Community Service Society of New York, 1993), 26–27.

59. "This Land Is Ours Demonstration," *Quality of Life in Loisaida*, July–August 1982, 3.

60. Ibid.

61. Ani Hurwitz, "New Alternatives for City-Owned Property," *City Limits*, February 1982, 15, https://www.scribd.com/document/79598691/City-Limits-Magazine -February-1982-Issue, accessed August 22, 2018.

62. Lawson et al., *Tenant Movement.*

63. "This Land Is Ours Demonstration," 3.

64. Hurwitz, "New Alternatives," 15.

65. Ibid.

66. Miranda J. Martinez, *Power at the Roots: Gentrification, Community Gardens, and the Puerto Ricans of the Lower East Side* (Lanham, Md.: Rowman and Littlefield, 2010), 16, emphasis added.

67. Jim Mendell, "Tenants Claim Victory in Lower East Side Tug-of-War," *City Limits*, February 1982, 4, https://www.scribd.com/document/79598691/City-Limits -Magazine-February-1982-Issue, accessed August 22, 2018.

CHAPTER 4. LOISAIDA COMMUNITY MURALS AS ACTIVISM

A version of this chapter originally appeared in the *Journal of Urban History* 44, no. 3 (May 2018), 519–532, https://doi.org/10.1177/0096144217699173. The epigraph is from Tomie Arai, interview by Hannah Jeffery, June 11, 2016. I want to thank Hannah Jeffery for sharing her interviews with me and giving me permission to cite her interviewees.

1. Rubén G. Mendoza and Cruz C. Torres, "Hispanic Community Murals and Social Technology," in *Handbook of Hispanic Cultures in the United States: Anthropology*, ed. Nicolás Kanellos and Claudio Esteva-Fabregat (Houston: Arte Público Press, 1994), 78.

2. Elsa B. Cardalda Sánchez and Amílcar Tirado Avilés, "Ambiguous Identities! The Affirmation of Puertorriqueñidad in the Community Murals of New York City," in *Mambo Montage: The Latinization of New York*, ed. Augustín Laó-Montes and Arlene Dávila (New York: Columbia University Press, 2001), 263–271.

3. Eva Cockcroft, John Pitman Weber, and James Cockcroft, *Toward a People's Art: The Contemporary Mural Movement* (New York: E. P. Dutton, 1977), 3.

4. Despite being published in 1984, Alan W. Barnett's *Community Murals: The People's Art* (New York: Cornwall Books, 1984) still provides the most expansive history of muralism in the United States, filling over three hundred pages in an oversized book format. However, most of this is devoted to the community murals of the 1960s and 1970s. He does describe and connect various influences, particularly the New Deal murals and the tradition of street art in Puerto Rico. Though more specifically focused on California, Guisela Latorre's *Walls of Empowerment: Chicana/o Indigenist Murals of California* (2008) and Timothy W. Drescher's *San Francisco Bay Area Murals: Communities Create Their Muses 1904–1997* (1998) both detail the influences of African American, indigenous, and Latino traditions in the emergence of murals especially in California but also in other southern mural hub cities such as Albuquerque, Houston, and New Orleans. Barnett also analyzes the mural scenes of these cities and their local particularities. There are, of course, plenty of studies on New Deal art itself, such as Jonathan Harris's *Federal Art and National Culture: The Politics of Identity in New Deal America* (1995) and Stacy I. Morgan's *Rethinking Social Realism: African American Art and Literature, 1930–1953* (2004), but their foci on New Deal art leaves out the continuities and connections with regard to community muralism in the latter decades of the twentieth century. Lastly, in their short contribution to the *Handbook of Hispanic Culture in the United States: Anthropology* (1994), Rubén G. Mendoza and Cruz C. Torres touch on the influences of Spanish *conquistadores* as well as Aztec, Maya, and Taíno people, whose histories and cultural artifacts featured frequently in Puerto Rican, Chicano, and otherwise Latino community murals. In the case of community muralism in the Lower East Side, the two key texts are Cockcroft, Weber, and Cockcroft, *Toward a People's Art*; and Janet Braun-Reinitz and Jane Weissman, *On the Wall: Four Decades of Community Murals in New York City* (Jackson: University Press of Mississippi, 2009). *Toward a People's Art* includes a chapter on Cityarts Workshop (CAW), which was the

primary organization for mural activities on the Lower East Side and, to some degree, throughout the city in the 1970s and early 1980s. The chapter, written by founder Susan Shapiro-Kiok, tells the story of a youth art education program in the Alfred E. Smith housing development near the Brooklyn Bridge in Manhattan, which quickly became an artist's workshop with future CAW director Susan Caruso-Green and muralist James Jannuzzi becoming the first members alongside Shapiro-Kiok.

5. Braun-Reinitz and Weissman, *On the Wall*, 130. See also a statement by muralist Maria Domínguez on why she cofounded the new mural group Artmakers alongside Eva Cockcroft, Camille Perrottet, A. G. Joe Stephenson, and Leslie Bender as a result of the leadership and vision change of CAW in Elsa B. Cardalda's *The Writing on the Wall (Soul): Puerto Rican Murals and Social Representations in New York City* (Hato Rey, Puerto Rico: Publicaciones Puertorriqueñas, 2009): "I sided with the group that left, they were older, they were much older and they were from a different radical time, they were early sixties and mid sixties, they were from that movement so I was young and I was in school but it amazed me to say well, I agree with that and I want to be part of that. So I sided with them and then I went with them and created a group called Art Makers [*sic*]" (87).

6. Ibid., 5.

7. This chapter does not delve into questions of Puerto Rican identity, which have been explored elsewhere already and which come to the forefront in chapter 6. See Sánchez and Avilés, "Ambigious Identities!"

8. See Miranda J. Martinez, *Power at the Roots: Gentrification, Community Gardens, and the Puerto Ricans of the Lower East Side* (Lanham, Md.: Lexington Books, 2010).

9. Susan Caruso-Green, Alfredo Hernández, and Chino García to Mary Slodki, April 13, 1977, CAWA. This letter serves as a written memorandum of understanding between the involved parties, highlighting community involvement in both the design and the painting of the mural.

10. Cityarts, "New York-New Jersey Murals Listing," CAWA, emphasis added.

11. Cockcroft, Weber, and Cockcroft, *Toward a People's Art*, 72–73.

12. For more details on the *La Lucha Continua* project, not just this one mural, see chapter 5 in Braun-Reinitz and Weissman, *On the Wall*. Weissman was one of the leading codirectors of the entire project alongside Eva Cockcroft.

13. Braun-Reinitz and Weissman, *On the Wall*, 93.

14. Ibid., 92–93.

15. Cockcroft, Weber, and Cockcroft, *Toward a People's Art*, 30.

16. Barnett, *Community Murals*, 322.

17. Cityarts, "A Two Block Long Mural Series Nears Completion on Avenue C," August 1982, CAWA.

18. Ibid.

19. Mary M. McCarthy, "The Merchants of Avenue C," *Quality of Life in Loisaida*, February 1980, 5–6.

20. Office of the Manhattan Borough President Andrew Stein, "Avenue C Revitalization Project," CAWA.

21. Ibid., emphasis added.

22. Barnett, *Community Murals*, 386.

23. Ibid.

24. Maria Domínguez, interview by author, April 28, 2016.

25. McCarthy, "Merchants of Avenue C," 6. A letter from Housing Commissioner Anthony Gliedman to Deputy Mayor Nathan Leventhal from January 17, 1980, shows that the community was supposedly in favor of the construction of Pathmark in this area, but the local neighborhood magazine and meetings such as the one on January 10 tell a different story. See Edward Koch Mayoral Records, Box 175, Folder 1, Municipal Archives, New York City Department of Records, New York.

26. Ricardo Guillermo, "Avenue C Commercial Revitalization," *Quality of Life in Loisaida*, February 1980.

27. Michael Neill, "On Avenue C, an Illusion of Life," *Daily News*, July 9, 1982.

28. M. C. Heffernan, "Hard to Believe," *East Villager*, July 15–31, 1982.

29. Ibid.

30. Brent Sharman, "Gentrification New Trend in Loisaida," *Quality of Life in Loisaida*, February 1980.

31. Cityarts, "Avenue C Mural," CAWA.

32. Barnett, *Community Murals*, 423.

33. Ibid., 426. Barnett provides an excellent analysis of funding sources—city, state, federal—in chapter 8.

34. According to a 2005 interview with then–New York commissioner of youth and community development Jeanne Mullgrav, the "Department of Employment was dissolved [in 2003] and the adult portfolio went to the Department of Small Business Services and the youth portfolio went to this department [Department of Youth & Community Development]" (12). See, for the full interview, Gregory DeFreitas, "New York's Youth Employment Problems and Policies: A Conversation with the NYC Commissioner of Youth & Community Development," *Regional Labor Review* 7, no. 2 (Spring/Summer 2005): 9–17.

35. Cockcroft, Weber, and Cockcroft, *Toward a People's Art*, 214.

36. Comprehensive Employment and Training Act, 95–524, *U.S. Statues at Large* 92 (1978): 2001. Of course, similar programs were part of many similar federal programs related to President Johnson's 1960s antipoverty programs or 1970s job training programs.

37. Neill, "On Avenue C."

38. Anne E. Bowler and Blaine McBurney, "Gentrification and the Avant-Garde in New York's East Village," in *Paying the Piper: Causes and Consequences of Art Patronage*, ed. Judith Huggins Balfe (Urbana: University of Illinois Press, 1993), 167.

39. Ibid. According to the authors, circa 60 percent of the area's housing stock was city owned by the late 1970s.

40. Ibid.

41. Anthony Gliedman to Mayor Edward Koch, January 15, 1980, Edward Koch Mayoral Records, Box 175, Folder 1, Municipal Archives, New York City Department of Records, New York.

42. Bonnie Greer, interview in "You Can Do It: Artist Housing Issue Defeated," *Quality of Life in Loisaida*, March–April, 1983, 5.

43. "The Mayor Brings Out His Plan—Not to Be Confused with the Community Plan," *Quality of Life in Loisaida*, September–October 1984, 4.

44. Bowler and McBurney, "Gentrification and the Avant-Garde," 167.

45. "Here It Is: The JPC Plan," *Quality of Life in Loisaida*, July–August 1984, 11.

46. "March to Save the Lower East Side, June 23," *Quality of Life in Loisaida*, July–August 1984, 14.

47. Neill, "On Avenue C."

48. Melvin Delgado, *Death at an Early Age and the Urban Scene: The Case for Memorial Murals and Community Healing* (Westport, Conn.: Praeger, 2003), 71.

49. *You Know . . . The Struggle*, dir. Ainslie Binder, Silviana Calderero, and Sarah Goodyear (New York: 1988), https://www.youtube.com/watch?v=anjx_nhkJfM, accessed August 22, 2018.

50. Neil Smith, *The New Frontier: Gentrification and the Revanchist City* (London: Routledge, 1996), 21.

51. Barnett, *Community Murals*, 356.

52. Ibid., 381.

53. Susan Shapiro-Kiok, "Cityarts Workshop: Out of the Gallery and into the Streets," in Cockcroft, Weber, and Cockcroft, *Toward a People's Art*, 172.

54. Ibid.

55. Ibid., 174–175.

56. Susan Shapiro-Kiok, interview by Hannah Jeffery, June 6, 2016.

57. Barnett, *Community Murals*, 57.

58. Shapiro-Kiok, "Cityarts Workshop," 175.

59. Ibid., 176.

60. Shapiro-Kiok, interview by Jeffery.

61. Cityarts, "Service to Youth," CAWA.

62. Paulo Freire, *Pedagogy of the Oppressed* (New York: Seabury Press, 1968), 90.

63. Ibid., 88.

64. Ibid., 90.

65. Shapiro-Kiok, "Cityarts Workshop," 182.

66. Braun-Reinitz and Weissman, *On the Wall*, 29.

67. Ibid.

68. Mark Rogovin, Marie Burton, and Holly Highfill, *Mural Manual: How to Paint Murals for the Classroom, Community Center, and Street Corner*, ed. Timothy Drescher (Boston: Beacon Press, 1975), 55, emphasis in original.

69. Delgado, *Death at an Early Age*, 77.

70. Braun-Reinitz and Weissman, *On the Wall*, 29.

71. Ibid.

72. Susan Caruso-Green, interview by Hannah Jeffery, June 10, 2016.

73. James Jannuzzi, quoted in Braun-Reinitz and Weissman, *On the Wall*, 29.

74. Braun-Reinitz and Weissman, *On the Wall*, 10.

75. Economic Opportunity Act of 1964, 88–452, *U.S. Statues at Large* 78 (1964): 508.

76. Ibid., 509, emphasis in original.

77. Ibid., 512.

78. Comptroller General of the United States, "Restructured Neighborhood Youth Corps Out-of-School Program in Urban Areas," *United States Department of Labor* (Washington, D.C.: U.S. General Accounting Office, 1974), 1.

79. Ibid., 4.

80. Maura E. Greany, "The Power of the Urban Canvas: Paint, Politics, and Mural Art Policy," *New England Journal of Public Policy* 18, no. 1 (2002): 22.

81. Ibid., 24.

82. Cockcroft, Weber, and Cockcroft, *Toward a People's Art*, 116.

83. Cityarts, "New York–New Jersey Murals Listing," CAWA.

84. Donna E. Shalala and Carol Bellamy, "A State Saves a City: The New York Case," *Duke Law Journal* 6 (1976): 1129.

85. Shapiro-Kiok, interview by Jeffery.

86. Both the Charas archive and the CAW archive contain myriad documents on aspects of fund-raising and grant applications.

87. Barnett, *Community Murals*, 426.

88. Ibid., 427–428.

89. Jamie Peck, *Work Place: The Social Regulation of Labor Markets* (New York: Guilford Press, 1996), 186, emphasis in original.

90. Arai, interview by Jeffery.

91. Maria Domínguez, quoted in Cardalda, *Writing on the Wall (Soul)*.

92. Delgado, *Death at an Early Age*, 66.

93. *You Know . . . The Struggle*, emphasis added.

CHAPTER 5. THE BATTLE AGAINST GENTRIFICATION

1. Charas, "Charas the Dream," CP.

2. Charas, "A Short History of Charas/El Bohío," CP.

3. Chino García, quoted in Josie Rolon, "Doing More with Less," *WIN Magazine*, December 20, 1979, 13, emphasis added.

4. Conference flyer, "Urban Alternatives: Towards a New Urbanism," CP.

5. Ibid.

6. In a *New York Times* article from April 27, 2017, on art galleries in the Lower East Side, author Holland Cotter writes that the "1980s art scene lasted just long enough to get the gentrification ball rolling and significantly alter the landscape, not least the ethnic mix" ("10 Galleries to Visit Now on the Lower East Side"). Essentially, the author is summing up in one sentence an entire process of raising rents and driving out lower-income residents—most of them Puerto Ricans. As such, Puerto Ricans increasingly became a minority population in Loisaida as more wealthy—and often white—tenants moved in. Of course, this was a different generation of white tenants than the ones who fled to the suburbs in the first place in the 1950s and 1960s. In many ways, the 1980s art scene in Loisaida, just like in similar urban neighborhoods around the United States, made inner-city living attractive and hip again.

7. Ibid.

8. García, quoted in Rolon, "Doing More with Less," 13, emphasis added.

9. City of New York Landmarks Preservation Commission, "(Former) Public School 64," June 20, 2006, 6.

10. Ibid., 2.

11. Ibid.

12. Ibid., 13.

13. Ibid.

14. Carlos Perkins to Steve Reichstein (Department of General Services), December 13, 1982, CP.

15. Marshall Spatz (Department of General Services) to John and Jane Doe, May 24, 1984, CP.

16. Chino García to Marshall Spatz (Department of General Services), June 21, 1984, CP.

17. Jack Tannenbaum, "Charas Core Group Retreat," September 26, 1989, CP.

18. Spatz to Doe and Doe.

19. El Bohío Public Development Corporation, "El Bohío Information Sheet," January 1983, CP.

20. El Bohío Public Development Corporation, "Application for Recognition of Exemption under Section 501(c)(3) of the Internal Revenue Code," January 10, 1983, CP.

21. Barbara Y. Newsom and Adele Z. Silver, eds., *The Art Museum as Educator: A Collection of Studies as Guides to Practice and Policy* (Berkeley: University of California Press, 1978), 181.

22. Seven Loaves, "Seven Loaves," Seven Loaves (Organization), MoMA Queens PAD/D Archive, New York.

23. Newsom and Silver, *Art Museum as Educator*, 181.

24. Steven M. Schwartz, "Feasibility Study: Submitted to the New York State Urban Development Corporation," April 7, 1992, 11, CP.

25. El Bohío Public Development Corporation, "El Bohío Information Sheet," 6. CP.

26. Charas, "By-Laws of El Bohío Public Development Corporation," February 5, 1986, 8–9, CP.

27. Charas, "Introduction," CP.

28. Brian Maxwell, "Art and Activism in Loisaida," *River to River*, October 29, 1997, CP.

29. Chino García, quoted in Brian Maxwell, "Art and Activism in Loisaida," *River to River*, October 29, 1997, CP.

30. García was not the only one invoking the word "genocide." While García refers to the displacement of all lower-income residents in Loisaida, Puerto Rican artist Juan Sánchez exhibited a painting in La Galería en El Bohío in 1988 called *Huellas: Avanzada Estética por la Liberación Nacional*, which highlights the cultural genocide of Puerto Ricans and the footprints it leaves (Puerto Rican Cultural Center Collection, University of Illinois at Chicago Library).

31. Perkins to Reichstein.

32. García, quoted in Maxwell, "Art and Activism."

33. Perry Good, "Art Explosion in Loisaida: The Survival Show," *Quality of Life in Loisaida*, July–August 1981, 2.

34. Carolyn J. Curran, "Marketing Plan for Charas Inc.," April 1986, 2, CP.

35. Seven Loaves, "9th Street Survival Show," Seven Loaves (Organization), MoMA Queens PAD/D Archive, New York.

36. Ibid.

37. Good, "Art Explosion," 3.

38. Richard Purcell, "A Brief Consideration of the Hip-Hop Biopic," in *21st Century Perspectives on Music, Technology, and Culture: Listening Spaces*, ed. Richard Purcell and Richard Randall (New York: Palgrave Macmillan, 2016), 90.

39. Ibid.

40. Ibid., 91.

41. Fred Good, "The Origins of Loisaida," in *Resistance: A Radical Social and Political History of the Lower East Side*, ed. Clayton Patterson (New York: Seven Stories Press, 2007), 34.

42. Alfredo Irizarry, "Alfredo Irizarry: Profile," in Patterson, *Resistance*, 506.

43. Kathleen Hulser, "Films Charas Brings Cinema to Loisaida," *Villager*, September 9, 1982, CP.

44. Curran, "Marketing Plan," 2.

45. Ibid., 6.

46. Doris Kornish, quoted in Barry Walters, "Films Charas: Way Down East," *Village Voice*, July 26, 1988, CP.

47. Walters, "Films Charas."

48. Kornish, quoted in Walters, "Films Charas."

49. Kevin Duggan, quoted in Walters, "Films Charas."

50. Charas, "Lower East Side on Film," 1984, CP.

51. Ronald O'Rourke, "Vieques, Puerto Rico Naval Training Range: Background and Issues for Congress," *Congressional Research Service*, August 20, 2004, 2.

52. Ibid.

53. César J. Ayala, "From Sugar Plantations to Military Bases: The U.S. Navy's Expropriations in Vieques, Puerto Rico, 1940–1945," *CENTRO Journal* 13, no. 1 (Spring 2001): 24.

54. Charas, "Films Charas Community Film Program," 1987, CP.

55. Puerto Rico is also called Borinquen after the Taíno name for the island.

56. Lopez Communications, "Vieques Film Now Available for Pre-release Screening," CP.

57. According to a statement by the official Vieques Support Campaign (VSC), "Those youth [the attackers in 2000] learned how to behave toward women at an early age from a society that promotes violence against women from the top on down—from Bill Clinton and his personal escapades to the military brass burying incidents of gang rape of women within the armed forces, to the basic inequities that women live with every day, from unequal pay to job discrimination. The horrible incident also gave the opportunity for the Mayor and the notorious NYPD to continue their racist practices. Giuliani doesn't care about women. His history of cutting city benefits that mainly aid women—child care, food stamps, not to mention demolishing public housing right here in New York City—prove that. Mayor Giuliani's attacks on the parade, and on Boricuas are racist and promote no justice for the women attacked" (quoted in "New York: Police vs. the Puerto Rican Day Parade," *Revolutionary Worker*, June 24, 2001).

58. torresD, "Vieques Support Movement Excluded from the Puerto Rican Day

Parade: Vieques Support Campaign Statement and Call to Action," posted on *Google Groups soc.culture.usa*, June 5, 2001, https://groups.google.com/forum/#!msg/soc .culture.usa/blFEkqPio_w/zb-DfJdHt7EJ, accessed August 22, 2018.

59. Charas, "35th Anniversary 1965–2000," 2000, CP.

60. Ayala, "From Sugar Plantations," 24.

61. A. Kronstadt, "A Short History of the Tompkins Square Neighborhood Revolt: 1988 to 1991," in Patterson, *Resistance*, 291.

62. Ibid., 292.

63. Clayton Patterson's community history on the Lower East Side includes a whole section on Tompkins Square Park with seven articles covering specific aspects such as police violence and the media coverage. Similarly, Janet L. Abu-Lughod's edited collection, *From Urban Village to East Village: The Battle for New York's Lower East Side* (Cambridge, Mass.: Blackwell, 1994), also includes several articles on the park and the ensuing wave of protests between the residents and the police. Beyond textual treatments on the riots, Patterson filmed the August 6 clash and edited two versions: a 90-minute version and a 213-minute original. The shorter version, *Tompkins Square Protect Police Riot*, August 1988, is available online at http://patterson.no-art.info/video /1988_tompkins.html, accessed August 22, 2018.

64. Charas, "Press Release: 'Free Society' plus 'Tompkins Square Park Riot," 1988, CP. Capitalization original.

65. "Yes, a Police Riot," *New York Times*, August 26, 1988.

66. Charas, "Press Release."

67. Paul Garrin, "The 1988 Tompkins Square Police Riot—A Video Point of View," *Tactical Media Files*, April 12, 2011, http://www.tacticalmediafiles.net/articles/3460/The -1988-Tompkins-Square-Police-Riot-_-A-Video-Point-of-View, accessed August 22, 2018.

68. Richard Porton, "Guerilla Video and the Battle of Tompkins Square Park," in Patterson, *Resistance*, 450.

69. Amy Starecheski, *Ours to Lose: When Squatters Became Homeowners in New York City* (Chicago: University of Chicago Press, 2016), 54.

70. García, quoted in Maxwell, "Art and Activism."

71. Charas, "Community and Cultural Center," 1996, CP.

72. Maura McDermott, *Villager*, October 2, 1996.

73. Chino García to Randy Mastro, January 29, 1997.

74. Chino García to Randy Mastro, February 28, 1997.

75. Marc Ferris, "Gregg Singer and the City: P.S. 64 Cooperation a Crumbling Façade," *Real Deal*, October 31, 2007.

76. The City of New York Department of Finance to Adopt-a-Building, Inc. and El Bohío Public Development Corporation, August 24, 2001.

77. Charas, "Community Unity March," 1997, CP.

78. Ibid., emphasis in original.

79. "Loisaida Unity March," 1997, CP.

80. Loisaida Center, "Our History," *Loisaida Center*, http://www.loisaida.org, accessed August 22, 2018.

81. Some reports on the ongoing events around the plans for El Bohío in the 2010s

include "Viva Old P.S. 64," *Villager*, October 19, 2017, http://thevillager.com/2017/10/19 /viva-old-p-s-64, accessed October 20, 2018; Harry Bubbins, "Twenty Years Later, A Community Center Is Still Empty," *Greenwich Village Society for Historic Preservation*, July 19, 2018, https://gvshp.org/blog/2018/07/19/twenty-years-later-a-community -center-is-still-empty, accessed June 2, 2019; Sarah Ferguson, "City to Old P.S. 64 Owner: Fix It, or Face Fines," *Villager*, March 15, 2019, https://www.thevillager.com /2019/03/city-to-old-p-s-64-owner-fix-it-or-face-fines, accessed June 2, 2019.

CHAPTER 6. THE RESIDENT DISSIDENTS OF EL SPIRIT REPUBLIC DE PUERTO RICO

A version of this chapter originally appeared in *Anglistica/AION* 20, no. 1 (November 2017).

1. Ronald Fernández, *Prisoners of Colonialism: The Struggle for Justice in Puerto Rico* (Monroe: Common Courage Press, 1994), 205.

2. John M. Broder, "12 Imprisoned Puerto Ricans Accept Clemency Conditions," *New York Times*, September 8, 1999.

3. Ibid.

4. Ibid.

5. Ibid. Giuliani was notoriously tough on terrorism both before and after the attacks on September 11, 2001.

6. Vagabond Beaumont, "From the Other Side of Between Two Worlds," *nothing-tobegainedhere*, March 2, 2015, https://nothingtobegainedhere.wordpress.com/2015/03 /02/from-the-other-side-of-between-two-worlds, accessed August 22, 2018.

7. "Dylcia Pagan Benefit," Box 70, Folder 8, PPP.

8. Carmen T. Whalen, "Colonialism, Citizenship, and the Making of the Puerto Rican Diaspora: An Introduction," in *The Puerto Rican Diaspora: Historical Perspectives*, ed. Carmen Teresa Whalen and Víctor Vázquez-Hernández (Philadelphia: Temple University Press, 2005), 13.

9. Adál Maldonado, Pedro Pietri, and Gloria Rodriguez to Raul Julia, Box 70, Folder 8, PPP.

10. Besides Maldonado, Pietri, and Figueroa, other artists and friends who worked on El Republic at one time or another include Jesús Papoleto Meléndez, Doctor Willie Pietri, Joe Pietri, Carmen Diaz Pietri, Mariposa Fernández, Sheila Candelario, Ricardo León Peña Villa, and Tato Laviera.

11. Adál Maldonado, "El Passport," *El Puerto Rican Embassy*, http://www .elpuertoricanembassy.org, accessed August 22, 2018.

12. Pietri, "El Spanglish National Anthem."

13. Benedict Anderson, *Imagined Communities: Reflections on the Origin and Spread of Nationalism* (London: Verso, 2006), 6.

14. Renato Rosaldo and William V. Flores, "Identity, Conflict, and Evolving Latino Communities: Cultural Citizenship in San Jose, California," in *Latino Cultural Citizenship: Claiming Identity, Space, and Rights*, ed. William V. Flores and Rina Benmayor (Boston: Beacon Press, 1997), 93.

15. Jorge Duany, *The Puerto Rican Nation on the Move: Identities on the Island and in the United States* (Chapel Hill: University of North Carolina Press, 2002), 37.

16. Ibid., 3.

17. Ibid., 4.

18. Ibid., 16.

19. United States Court of Appeals, First Circuit, Gregorio Igartúa, et al., Plaintiffs, Appellants, v. United States of America, et al., Defendants, Appellees, 417 F.3d 145 (en banc), No. 09–2186.

20. Abby Ohlheiser, "Is Puerto Rico on Its Way to Becoming the 51st State? Possibly," *Slate*, November 7, 2012, http://www.slate.com/blogs/the_slatest/2012/11/07/puerto_rico_statehood_referendum_2012_majority_support_of_status_change.html, accessed August 22, 2018.

21. Juan Flores, *From Bomba to Hip-Hop: Puerto Rican Culture and Latino Identity* (New York: Columbia University Press, 2000), 35.

22. Whalen, "Colonialism, Citizenship, and the Making," 13.

23. Rina Benmayor, Rosa M. Torruellas, and Ana L. Juarbe, "Claiming Cultural Citizenship in East Harlem: 'Si Esto Puede Ayudar a la Comunidad Mía . . . ,'" in W. V. Flores and Benmayor, *Latino Cultural Citizenship*.

24. This chapter focuses on activism in the cultural arena rather than political activities by groups such as the Young Lords. See, for example, Yasmin Ramírez's PhD thesis, "Nuyorican Vanguards, Political Actions, Poetic Visions: A History of Puerto Rican Artists in New York, 1964–1984" (City University of New York, 2005).

25. William V. Flores and Rina Benmayor, "Constructing Cultural Citizenship," in Flores and Benmayor, *Latino Cultural Citizenship*, 6.

26. IUP Cultural Studies Working Group, "Draft Concept Paper on Cultural Citizenship," unpublished working concept paper no. 2 (Stanford, Calif.: Center for Chicano Research, 1988), quoted in Flores and Benmayor, "Constructing Cultural Citizenship," 12.

27. Rosaldo and Flores, "Identity, Conflict, and Evolving Latino Communities," 57.

28. Whalen, "Colonialism, Citizenship, and the Making," 41–42.

29. Rosaldo and Flores, "Identity, Conflict, and Evolving Latino Communities," 61.

30. Ibid.

31. Duany, *Puerto Rican Nation*, 32.

32. Kenkeleba House, "Press Release," June 10, 1994, Box 71, Folder 1, PPP.

33. Urayoán Noel, "On Out of Focus Nuyoricans, Noricuas, and Performance Identities," *Liminalities: A Journal of Performance Studies* 10, no. 3/4 (2014): 3.

34. Kenkeleba House, "Press Release."

35. Ibid.

36. Adál Maldonado, interview by Berta Jottar, *CEPA Gallery*, http://www.old.cepagallery.org/exhibitions/Unlimited2/adal.html, accessed August 22, 2018.

37. Adál Maldonado, e-mail message to author, January 14, 2017.

38. Critics include the investigative reporter Richard de Mille as well as anthropologists who studied the Yaqui Indian culture from which Castaneda claims to take his guidance. See, for example, pages 24 and 25 in Jane Holden Kelley, *Yaqui Women: Contemporary Life Histories* (Lincoln: University of Nebraska Press, 1978).

39. Maldonado, e-mail message.

40. Ibid.

41. Anonymous source, quoted in Marina Roseman, "The New Rican Village: Artists in Control of the Image-Making Machinery," *Latin American Music Review / Revista de Múisca Lationamericana* 4, no. 1 (1983): 135, emphasis added.

42. Ed Morales, "Eddie Figueroa's Spirit Republic Alternative to the Young Lords," *EdMorales.net*, July 25, 2015, https://edmorales.net/2015/07/25/eddie-figueroas-spirit -republic-alternative-to-the-young-lords, accessed August 22, 2018, emphasis added.

43. Figueroa, quoted in "Eddie Figueroa's Spirit Republic."

44. Morales, "Eddie Figueroa's Spirit Republic."

45. Figueroa, quoted in "Eddie Figueroa's Spirit Republic."

46. Pedro Pietri, "Poem/Prologue," in *Out of Focus Nuyoricans* (Hollis, N.H.: Puritan Press, 2004).

47. Maldonado, e-mail message.

48. Ibid.

49. Ibid.

50. Ibid.

51. Ibid.

52. Adál Maldonado to Alberto Cappas, Box 70, Folder 8, Centro Archives and Library, PPP.

53. Noel, "On Out of Focus," 3.

54. As of August 2018, the official website, ElPuertoRicanEmbassy.org, is available but frequently goes offline for long periods.

55. Maldonado, e-mail message.

56. Maldonado, interview by Jottar.

57. Ibid., 6, emphasis added.

58. Some ephemera for selected events can be found in the Pedro Pietri Papers.

59. James Estrin, "Puerto Rican Identity, In and Out of Focus," *New York Times*, August 28, 2012. I was issued my own passport when I contacted Maldonado in 2015.

60. Maldonado, e-mail message.

61. Ibid.

62. Jose Luis Falconi, "Blurriness in Focus," in *Out of Focus Nuyoricans*.

63. Urayoán Noel, *In Visible Movement: Nuyorican Poetry from the Sixties to Slam* (Iowa City: University of Iowa Press, 2014), 70.

64. Pedro Pietri, "Notes on El Puerto Rican Embassy," 1994, Box 70, Folder 8, PPP.

65. Maldonado, interview by Jottar.

66. Pietri, "Notes on El Puerto Rican Embassy."

67. Luckily, the records of the performances are not just kept on sheets of paper in institutional archives but are also collected and cut together by Maldonado in a video on his YouTube channel, https://www.youtube.com/watch?v=F82EmeLrrL4, accessed August 22, 2018.

68. Pietri, "Poem/Prologue."

69. J. Flores, *From Bomba to Hip Hop*, 58.

70. Ibid.

71. Pietri, "El Spanglish National Anthem."

72. Austin Arts Center, "El Spanglish National Anthem," 1998, Box 1, Folder 2, PPP.

73. Maldonado, e-mail message.

74. Diana Taylor, *The Archive and the Repertoire: Performing Cultural Memory in the Americas* (Durham, N.C.: Duke University Press, 2003), 2.

75. Ibid., 19, emphasis added.

76. Ibid., 21.

77. Ibid., 20.

78. David Barstow, "Giuliani Is Ordered to Halt Attacks against Museum," *New York Times*, November 2, 1999.

79. Ibid.

80. Albor Ruiz, "Rudy on Art: It's Theater of the Absurd," *New York Daily News*, April 2, 2001.

81. Ibid.

82. "Dylcia Pagan Benefit." The full version of *Delito Cha Cha Cha* can be found on Adál Maldonado's YouTube channel, https://www.youtube.com/watch?v=sidhTjoqYvY, accessed August 22, 2018.

83. Eddie Figueroa, quoted in Morales, "Eddie Figueroa's Spirit Republic."

84. Félix V. Matos Rodríguez, "Saving the Parcela: A Short History of Boston's Puerto Rican Community," in *The Puerto Rican Diaspora: Historical Perspectives*, ed. Carmen Teresa Whalen and Víctor Vázquez-Hernández (Philadelphia: Temple University Press, 2005), 200–201.

85. The legacy of El Republic continues to be a presence for Puerto Rican activists as evidenced by a 2015 New York exhibition on the Young Lords, which includes exhibition space for the work of Figueroa, Pietri, and Maldonado. Connie Kargbo, "Puerto Rican Radical Group Young Lords Retake NYC in Museum Exhibit," *PBS Newshour*, September 19, 2015, http://www.pbs.org/newshour/art/puerto-rican-radical-group -young-lords-retake-new-york-city-multi-museum-exhibit, accessed August 22, 2018.

86. IUP Cultural Studies Working Group, "Draft Concept Paper," quoted in W. V. Flores and Benmayor, "Constructing Cultural Citizenship," 13.

87. "Don't Waste Waste," *Quality of Life in Loisaida*, June–July 1978, 6.

88. *Viva Loisaida*, dir. Marlis Momber (New York: Gruppe Dokumentation, 1978).

89. Chino García, quoted in Josie Rolon, "Doing More with Less," *WIN Magazine*, December 20, 1979, 13.

CONCLUSION. THE JOYS OF ACTIVISM

1. Kai Wright, Sophia Paliza Carre, and Karen Frillmann, "These 'Witches' Are Empowering the Next Generation," *United States of Anxiety*, June 20, 2017, http://www .wnyc.org/story/episode-8-brujas, accessed August 22, 2018.

2. Brujas, "Launch BRUJAS x 1971 P.E. Streetwear!" *Kickstarter*, October 2016, https://www.kickstarter.com/projects/582051340/launch-brujas-x-1971-pe-streetwear /description, accessed August 22, 2018.

3. Wright, Carre, and Frillmann, "These 'Witches' Are Empowering."

4. Brujas, "Launch BRUJAS."

5. Isabelle "Izzi" Nastasia, quoted in Samuel Hine, "Meet Brujas, the Bronx Skate Crew Making Streetwear for Post-Election America," *GQ Magazine*, November 17,

2016, http://www.gq.com/story/brujas-1971-streetwear-skate-crew, accessed August 22, 2018.

6. Antonia Pérez, quoted in Anna Bressanin, "Meet the Latina Skate 'Witches' of the Bronx," *BBC*, December 10, 2015, http://www.bbc.co.uk/news/av/magazine-35064718 /meet-the-latina-skate-witches-of-the-bronx, accessed August 22, 2018.

7. James M. Jasper, *The Art of Moral Protest: Culture, Biography, and Creativity in Social Movements* (Chicago: University of Chicago Press, 1997).

8. Ibid., 114.

9. Ibid.

10. Sara O'Keeffe, quoted in "Meet Brujas," emphasis added.

11. Wright, Carre, and Frillmann, "These 'Witches' Are Empowering."

12. Alynda Segarra, quoted in Richard Villegas, "How the Young Lords Inspired the Political Mission of Hurray for the Riff Raff's Nosotros Fest," *Remezcla*, July 26, 2017, http://remezcla.com/features/music/hurray-for-the-riff-raff-young-lords-nosotros -fest, accessed August 22, 2018.

13. Christopher Mele, *Selling the Lower East Side: Culture, Real Estate, and Resistance in New York City* (Minneapolis: University of Minnesota Press, 2000).

14. Kate Hodal, "Puerto Rico Files for Bankruptcy in Last-Ditch Attempt to Sustain Public Services," *Guardian*, May 5, 2017, https://www.theguardian.com/global -development/2017/may/05/puerto-rico-files-for-bankruptcy-in-last-ditch-attempt-to -sustain-public-services, accessed August 22, 2018.

15. Mike Schneider, "Some Puerto Ricans Struggle to Find Careers in Florida," *Associated Press*, July 5, 2017, https://apnews.com/d5oab002cbf144f881ca877cd951ec34, accessed August 22, 2018.

16. Jenny Jarvie, "Puerto Ricans Fleeing Their Hurricane-Ravaged Island Are Pouring into the U.S. Mainland," *Los Angeles Times*, October 10, 2017, http://www.latimes .com/nation/la-na-puerto-rico-orlando-20171010-story.html, accessed October 26, 2018.

17. John Leland, "East Village Shrine to Riots and Radicals," *New York Times*, December 8, 2012, http://www.nytimes.com/2012/12/09/nyregion/the-museum-of -reclaimed-urban-space-enshrines-the-east-village-struggle.html?mcubz=2, accessed August 22, 2018.

INDEX

GEOGRAPHIES OF JUSTICE AND SOCIAL TRANSFORMATION

www.ingramcontent.com/pod-product-compliance
Lightning Source LLC
Chambersburg PA
CBHW010139270326
41926CB00022B/4503